DETROIT PUBLIC LIBRARY

3 5674 04324291 7

W9-BXE-045

CliffsTestPrep®

U.S. Citizenship Test

by

Edward Swick

KNAPP BRANCH LIBRARY
13330 CONANT
DETROIT, MI 48212
852-4283

WILEY

Wiley Publishing, Inc.

MAY 06

About the Author

Edward Swick has been an ESL and foreign language teacher for more than 30 years. After studying at the University of Hamburg in Germany as a Fulbright scholar, he completed his Master's Degree in German, Russian, and English at Southern Illinois University. He now resides in Chicago, where he works full time on ESL and foreign language instructional materials.

Publisher's Acknowledgments

Editorial

Project Editor: Kelly D. Henthorne

Acquisitions Editor: Greg Tubach

Production

Proofreader: Debbye Butler

Wiley Publishing, Inc. Composition Services

CliffsTestPrep® U.S. Citizenship Test

Published by:
Wiley Publishing, Inc.
111 River Street
Hoboken, NJ 07030-5774
www.wiley.com

Copyright © 2005 Wiley, Hoboken, NJ

Published by Wiley, Hoboken, NJ
Published simultaneously in Canada

Library of Congress Cataloging-in-Publication Data

Swick, Edward.
 CliffsTestPrep U.S. citizenship test / by Edward Swick.
  p. cm. -- (CliffsTestPrep)
 ISBN-13: 978-0-7645-7693-5 (pbk.)
 ISBN-10: 0-7645-7693-3

1. Citizenship--United States--Examinations, questions, etc. 2. Citizenship--United States--Examinations--Study guides. I. Title: U.S. citizenship test. II. Title: U.S. citizenship test. III. Title. IV. Series.
 JK1758.S98 2005
 323.6'23'0973--dc22

                                2005011637

ISBN-13: 978-0-7645-7693-5

ISBN-10: 0-7645-7693-3

Printed in the United States of America

10 9 8 7 6 5 4 3 2 1

1B/QR/QX/QV/IN

Note: If you purchased this book without a cover, you should be aware that this book is stolen property. It was reported as "unsold and destroyed" to the publisher, and neither the author nor the publisher has received any payment for this "stripped book."

NO PART OF THIS PUBLICATION MAY BE REPRODUCED, STORED IN A RETRIEVAL SYSTEM, OR TRANSMITTED IN ANY FORM OR BY ANY MEANS, ELECTRONIC, MECHANICAL, PHOTOCOPYING, RECORDING, SCANNING, OR OTHERWISE, EXCEPT AS PERMITTED UNDER SECTIONS 107 OR 108 OF THE 1976 UNITED STATES COPYRIGHT ACT, WITHOUT EITHER THE PRIOR WRITTEN PERMISSION OF THE PUBLISHER, OR AUTHORIZATION THROUGH PAYMENT OF THE APPROPRIATE PER-COPY FEE TO THE COPYRIGHT CLEARANCE CENTER, 222 ROSEWOOD DRIVE, DANVERS, MA 01923, 978-750-8400, FAX 978-646-8600, OR ON THE WEB AT WWW.COPYRIGHT.COM. REQUESTS TO THE PUBLISHER FOR PERMISSION SHOULD BE ADDRESSED TO THE LEGAL DEPARTMENT, WILEY PUBLISHING, INC., 10475 CROSSPOINT BLVD., INDIANAPOLIS, IN 46256, 317-572-3447, OR FAX 317-572-4355.

THE PUBLISHER AND THE AUTHOR MAKE NO REPRESENTATIONS OR WARRANTIES WITH RESPECT TO THE ACCURACY OR COMPLETENESS OF THE CONTENTS OF THIS WORK AND SPECIFICALLY DISCLAIM ALL WARRANTIES, INCLUDING WITHOUT LIMITATION WARRANTIES OF FITNESS FOR A PARTICULAR PURPOSE. NO WARRANTY MAY BE CREATED OR EXTENDED BY SALES OR PROMOTIONAL MATERIALS. THE ADVICE AND STRATEGIES CONTAINED HEREIN MAY NOT BE SUITABLE FOR EVERY SITUATION. THIS WORK IS SOLD WITH THE UNDERSTANDING THAT THE PUBLISHER IS NOT ENGAGED IN RENDERING LEGAL, ACCOUNTING, OR OTHER PROFESSIONAL SERVICES. IF PROFESSIONAL ASSISTANCE IS REQUIRED, THE SERVICES OF A COMPETENT PROFESSIONAL PERSON SHOULD BE SOUGHT. NEITHER THE PUBLISHER NOR THE AUTHOR SHALL BE LIABLE FOR DAMAGES ARISING HEREFROM. THE FACT THAT AN ORGANIZATION OR WEBSITE IS REFERRED TO IN THIS WORK AS A CITATION AND/OR A POTENTIAL SOURCE OF FURTHER INFORMATION DOES NOT MEAN THAT THE AUTHOR OR THE PUBLISHER ENDORSES THE INFORMATION THE ORGANIZATION OR WEBSITE MAY PROVIDE OR RECOMMENDATIONS IT MAY MAKE. FURTHER, READERS SHOULD BE AWARE THAT INTERNET WEBSITES LISTED IN THIS WORK MAY HAVE CHANGED OR DISAPPEARED BETWEEN WHEN THIS WORK WAS WRITTEN AND WHEN IT IS READ.

Trademarks: Wiley, the Wiley Publishing logo, CliffsNotes, the CliffsNotes logo, Cliffs, CliffsAP, CliffsComplete, CliffsQuickReview, CliffsStudySolver, CliffsTestPrep, CliffsNote-a-Day, cliffsnotes.com, and all related trademarks, logos, and trade dress are trademarks or registered trademarks of John Wiley & Sons, Inc. and/or its affiliates. All other trademarks are the property of their respective owners. Wiley Publishing, Inc. is not associated with any product or vendor mentioned in this book.

For general information on our other products and services or to obtain technical support, please contact our Customer Care Department within the U.S. at 800-762-2974, outside the U.S. at 317-572-3993, or fax 317-572-4002.

Wiley also publishes its books in a variety of electronic formats. Some content that appears in print may not be available in electronic books. For more information about Wiley products, please visit our web site at www.wiley.com.

WILEY

Table of Contents

The Geography of the United States

The United States of America is located in the center of the continent of North America. Canada borders the United States in the north, and Mexico borders the United States in the southwest. The Gulf of Mexico makes up the southern coastline of the country from Texas to Florida. The Atlantic Ocean is off the east coast, and the Pacific Ocean is off the west coast.

There are 50 states in the American union. Forty-eight states are located between Canada and Mexico. They are called the 48 *contiguous* states. Alaska, the largest state, is northwest of Canada. The state of Hawaii is in the Pacific Ocean about 2,800 miles west of North America.

The United States also has several possessions and territories, which are located in the Pacific Ocean and the Caribbean Sea.

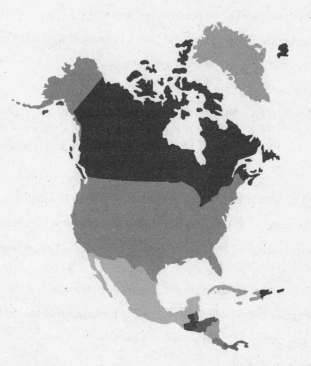

Do you see Alaska on the map?

Do you know where the Atlantic Ocean is?

Do you live in the north, south, east, or west of the United States?

Can you find your part of the country on the map?

If you are a resident of the United States of America, you might be eligible to become a citizen. But how? The answer is coming up.

Who Can Become an American Citizen?

The INS (Immigration and Naturalization Service) is now called the USCIS (United States Citizenship and Immigration Services). You can contact your local USCIS office to learn whether you are eligible to apply for citizenship. If you have access to the Internet, you can get helpful information at the USCIS Web site:

http://uscis.gov

Although you can consult an immigration lawyer to help you to understand the legal process thoroughly and to know your exact eligibility status, the USCIS has a worksheet to help you learn whether you are eligible to apply for citizenship. The questions on that worksheet are listed here. Answer the questions carefully to learn whether you can apply for citizenship now.

Eligibility Worksheet

Circle the word *YES* if the sentence is true. Circle *NO* if the sentence is not true.

1. I am at least 18 years old.

      YES   NO   If you circled NO, you are not eligible now.

2. I am a Permanent Resident of the United States and have a Permanent Resident Card.

      YES   NO   If you circled NO, you are not eligible now.

3. I have been a Permanent Resident for:

     a. 5 years or more.   YES   NO   If you circled NO, you are not eligible now.
     b. less than 3 years.   YES   NO   If you circled YES, you are not eligible now.
     c. 3 to 5 years   YES   NO   If you circled YES, go now to Attachment A to learn about exceptions.

4. During the last 5 years, I have NOT been out of the United States for 30 months or more.

      YES   NO   If you circled NO, you are not eligible now. Go now to Attachment B for exceptions.

5. Since becoming a permanent resident, I have not taken a trip out of the United States that lasted for 1 year or more.

      YES   NO   If you circled NO, you are not eligible now. Go now to Attachment C for exceptions.

6. I have resided in the district or state in which I am applying for citizenship for the last 3 months.

      YES   NO   If you circled NO, you are not eligible now.

7. I can read, write, and speak basic English.

      YES   NO   If you circled NO, you are not eligible now. Go now to Attachment D for exceptions.

8. I can pass the civics test.

      YES   NO   If you circled NO, you are not eligible now.

9. I am a person of good moral character.

      YES   NO   If you circled NO, you are not eligible now.

10. One of the following is true:

   a. I am a female, **OR**

   b. I am a male registered with the Selective Service, **OR**

   c. I am a male who did not enter the United States under any status until my 26th birthday, **OR**

   d. I am a male who was born before January 1, 1960, **OR**

   e. I am a male who was in the United States between the ages of 18 and 26 but who did not register with the Selective Service, and I will send a "Status Information Letter" explaining why with my application.

   YES   NO   If you circled NO, you are not eligible now.

11. I have never deserted from the U.S. Armed Forces.

   YES   NO   If you circled NO, you are not eligible now.

12. I have never received an exemption or discharge from the U.S. Armed Forces on the grounds that I am an alien.

   YES   NO   If you circled NO, you are not eligible now.

13. I am willing to perform either military **OR** civilian service for the United States if required by law. (If your religious beliefs prohibit you from performing military service, you must be willing to perform non-military service.)

   YES   NO   If you circled NO, you are not eligible now.

14. I will support the U.S. Constitution.

   YES   NO   If you circled NO, you are not eligible now.

15. I understand and am willing to take an oath of allegiance to the United States.

   YES   NO   If you circled NO, you are not eligible now.

Attachment A

I have been a Permanent Resident for 3 to 5 years.

A1. I am married to and living with a U.S. citizen.

   YES   NO   If you circled NO, you are not eligible now.

A2. I have been married to that U.S. citizen for at least the last 3 years.

   YES   NO   If you circled NO, you are not eligible now.

A3. My spouse has been a U.S. citizen for at least the last 3 years.

   YES   NO   If you circled NO, you are not eligible now.

A4. During the past 3 years, I have not been out of the country for 18 months or more.

   YES   NO   If you circled NO, you are not eligible now.

If you answered YES to all 4 questions, go to **Question 5.**

Attachment B

I have been out of the country for 30 months or more.

B1. I am:

    a. a person who has served on board a vessel operated by or registered in the United States, **OR**

    b. an employee or an individual under contract to the U.S. Government, **OR**

    c. a person who performs ministerial or priestly functions for a religious denomination or an interdenominational organization with a valid presence in the United States.

      YES NO   If you circled NO, you are not eligible now. If you answered YES, go to **Question 5.**

Attachment C

I have been out of the country for 1 year or more.

C1. Since becoming a permanent resident, I have not taken a trip out of the United States that lasted for 1 year or more without an approved "Application to Preserve Residence for Naturalization Purposes." (Form N-470)

      YES NO   If you circled NO, you are not eligible now. If you answered YES, go to **Question 6.**

Attachment D

I cannot read, write, or speak Basic English.

D1. I am over 50 and have lived in the United States for at least 20 years since I became a permanent resident, **OR**

      YES NO   If you circled NO, you are not eligible now.

D2. I am over 55 and have been living in the United States for at least 15 years since I became a permanent resident, **OR**

      YES NO   If you circled NO, you are not eligible now.

D3. I have a disability that prevents me from fulfilling this requirement and will be filing a "Medical Certification for Disability Exceptions" completed and signed by a doctor with my application. (Form N-648)

      YES NO   If you circled NO, you are not eligible now.

Worksheet courtesy of USCIS.

If you now believe that you are eligible for naturalization, you can call the USCIS Forms Line (1-800-870-3676) to request an application (Form N-400) or download the N-400 from the USCIS Web site. A final decision regarding your naturalization as a citizen will be made after you submit an application, take a citizenship test, and are interviewed.

If you have questions regarding your eligibility, you should read "A Guide to Naturalization." You may also want to get advice from an immigrant assistance organization or immigration attorney.

Special Consideration for Military Personnel

If you are serving or have served in one of the branches of the U.S. Armed Forces—Army, Navy, Marine Corps, Air Force, Coast Guard, Certain Reserve components of the National Guard, Selected Reserve, or the Ready Reserve—you may be eligible to apply for citizenship under the special provisions of the Immigration and Nationality Act (INA). Special consideration will be given to military personnel who have served or are serving during "authorized periods of conflict" including the post-September 11, 2001, period and the War on Terrorism. To learn more, you should contact your military point-of-contact or a local USCIS office.

Inquire through your chain of command to locate the office that can guide you through your application. After your Request for Certification of Military or Naval Service (Form N-426) has been certified, it will be sent together with your N-400 and G325B to the service center:

> Nebraska Service Center
> PO Box 87426
> Lincoln, NE 68501-7426

The N-400 is the application for naturalization, and the G325B is your biographical information. You can obtain these forms from the USCIS Web site (http://uscis.gov), or you can telephone 1-800-870-3676 to request the handbook called "Guide to Naturalization" and the "Military Packet" of forms.

After the service center has reviewed your application and carried out the required security check, your information will be sent to the district office closest to where you live. That district office will set up a date and time for your interview and for your civics test and English evaluation.

The USCIS also awards posthumous citizenship on active-duty military personnel. This special consideration is for men and women who have died while serving in the U.S. Armed Forces. Family members of the deceased military personnel may also be eligible for special consideration. You should contact your military point-of-contact or the nearest USCIS office for further information.

What Are the Steps on the Road to Citizenship?

You have already taken the first step: You used the Eligibility Worksheet to learn whether you are eligible to apply for naturalization. After you know that you are eligible, you can begin the application process. The Application for Naturalization (Form N-400) and all other forms are available from your local USCIS office or online at the USCIS Web site, http://uscis.gov. Military personnel should get Form M-599, which is special information for people who are serving or have served in the U.S. Armed Forces.

These are the remaining steps to take on the road to citizenship:

- Fill out Form N-400 and file it with your local USCIS district office.
- As of April, 2004, the application fee that must accompany Form N-400 is $320.
- As of April, 2004, the fee for fingerprinting is $70. Do not submit the fingerprinting fee with your Application for Naturalization. The USCIS will arrange an appointment for your fingerprinting and inform you where and when to pay the fee.
- The USCIS requires applicants for citizenship to show that they have the skills to read, write, understand, and speak basic English. Be prepared to take a written and oral test to demonstrate what you know about English.
- The USCIS requires applicants for citizenship to show an understanding of American civics. Be prepared to be tested on American history and government.
- The USCIS requires applicants for citizenship to answer questions in an oral interview. Be prepared for questions about your Application for Naturalization (Form N-400), America and its history and government, or about your personal life.
- You must be of good moral character, adhere to the principles of the U.S. Constitution, and have a favorable disposition toward the United States.
- The USCIS requires applicants for citizenship to take an oath of allegiance to the United States. This will occur at the citizenship swearing-in ceremony at the end of the naturalization process. Then you will have all the rights, responsibilities, and benefits of all other American citizens.

How Do I Prepare for the Citizenship Test?

You are preparing for the citizenship test now. By using this book, you will find information and practice that will get you ready for testing on a variety of subjects that you will find in the USCIS citizenship test.

The USCIS test is designed for people who are not native speakers of English. But the test questions assume that the people being tested have a basic knowledge of English. As you prepare for the test, you should have two goals: 1) to improve your English and 2) to learn about the history and government of the United States. This book will guide you in both.

There will not be a lot of emphasis on English grammar and structure. Instead, you will find useful "tips" that will help you to correct misunderstandings about the language and to improve your general skill level. The USCIS citizenship test is not a test of specific grammatical concepts in English. It is a test to determine whether or not you have the basic skills to communicate. Therefore, this book will give you experience and practice that will help you to develop your communication skills.

The greater emphasis in this book will be on history and government and how these topics are covered in the USCIS citizenship test. You will find explanations about and abundant practice with the history of the United States. You will find answers to questions like these:

- How did the United States begin?
- Who are the important historical figures?
- What are the important historical events?
- How is American freedom and democracy protected?
- How does the American Constitution work?
- What are my rights and responsibilities as a citizen?

And you will find answers to questions about government like these:

- What is the Declaration of Independence?
- What are the parts of the Constitution?
- What is the job of the Executive Branch of government?
- What is the job of the Legislative Branch of government?
- What is the job of the Judicial Branch of government?
- How does state government work?

Speaking, Understanding, Reading, and Writing English

To be a good citizen of the United States, you need to know English. It is the language used by most people in the United States. Although there is no "official language" of the country, a basic knowledge of English is required to become a citizen. That is the reason for the oral interview and for parts of the written test: to determine whether or not you can speak and understand English and whether or not you can read and write adequately in English.

A good citizen reads newspapers and magazines to know what is going on in the country. A good citizen listens to radio broadcasts and watches television to get the latest news. A good citizen has to be informed. And knowing basic English is the key to the information that will make you a good citizen and a well-informed voter.

If you were not born a native English speaker, you may believe that your English is poor. Do not let that worry you. **To become an American citizen, you do not have to speak and write perfect English.** Many Americans speak using incorrect grammar. Many have foreign accents. That's actually a part of America, for this country is a *nation of immigrants*. Your goal for yourself while using this book should be to improve your level of English and to go to the USCIS citizenship test prepared to speak and write as best you can.

A Special Word About the Personal Interview

The personal interview will be between you and an USCIS officer. The officer will look through your Application for Naturalization (Form N-400) to see that everything is in order. Then the USCIS officer will begin questioning you to find out whether you are ready to become a citizen. The officer wants to know whether you have knowledge of American history and government. Do you know who the President is? Do you know what the American flag looks like? Can you understand English when spoken to? Can you write simple sentences?

In rare cases, applicants are asked complicated questions or questions that require knowing a lengthy answer, such as, "Can you name the original 13 colonies?" But remember, that's rare. More often, the USCIS officer will ask about things that most ordinary Americans know about: "Who is the Vice President of the United States?" "How many stars are in the flag?" "What branch of government makes the laws?" "Why do we celebrate the Fourth of July?"

You will probably also hear questions that refer to your personal life: "Are you married?" "How long have you been divorced?" "Have you ever been arrested?" "What kind of work do you do?" "How many children do you have?"

The USCIS officer will ask you to write some sentences. The officer will say the sentences, and you will write them. For example:

> **Officer:** "I have two children, a boy and a girl."
> **You write:** *I have two children, a boy and a girl.*
> **Officer:** "I always vote in every election."
> **You write:** *I always vote in every election.*
> **Officer:** "The President must be born in the U.S."
> **You write:** *The President must be born in the U.S.*
> **Officer:** "There are three branches of government."
> **You write:** *There are three branches of government.*

At some point in the interview, the officer may ask you to read a few lines from your Application for Naturalization (Form N-400). Or he or she may give you a sheet of paper with a few sentences on it. The officer will ask you to read what is on the paper. It will look something like this:

> *I have been living in the United States for ten years. I want to be a good citizen. A good citizen votes in elections. A good citizen is also a good neighbor. Speaking and writing English is a part of being an American.*

Remember that these are only examples of what your oral interview might be like. Each USCIS officer is an individual and will give his or her individual touch to the interview.

If you pass the oral interview, you will be notified at a later time about the date and place of the swearing-in ceremony. At the swearing-in ceremony, you will be asked to take this oath of allegiance to the United States of America:

> "I hereby declare, on oath, that I absolutely and entirely renounce and abjure all allegiance and fidelity to any foreign prince, potentate, state, or sovereignty of whom or which I have heretofore been a subject or citizen; that I will support and defend the Constitution and laws of the United States of America against all enemies, foreign and domestic; that I will bear true faith and allegiance to the same; that I will bear arms on behalf of the United States when required by the law; that I will perform noncombatant service in the Armed Forces of the United States when required by the law; that I will perform work of national importance under civilian direction when required by the law; and that I take this obligation freely without any mental reservation or purpose of evasion; so help me God."

In special cases, USCIS may allow the oath to be taken without the clause:

> ". . .that I will bear arms on behalf of the United States when required by law; that I will perform noncombatant service in the Armed Forces of the United States when required by law. . ."

Some Important Information about the Written and Oral Tests

Some applicants for naturalization will be exempt from the citizenship test requirements.

If on the date of filing an applicant is over 55 years of age and has been a permanent resident for 15 years or more, he or she will be exempt from the test to demonstrate the ability to read, write, speak, and understand basic English.

If on the date of filing an applicant is over 50 years of age and has been a permanent resident for 20 years or more, he or she will be exempt from the test to demonstrate the ability to read, write, speak, and understand basic English.

If on the date of filing an applicant has a mental or physical impairment that affects the applicant's ability to learn English, he or she will be exempt from the test to demonstrate the ability to read, write, speak, and understand basic English.

If on the date of filing an applicant is over 65 years of age and has been a permanent resident for 20 years or more, he or she will be given special consideration in satisfying the requirement of demonstrating a knowledge and understanding of American history and government.

If on the date of filing an applicant has a mental or physical impairment that affects the applicant's ability to learn American history and government, he or she will be given special consideration in satisfying the requirement of demonstrating a knowledge and understanding of American history and government.

Contact your local USCIS office to learn whether you qualify for one of these exemptions.

Types of Test Items

Part of preparing for the USCIS written citizenship test is having an understanding of the different kinds of test items. One part of testing will be reading. Another part of testing will check your ability to write. And the third part of testing will cover history and government. To achieve these three things (reading, writing, and civics), the citizenship test can consist of different kinds of test items.

In order to demonstrate the different kinds of test items, let us begin with a brief sample passage for reading:

> Christopher Columbus sailed from Spain in 1492. He was looking for a western route to Asia. After a long and dangerous journey across the Atlantic Ocean, he landed in the New World. Instead of Asia, he had discovered the Americas.

Let us use this passage to demonstrate the different kinds of test items. The answers to the questions will be found in the preceding passage.

Written or Oral Question-Answer Items

Questions	Answers
Who sailed from Spain in 1492?	Columbus
What was he looking for?	Asia
What was long and dangerous?	the journey
What did Columbus discover?	the Americas

Sentence Writing

Rewrite the sentence in the first blank. Write it in the second blank from memory.

He sailed from Spain in 1492.

<u>He sailed from Spain in 1492.</u>
<u>He sailed from Spain in 1492.</u>

Columbus landed in the New World.

<u>Columbus landed in the New World.</u>
<u>Columbus landed in the New World.</u>

Multiple Choice Questions

Circle the letter of the word or phrase that answers the question.

1. In what year did Columbus sail from Spain?

   a. 1066
   b. 1492
   c. 1776
   d. 1812

1. b is the correct answer.

2. What was Columbus looking for?

   a. the Atlantic Ocean
   b. Spain
   c. a western route to Asia
   d. the Americas

2. c is the correct answer.

3. What did Columbus discover?

   a. the New World
   b. Asia
   c. a western route to Asia
   d. a dangerous journey

3. a is the correct answer.

Multiple Choice Completion

Circle the letter of the word or phrase that best completes each sentence.

---

1. Columbus sailed from _____ in 1492.

    a. the Atlantic Ocean

    b. Spain

    c. Asia

    d. the Americas

---

1. b is the correct answer.

---

2. He _____ in the New World.

    a. journey

    b. route

    c. landed

    d. discovered

---

2. c is the correct answer.

---

3. _____ of Asia, he discovered the Americas.

    a. Instead

    b. Dangerous

    c. Across

    d. Looking for

---

3. a is the correct answer.

Completions

Fill in the blank with any appropriate word from the above passage.

1. _____ sailed from Spain. *(Columbus)*

2. Instead of Asia, he had _____ the Americas. *(discovered)*

3. After a long and _____ journey, he landed in the New World. *(dangerous)*

Substitutions

In the blank write the word from the above passage that can replace the underlined word.

1. Columbus <u>found</u> the Americas.   *discovered*

2. The <u>trip</u> across the Atlantic was long and dangerous.   *journey*

3. After a long journey, he <u>arrived</u> in the New World.   *landed*

When you understand what the test item is looking for, you are on the right track to answering the item correctly. In this book, you will have many opportunities to practice different types of question items. These different types of question items have an important purpose: They give you a way of looking at new information or a new idea *from different angles*. Consider how the same information in the above passage was examined differently by the different types of question items. For example:

Christopher Columbus sailed from Spain in 1492.

1. Who sailed from Spain in 1492?

2. Columbus sailed from _____ in 1492.

    a.   the Atlantic Ocean
    b.   Spain
    c.   Asia
    d.   the Americas

3. He sailed from Spain in 1492.

He sailed from Spain in 1492.

He sailed from Spain in 1492.

4. In what year did Columbus sail from Spain?

    a.   1066
    b.   1492
    c.   1776
    d.   1812

5. _____ sailed from Spain.   *(Columbus)*

The idea of looking at information *from different angles* can help you to learn the new information and, at the same time, make that information useful to you and easier to remember.

You are now about to begin your journey on the road to American citizenship. Learn all you can. Practice what you learn. Then at the end of this book take the three practice tests to determine whether you are ready for the USCIS citizenship test.

The Pre-Test

This pre-test will help you to learn how much you know about American history and government now. (American history and government are often called *civics*.) This pre-test should give you an idea of what topics you are strong in and what topics you need to review. Whether you do well or poorly on the pre-test, it is important to go through this book and learn and practice as much as you can. Your goal should be to improve on what you already know and to learn what you do not know.

There are 50 items in the pre-test. Some are multiple-choice questions; you will have to fill in the blank in others; and some items are direct questions that require you to write an answer. At the end of the pre-test, use the Answer Key at the back of the book to check your answers.

Part One

Circle the letter of the word or phrase that *completes the sentence*.

> Example: The American flag is red, white, and _____.
>
> **a.** green
> **b.** blue
> **c.** yellow
> **d.** pink

1. There are _____ stars on the American flag.

   a. 40
   b. 48
   c. 50
   d. 55

2. There are _____ stripes on the American flag.

   a. 13
   b. 14
   c. 20
   d. 50

3. There are _____ states in the United States.

   a. 13
   b. 14
   c. 20
   d. 50

4. During the Revolutionary War, we fought against _____.

   a. Spain
   b. Canada
   c. England
   d. France

5. America declared its independence on _____.

    a. July 4
    b. June 1
    c. November 7
    d. May 1

6. A change to the Constitution is called an _____.

    a. amendment
    b. reason
    c. article
    d. government

7. There are _____ branches of the American government.

    a. two
    b. three
    c. five
    d. six

8. The Legislative Branch is made up of the House of Representatives and the _____.

    a. Judicial Branch
    b. Capitol
    c. Presidency
    d. Senate

9. The _____ make(s) the laws of the land.

    a. Executive Branch
    b. President
    c. Congress
    d. states

10. The head of the Executive Branch is _____.

    a. the President
    b. the Senate
    c. the Judicial Branch
    d. Congress

11. _____ is not one of the original 13 colonies.

    a. New Jersey
    b. New York
    c. Virginia
    d. California

12. Martin Luther King, Jr., was _____.

    a. one of the Founding Fathers
    b. a civil rights leader
    c. a former vice president
    d. a senator from Pennsylvania

13. A president can serve for only _____ terms.

    a. two
    b. three
    c. four
    d. five

14. _____ decides whether a law is constitutional.

    a. The President
    b. The Supreme Court
    c. Congress
    d. Each state

15. The duty of Congress is to make the _____.

    a. veto
    b. government
    c. laws
    d. Constitution

16. The first 10 amendments to the Constitution are called _____.

    a. the Bill of Rights
    b. a constitutional convention
    c. the Articles of Confederation
    d. the Declaration of Independence

17. The introduction to the Constitution is called the _____.

    a. Articles
    b. Veto
    c. Bill of Rights
    d. Preamble

18. There are _____ senators in the Congress.

    a. 25
    b. 50
    c. 75
    d. 100

19. The minimum voting age in the United States is _____.

    a. 18
    b. 20
    c. 21
    d. 25

20. _____ helped the Pilgrims in colonial America.

    a. Congress
    b. Parliament
    c. The English king
    d. Native Americans

Part Two

In the blank provided, complete each sentence with an appropriate word or phrase.

> Example: The American flag is red, white and, __*blue*__ .

21. The _____ advises the president.

22. The Declaration of Independence was written in _____ .

23. A new president is inaugurated in the month of _____ .

24. The U.S. Capitol is where _____ meets.

25. The people's rights are guaranteed in the Constitution by the _____ .

26. The slaves were freed by President _____ .

27. There are _____ white stars on the American flag.

28. The chief executive of a state is called the _____ .

29. Our national anthem is called *The Star* _____ .

30. The main writer of the Declaration of Independence was _____ .

31. The first president was _____ .

32. Only the _____ has the power to declare war.

33. _____ and _____ are the newest states in the Union.

34. _____ is the capital city of the United States.

35. Congress is elected by the _____ .

Part Three

In the blank provided, write a brief answer to each question.

> Example: What are the colors of the American Flag?
>
> __*red, white, and blue*__

36. Who is the President of the United States now?

    _____

37. Who sailed to the New World aboard the *Mayflower*?

    _____

38. How many justices are there on the Supreme Court?

_____

39. How many years long is a president's term of office?

_____

40. What are the colors of the stripes of the American flag?

_____

41. Who becomes President if the President of the United States dies?

_____

42. What do the stars on the American flag mean?

_____

43. What is the date of Independence Day?

_____

44. Name a country that was an enemy in World War II.

_____

45. Who is the Vice President of the United States now?

_____

46. What does the Legislative Branch of government do?

_____

47. For how many years do we elect a senator?

_____

48. How many representatives are in the House of Representatives?

_____

49. What is the capital city of your state?

_____

50. Who is the governor of your state?

_____

Now go to the Answer Key at the back of the book and check your answers. Count the number you have correct. Then multiply that number by **2**. This will give you your percentage of accuracy.

number of correct answers $\times$ 2 = % correct

Remember your percentage of accuracy. Compare it to the scores you get on the three Practice Tests after you finish reviewing the subject areas within this book.

The New World

How Did America Begin?

North and South America were unknown to the rest of the world until the end of the fifteenth century. When Europeans sailed from Europe to Asia, they first had to sail around Africa. This made the journey very long and very dangerous. People began to wonder whether there was a shorter route to Asia. A few believed that sailing west from Europe would be the shortest route. When Columbus attempted this, instead of Asia he found a new land—the Americas.

Not everyone agrees about who discovered the New World first. Some say it was a Scandinavian, Leif Erickson, around 1000 A.D. Many believe it was Christopher Columbus. He was sent in 1492 by the Spanish king and queen to find a western route to Asia. Instead, he found islands that today we call the West Indies.

Because some believed he had landed in India, the people who lived on these islands were called Indians. Today, we often use the word *Indians* to describe the native residents of the New World. But a more proper term is *Native Americans.*

If Columbus or Erickson discovered the New World, why is it called *America*? The answer to that question is simple: An Italian sailor, Amerigo Vespucci, traveled to the New World after Columbus. His name became connected with the new land, and today we call the regions of the western hemisphere North America, Central America, and South America.

A few decades after Columbus' discovery, people began traveling to America to find their fortune there or just to begin a new life. The English Pilgrims landed at Plymouth, Massachusetts, in 1620 and started a settlement there. They were looking for religious freedom. They struggled through cold winters and hot summers, but with the help of Native Americans, their community survived and began to grow.

They celebrated their good harvest with a feast of thanksgiving. That tradition continues today. All Americans celebrate Thanksgiving on the fourth Thursday of November.

Important Words

Learn the meaning of these new words. Say a sentence using each new word.

unknown = no one knows about this	"The answer is unknown to me."
century = 100 years	"My family has lived here for a century."
sail = travel by ship	"Columbus sailed west."
journey = a trip	"The journey from Spain was long."
dangerous = unsafe and difficult	"Life was dangerous in the new land."
attempt = try	"They attempted to travel across the Atlantic."
instead of = in place of something	"I bought a truck instead of a car."
discover = find	"Who discovered America?"
route = road, way	"I travel this route to work."
island = land surrounded by water	"Puerto Rico is an island."
resident = a person who lives somewhere	"I am a resident of the United States."
western hemisphere = continents of the New World	"Canada is in the western hemisphere."
decade = 10 years	"I lived in Mexico two decades ago."
community = town, neighborhood	"My community is on the east side of the city."

harvest = things grown on farms (noun); to pick the things grown on farms (verb)

survive = live through

north, south, east, and west = the four points on a compass

"Farmers take the corn harvest in the fall." or "Farmers harvest the corn in the fall."

"My son survived a terrible accident."

"Which direction should we go? North, south, east, or west?"

Write Your New Words

In the blank of the first sentence, write the missing word. In the second sentence, write the same word from memory.

1. North America was unknown to the world.

    North America was _____ to the world.

    North America was _____ to the world.

2. Europeans sailed around Africa to Asia.

    Europeans _____ around Africa to Asia.

    Europeans _____ around Africa to Asia.

3. Some believed it was the shortest route.

    Some believed it was the shortest _____.

    Some believed it was the shortest _____.

4. Columbus found a new land instead of Asia.

    Columbus found a new land _____ of Asia.

    Columbus found a new land _____ of Asia.

5. Today, we call these regions the western hemisphere.

    Today, we call these regions the western _____.

    Today, we call these regions the western _____.

6. Did Columbus discover America?

    Did Columbus _____ America?

    Did Columbus _____ America?

7. We are residents of California.

    We are _____ of California.

    We are _____ of California.

8. I lived here for more than a decade.

    I lived here for more than a _____.

    I lived here for more than a _____.

9. The harvest was good this year.

The _____ was good this year.

The _____ was good this year.

10. They were looking for religious freedom.

They were looking for _____ freedom.

They were looking for _____ freedom.

Important Questions and Answers

1. What was unknown to the world in the fifteenth century? (North and South America)

2. Around what continent did Europeans sail to Asia? (Africa)

3. What kind of route to Asia did people want? (a shorter route)

4. What did Columbus discover when he sailed west? (a new land, the New World)

5. What is a better term for *Indians*? (Native Americans)

6. Why is the New World called *America*? (It is named for Amerigo Vespucci, a sailor.)

7. Why did people begin traveling to the New World? (to begin a new life, to find their fortune)

8. When did Columbus sail to the New World? (in 1492, fourteen ninety-two)

9. In what hemisphere is America located? (western)

10. Who landed at Plymouth, Massachusetts, in 1620? (Pilgrims)

11. What were the Pilgrims looking for in the New World? (religious freedom)

12. What holiday celebrates a good harvest? (Thanksgiving)

Is It TRUE or FALSE?

Say TRUE if the sentence is correct. Say FALSE if it is incorrect.

1. The shortest route to Asia was around South America.

2. The New World was unknown until the fifteenth century.

3. The journey to America was easy and pleasant.

4. Some believed that sailing west was the shortest route to Africa.

5. No one knows who discovered America first.

6. The Spanish king and queen sent Columbus to find a western route to Asia.

7. Instead of Asia, Columbus found the West Indies.

8. Columbus came to India in 1492.

9. North America is in the western hemisphere.

10. Native Americans helped the Pilgrims in many ways.

11. Native Americans were once called *Pilgrims*.

12. The Pilgrims found religious freedom in the new land.

13. Native Americans came to Plymouth, Massachusetts, in 1620.

14. Americans celebrate Thanksgiving in July.

Answers

1. False	8. False
2. True	9. True
3. False	10. True
4. False	11. False
5. True	12. True
6. True	13. False
7. True	14. False

Let's Look at Some Important Sentences

Circle the letter of the word or phrase that completes the sentence.

1. The New World was unknown until the fifteenth _____.

   a. community
   b. century
   c. journey
   d. attempt

2. The journey to America was _____.

   a. shortest
   b. around Africa
   c. dangerous
   d. east

3. The people in the West Indies were called _____.

   a. Indians
   b. Pilgrims
   c. sailors
   d. Scandinavians

4. Native Americans were the residents of the _____.

    a. Africa

    b. Spain

    c. Asia

    d. New World

5. The word _____ comes from a sailor's name.

    a. America

    b. Pilgrim

    c. Indian

    d. hemisphere

6. _____ is in the western hemisphere.

    a. Central America

    b. Spain

    c. Asia

    d. Europe

7. Columbus traveled to _____ in 1492.

    a. the hemisphere

    b. Spain

    c. the New World

    d. Plymouth

8. Pilgrims came from _____ and settled in Massachusetts.

    a. England

    b. Spain

    c. Central America

    d. the community

9. The Pilgrims' settlement was called _____.

    a. Plymouth

    b. West Indies

    c. North America

    d. Thanksgiving

10. _____ helped the Pilgrims survive the cold winters.

    a. English

    b. Amerigo Vespucci

    c. the king and queen

    d. Native Americans

11. Thanksgiving is a celebration of a good _____.

    a. journey

    b. route

    c. harvest

    d. decade

Answers

1. b
2. c
3. a
4. d
5. a
6. a

7. c
8. a
9. a
10. d
11. c

Let's Write the New Words

In the blank, write the word or phrase that completes the sentence. Look at the words in parentheses. They will help you.

1. Their ship slowly _____ into the west. (traveled by ship)

2. The New World was _____ for many centuries. (no one knows about this)

3. The _____ across the ocean took many weeks. (a trip)

4. It was _____ to sail to America in the fifteenth century. (unsafe and difficult)

5. He discovered a new land _____ Asia. (in place of something)

6. Many believe that Leif Erickson _____ America. (found)

7. I am now a _____ of this city. (a person living here)

8. She worked in this factory for more than a _____. (10 years)

9. Hawaii is a state made up of _____. (lands surrounded by water)

10. The Pilgrims had a religious _____. (town, neighborhood)

11. Native Americans helped them _____ the bad weather. (live through)

12. New York is in the north, and Miami is in the _____. (a point on the compass)

Answers

1. sailed
2. unknown
3. journey
4. dangerous
5. instead of
6. discovered

7. resident
8. decade
9. islands
10. community
11. survive
12. south

Life in Colonial America

Several European nations established colonies in North America. The Spanish were the first to come here, but soon after, England, the Netherlands, and France also had colonies here. Most of the colonies were located near the Atlantic coast. The first British colony in America was founded at Jamestown, Virginia, in 1607.

The Dutch founded New York. At that time it was called New Amsterdam, but when it became an English colony, it was renamed to New York.

The American colonists were dependent upon England for manufactured goods, and they sent back to Europe raw materials plus furs, tobacco, and cotton. The relationship worked well for a long time.

Most of the colonists were immigrants from Europe. Many slaves also had been brought from Africa. By 1770 there were about 2 million people in Great Britain's 13 colonies. Nearly 20 percent of them were African slaves.

The original 13 colonies were (from north to south):

Rhode Island	Pennsylvania
Connecticut	Maryland
New Hampshire	Virginia
Massachusetts	North Carolina
New York	South Carolina
New Jersey	Georgia
Delaware	

During the colonial period, Americans considered themselves Englishmen and subjects of the king. But the English parliament decided to impose special taxes on the colonists. This caused the relationship between America and England to change. Americans began to protest the new taxes. Parliament thought the Americans were being disobedient. And as the relationship between the two sides grew worse, violence began to break out.

One of the taxes the Americans hated was the tax on tea. One day when a cargo of English tea arrived in Boston harbor, a group of men boarded the ship and threw the tea into the harbor as a protest. This was called *the Boston Tea Party*.

Important Words

Learn the meaning of these new words. Say a sentence using each new word.

located = situated, found	"The factory is located in the city."
dependent upon = relying on	"Children are dependent upon their parents."
manufactured goods = things made in a factory	"Our company makes many kinds of manufactured goods."
raw materials = things used to make a new product	"Wood and steel are some of the raw materials we use."
relationship = connection or bond with someone	"The relationship between England and the colonies was growing weak."
found = set up, create	"The Dutch founded New Amsterdam."
rename = give a new name	"They renamed our school John F. Kennedy High School."
colonist = person sent to live in a new place	"The Pilgrims were early colonists of Massachusetts."
immigrant = newcomer from another country	"I came to America as an immigrant."
slave = servant in bondage	"There were slaves in America for many years."
original = the first one, genuine	"This is an original painting by Picasso."
parliament = legislature of England	"Parliament governed the colonies."

tax = money owed the government	"I pay my taxes every year."
protest = complain	"The colonists protested the unfair taxes."
violence = fury, dangerous and unlawful force	"Violence broke out in the streets."
harbor = port, anchorage	"There were two ships in the harbor."
cargo = goods on a ship	"The men threw the cargo into the harbor."

Write Your New Words

In the blank of the first sentence, write the missing word. In the second sentence, write the same word from memory.

1. The English established a settlement in Virginia.

   The English _____ a settlement in Virginia.
   The English _____ a settlement in Virginia.

2. The colonies were located on the coast.

   The colonies were _____ on the coast.
   The colonies were _____ on the coast.

3. New Amsterdam was renamed New York.

   New Amsterdam was _____ New York.
   New Amsterdam was _____ New York.

4. The first British colony was Jamestown.

   The first _____ colony was Jamestown.
   The first _____ colony was Jamestown.

5. They founded Plymouth colony.

   They _____ Plymouth colony.
   They _____ Plymouth colony.

6. Many colonists came to America.

   Many _____ came to America.
   Many _____ came to America.

7. The Americans were dependent upon England for many things.

   The Americans were _____ upon England for many things.
   The Americans were _____ upon England for many things.

8. The colonies sent back raw materials to Europe.

   The colonies sent back raw _____ to Europe.
   The colonies sent back raw _____ to Europe.

9. The Parliament imposed a tax.

   The _____ imposed a tax.

   The _____ imposed a tax.

10. I pay my taxes every year.

    I pay my _____ every year.

    I pay my _____ every year.

11. Twenty percent of the people were slaves.

    Twenty percent of the people were _____.

    Twenty percent of the people were _____.

12. There were 13 original English colonies.

    There were 13 _____ English colonies.

    There were 13 _____ English colonies.

13. Soon violence began to break out.

    Soon _____ began to break out.

    Soon _____ began to break out.

Important Questions and Answers

1. What nations established colonies in North America? (European nations)

2. What nation came first to North America? (Spain)

3. In what year did the English found Jamestown? (1607)

4. What was New York's original name? (New Amsterdam)

5. What did the colonists receive from England? (manufactured goods)

6. What did the colonists send to England? (raw materials, furs, tobacco, cotton)

7. From what continent did the American colonists come? (Europe)

8. What percent of the colonial population were African slaves? (twenty percent)

9. What did Parliament impose on tea? (a tax)

10. What happened when the relationship between England and the colonies grew worse? (violence broke out)

11. What was the Boston Tea Party? (a protest)

12. Where did the men throw the tea at the Boston Tea Party? (into the harbor)

Is It TRUE or FALSE?

Say TRUE if the sentence is correct. Say FALSE if it is incorrect.

1. African nations established colonies in North America.

2. The Spanish were the last to come to the New World.

3. France's first colony was called Jamestown.

4. New Amsterdam was renamed New York.

5. Most of the colonists in America were immigrants from Europe.

6. The American colonies depended upon France.

7. The colonies sent manufactured goods to England.

8. Great Britain had 13 colonies in North America.

9. The Americans imposed a tax on Parliament.

10. England thought the colonists were disobedient.

11. The colonists liked the tax on tea.

12. The relationship between the colonists and England grew worse.

13. Men boarded a ship in Boston harbor and threw the tea cargo into the water.

Answers

1. False
2. False
3. False
4. True
5. True
6. False
7. False

8. True
9. False
10. True
11. False
12. True
13. True

Let's Look at Some Important Sentences

Circle the letter of the word that completes the sentence.

1. Several nations _____ colonies in the New World.

   a. locate
   b. established
   c. brought
   d. sent back

2. Most colonies were located near the Atlantic _____.

    a. coast

    b. continent

    c. world

    d. harbor

3. A British colony called Jamestown was _____ in 1607.

    a. locate

    b. renamed

    c. dependent

    d. founded

4. New York was part of an English _____.

    a. parliament

    b. colony

    c. city

    d. protest

5. America _____ upon England for manufactured goods.

    a. helped

    b. sent

    c. depended

    d. buy

6. The colonies sent _____ to England.

    a. tobacco

    b. slaves

    c. immigrants

    d. tea

7. Nearly 20 percent of the population were _____.

    a. slaves

    b. immigrants

    c. Englishmen

    d. French

8. The English _____ imposed a tax on tea.

    a. Parliament

    b. immigrants

    c. slaves

    d. violence

9. The _____ between England and America began to change.

    a. protest

    b. colonial period

    c. taxes

    d. relationship

10. The English thought the colonists were _____.

    a. immigrants

    b. dependent

    c. disobedient

    d. subjects of the king

11. Soon _____ broke out in several towns.

    a. cargo

    b. violence

    c. raw materials

    d. taxes

12. The Boston Tea Party was a _____ against the tax on tea.

    a. party

    b. cargo

    c. celebration

    d. protest

Answers

1. b	**7.** a
2. a	**8.** a
3. d	**9.** d
4. b	**10.** c
5. c	**11.** b
6. a	**12.** d

Let's Write the Answers

In the blank, write the word or phrase that completes the sentence. Look at the words in parentheses. They will help you.

1. America received _____ from England. (things made in a factory)

2. The colonists were _____ England for many things. (relying on)

3. For a long time the _____ between England and America was good. (connection or bond with someone)

4. Jamestown was _____ near the Atlantic coast. (situated, found)

5. The Netherlands _____ New Amsterdam. (set up, created)

6. Many who lived in the colonies were _____. (servants in bondage)

7. _____ began to impose new taxes. (legislature of England)

8. The _____ hated the tax on tea. (persons sent to live in a new place)

9. Soon the colonies _____ the new taxes. (complained about)

10. _____ broke out in many places. (fury, dangerous and unlawful force)

11. The men threw the _____ into the harbor. (goods on a ship)

12. England imposed a heavy _____ on tea. (money owed the government)

13. *The Boston Tea Party* happened in Boston _____. (port, anchorage)

Answers

1. manufactured goods
2. dependent upon
3. relationship
4. located
5. founded
6. slaves
7. Parliament
8. colonists
9. protested
10. Violence
11. cargo
12. tax
13. Harbor

Some Tips About English

- English verbs in the present tense are easy. Only the third person singular (he, she, and it) has a different ending (-s). The only exception is the verb *to be*. Some examples follow:

	to be	*to come*	*to protest*	*to see*
I	am	come	protest	see
you	are	come	protest	see
he, she, it	is	comes	protests	sees
we	are	come	protest	see
they	are	come	protest	see

- Careful! There is a difference between *to find* and *to found*. *Find* means *to discover* or *to locate*:

  I *find* some money under the table.

  Who *found* my wallet?

  To found looks like the past tense of *to find*. But it is a different verb. *Found* means *to set up, establish* or *create*:

  The Pilgrims *founded* a settlement in Massachusetts.

  America was *founded* on principles of democracy.

  Notice that *find* is an irregular verb, and *found* is a regular verb. Look at them in the present and past tenses:

	Find	*Found*
Present Tense	I find, he finds	I found, he founds
Past Tense	I found, he found	I founded, he founded

- Some important words in this chapter are *irregular verbs*. Their past tense form does not follow the regular pattern. Regular verbs in the past tense end in *–ed*. Irregular verbs make other kinds of changes to form the past tense:

	Regular Verbs	*to be*	*to begin*
Present Tense	I help, he helps	I am, you are	I begin, he begins
		he is	
Past Tense	I helped, he helped	I was, you were	I began, he began
		he was	
	to send	*to grow*	*to know*
Present Tense	I send, he sends	I grow, he grows	I know, he knows
Past Tense	I sent, he sent	I grew, he grew	I knew, he knew
	to break	*to bring*	*to think*
Present Tense	I break, he breaks	I bring, he brings	I think, he thinks
Past Tense	I broke, he broke	I brought, he brought	I thought, he thought

The Declaration of Independence

1776 was a year of changes for the American colonies. On June 7, the Continental Congress met in Philadelphia and called for a resolution to declare independence from England. The Congress selected Thomas Jefferson, John Adams, Benjamin Franklin, Roger Sherman, and Robert Livingston to write the resolution. This committee of men worked on a draft of the Declaration of Independence for three weeks. Then, on June 28, the document was read in Congress.

There were debates about the language in the document and some revisions were made. Congress had not yet adopted the declaration when the British navy and army arrived in New York. Finally, on July 4, 1776, Congress adopted the Declaration of Independence. Delegates from the 13 colonies began to sign the document in August.

The first few lines of the second paragraph explain why Americans wished to be independent from England:

> We hold these truths to be self-evident, that all men are created equal, that they are endowed by their Creator with certain unalienable rights, that among these are life, liberty, and the pursuit of happiness. That to secure these rights, governments are instituted among men, deriving their just powers from the consent of the governed, that whenever any form of government becomes destructive of these ends, it is the right of the people to alter or to abolish it. . .

The declaration also says that the English king and his parliament made many mistakes in the colonies:

- They kept an army in the colonies in times of peace.
- They stopped American trade with the rest of the world.
- They imposed taxes without American agreement.
- They took away trial by jury.
- They abolished American laws.

The declaration ends with a statement by the delegates that they promised to wager everything in the struggle for independence:

> . . .we mutually pledge to each other our lives, our fortunes, and our sacred honor.

The English crown could not allow the colonists to become independent. England would force the colonies to obey. But the Americans would not obey, and war broke out.

Important Words

Learn the meaning of these new words. Say a sentence using each new word.

resolution = a statement, document	"They called for a new resolution."
declare = announce	"The colonies declared their independence."
select = choose, pick out	"The delegates selected the members of the committee."
committee = an official group of people	"There are five people on the committee."
draft = a written plan	"The draft is the first copy of the resolution."
debate = argument, to argue	"They debated the statements in the document."
revision = a change	"Jefferson wanted several revisions."
adopt = accept	"Congress adopted the declaration in 1776."

sign = write your name on a document	"Each delegate signed the declaration."
explain = tell why	"He explained why he did it."
equal = the same, even	"All men are created equal."
mistake = error, something done wrong	"Parliament made many mistakes."
trial = a case in court	"Her trial began in July."
jury = citizens who decide a court case	"She became a member of the jury."
abolish = end, destroy	"England abolished all trade with the colonies."
wager = make a bet	"I wagered five dollars in the card game."
allow = let, give permission	"Mother allowed him to stay at home."
force = make, compel	"Parliament forced them to pay taxes."
obey = listen to, comply with, yield	"The colonists did not obey the king."

Write Your New Words

In the blank of the first sentence, write the missing word. In the second sentence, write the word from memory.

1. 1776 was a year of great changes.

1776 was a year of great _____.

1776 was a year of great _____.

2. They called for a resolution to declare independence.

They called for a _____ to declare independence.

They called for a _____ to declare independence.

3. The committee consisted of five men.

The _____ consisted of five men.

The _____ consisted of five men.

4. They wrote a draft for the Declaration of Independence.

They wrote a draft for the _____ of Independence.

They wrote a draft for the _____ of Independence.

5. Congress debated the language in the document.

Congress _____ the language in the document.

Congress _____ the language in the document.

6. The declaration was adopted on July fourth.

The declaration was _____ on July fourth.

The declaration was _____ on July fourth.

7. In late summer, they began to sign the declaration.

   In late summer, they began to _____ the declaration.

   In late summer, they began to _____ the declaration.

8. The first lines explain why the colonies wanted independence.

   The first lines _____ why the colonies wanted independence.

   The first lines _____ why the colonies wanted independence.

9. The English crown made many mistakes.

   The English crown made many _____.

   The English crown made many _____.

10. The army stayed there in times of peace.

    The army stayed there in times of _____.

    The army stayed there in times of _____.

11. They imposed taxes without American agreement.

    They imposed _____ without American agreement.

    They imposed _____ without American agreement.

12. They wagered everything in the struggle for freedom.

    They wagered everything in the _____ for freedom.

    They wagered everything in the _____ for freedom.

13. England wanted to force the colonies to obey.

    England wanted to _____ the colonies to _____.

    England wanted to _____ the colonies to _____.

Important Questions and Answers

1. In what year were there great changes in the American colonies? (1776)

2. Who called for a resolution to declare independence? (Continental Congress)

3. Who wrote the draft for the Declaration of Independence? (Jefferson and a committee)

4. Who arrived in New York before Congress adopted the declaration? (British navy and army)

5. On what date did Congress adopt the Declaration of Independence? (July 4)

6. Who signed the declaration? (delegates from the colonies)

7. What is written in the second paragraph of the declaration? (why the colonies want independence)

8. Who is created equal? (all men)

9. Who kept an army in America in times of peace? (English Parliament, the king)

10. What did the delegates promise at the end of the declaration? (They will wager everything for freedom.)

Is It TRUE or FALSE?

Say TRUE if the sentence is correct. Say FALSE if it is incorrect.

1. 1776 was a year of changes for France.

2. The Continental Congress met in Boston.

3. Congress wanted a resolution to declare independence from England.

4. Thomas Jefferson and a committee wrote the Declaration of Independence.

5. Some members of Congress did not like the language of the declaration.

6. England had sent an army and a navy to Virginia.

7. Delegates from five colonies signed the declaration.

8. The declaration says that all men are created equal.

9. The king and parliament made no mistakes in America.

10. France stopped American trade with the rest of the world.

11. Congress promised to do everything in the struggle for freedom.

12. England allowed the colonies to become independent.

13. The colonies did not obey England, and war broke out.

Answers

1. False	8. True
2. False	9. False
3. True	10. False
4. True	11. True
5. True	12. False
6. False	13. True
7. False	

Let's Look at Some Important Sentences

Circle the letter of the word or phrase that completes the sentence.

1. 1776 was a year of changes for the American _____.

    a. delegates

    b. colonies

    c. trade

    d. war

2. _____ met in Philadelphia and called for a declaration.

    a. Congress

    b. The navy

    c. Parliament

    d. The army

3. A _____ worked on a draft of the Declaration of Independence.

    a. Congress

    b. colonist

    c. committee

    d. jury

4. There were _____ about the language of the resolution.

    a. delegates

    b. revisions

    c. drafts

    d. debates

5. On July, 4, 1776 Congress _____ the Declaration of Independence.

    a. adopted

    b. revision

    c. traded

    d. declared

6. The delegates _____ the declaration in August.

    a. allowed

    b. trial

    c. signed

    d. called

7. One paragraph _____ why they wanted independence.

    a. explained

    b. found

    c. wished

    d. wrote

8. The writers of the declaration believed that all men were created _____.

    a. freedom
    b. for the colonies
    c. independent
    d. equal

9. England had an army in the colonies in times of _____.

    a. peace
    b. the trial
    c. law
    d. a protest

10. England tried to _____ America's trade with other nations.

    a. struggle
    b. stop
    c. send
    d. adopt

11. Parliament abolished American _____.

    a. protest
    b. independence
    c. laws
    d. delegates to Congress

12. When the colonists did not _____, _____ broke out.

    a. allow, laws
    b. obey, war
    c. create, struggle
    d. trade, freedom

Answers

1. b	**7.** a
2. a	**8.** d
3. c	**9.** a
4. d	**10.** b
5. a	**11.** c
6. c	**12.** b

Let's Write the New Words

In the blank, write the word or phrase that completes the sentence. Look at the words in parentheses. They will help you.

1. Thomas Jefferson was _____ for the committee. (chosen, picked out)

2. They did not adopt the first _____ of the document. (the written plan)

3. Congress called for a _____ for independence. (a statement, document)

4. The delegates _____ the language of the document. (argued about)

5. Independence was _____ on July 4. (announced)

6. Congress _____ the declaration in 1776. (accepted)

7. The second paragraph _____ the mistakes England made. (tells why)

8. Benjamin Franklin was a member of the _____. (an official group of people)

9. The Americans did not _____ the king. (listen to, comply with, yield to)

10. They _____ the colonists to pay taxes. (made, compelled)

11. The delegates _____ everything they had. (made a bet)

12. I believe in _____ by jury. (a case in court)

13. The declaration says that all men are created _____. (the same, even)

14. Parliament _____ the American laws. (ended, destroyed)

15. England could not _____ the colonies to be independent. (let, give permission)

Answers

1. selected

2. draft

3. resolution

4. debated

5. declared

6. adopted

7. explains

8. committee

9. obey

10. forced

11. wagered

12. trial

13. equal

14. abolished

15. allow

The War for Independence

The *Revolutionary War* lasted for many years. Most of the fighting finally ended in 1781 with the defeat of British forces at Yorktown. But the Revolutionary War did not officially end until April of 1783 with the signing of a treaty in Paris.

The commander-in-chief of the Continental Army was General George Washington. He was a Virginia landowner and had a plantation called Mount Vernon. The plantation was located on the banks of the Potomac River. Because Washington had military experience in the French and Indian War, Congress chose him to lead the army.

But the war against England was not easy. The British army was well trained and well equipped. Much of the American army was made up of volunteers called minutemen. The soldiers often went without enough food and lacked proper clothing and equipment. In the winter of 1777–1778 Washington and his men were camped at Valley Forge. The cold and lack of food nearly destroyed the army. But they survived until spring and began to harass the British troops.

Washington knew he could not destroy the British army with a single attack. Instead, he would fall back when necessary and then strike at the enemy unexpectedly. This tactic slowly wore down the British. Finally, in 1781 there was an important battle at Yorktown. Washington's Continental Army had General Cornwallis and his British troops surrounded. Cornwallis had no choice but to surrender. Although there were a few small battles after the surrender, Cornwallis' defeat was the end of the Revolutionary War.

Important Words

Learn the meaning of these new words. Say a sentence using each new word.

fighting = battle, making war	"The fighting continued for 10 hours."
defeat = beat, conquer	"The enemy was defeated in 1781."
treaty = peace document	"The delegates signed the treaty in Paris."
landowner = a person who has land	"Washington was a rich landowner."
plantation = large farm	"He grew tobacco on his plantation."
banks = shore, area next to a river	"The house was on the banks of a river."
military = referring to an army or soldiers	"Who has enough military experience?"
volunteer = a soldier serving willingly	"The minutemen were volunteers."
trained = prepared, taught skills	"The British soldiers were trained better."
equipped = having equipment	"His troops were well equipped."
camp = live in tents	"The army camped at Valley Forge."
harass = torment, annoy	"The Americans began to harass the enemy."
attack = assault, fall upon	"The attack must be a surprise."
strike at = hit hard	"They struck at the enemy at night."
unexpectedly = as a surprise	"The attack came unexpectedly."
surrounded = in a ring, encircled	"Cornwallis was finally surrounded."
surrender = give up, yield	"The general did not want to surrender."

Write Your New Words

In the blank of the first sentence, write the missing word. In the second sentence, write the same word from memory.

1. The fighting did not end until 1781.

The _____ did not end until 1781.

The _____ did not end until 1781.

2. The Americans defeated them at Yorktown.

The Americans _____ them at Yorktown.

The Americans _____ them at Yorktown.

3. A treaty was signed in Paris.

A _____ was signed in Paris.

A _____ was signed in Paris.

4. Washington was a rich landowner.

Washington was a rich _____.

Washington was a rich _____.

5. His plantation was called Mount Vernon.

His _____ was called Mount Vernon.

His _____ was called Mount Vernon.

6. Washington, D.C. is located on the banks of the Potomac.

Washington, D.C. is located on the _____ of the Potomac.

Washington, D.C. is located on the _____ of the Potomac.

7. The general had a lot of military experience.

The general had a lot of _____ experience.

The general had a lot of _____ experience.

8. Some volunteers were called minutemen.

Some _____ were called minutemen.

Some _____ were called minutemen.

9. The army was poorly trained.

The army was poorly _____.

The army was poorly _____.

10. The British troops were well equipped.

The British troops were well _____.

The British troops were well _____.

11. The Americans camped at Valley Forge.

The Americans _____ at Valley Forge.

The Americans _____ at Valley Forge.

12. In spring they began to harass the English.

In spring they began to _____ the English.

In spring they began to _____ the English.

13. The attack began in the morning.

The _____ began in the morning.

The _____ began in the morning.

14. He wanted to strike at the enemy first.

He wanted to _____ the enemy first.

He wanted to _____ the enemy first.

15. The army appeared unexpectedly.

The army appeared _____.

The army appeared _____.

16. The British were surrounded.

The British were _____.

The British were _____.

17. Cornwallis had to surrender.

Cornwallis had to _____.

Cornwallis had to _____.

Important Questions and Answers

1. What war lasted for many years? (Revolutionary War)

2. In what year did most of the fighting end? (1781)

3. Whose forces were defeated at Yorktown? (British forces, Cornwallis' forces)

4. What was signed in Paris in 1783? (a treaty)

5. Who became commander-in-chief of the Continental Army? (George Washington)

6. What was Mount Vernon? (a plantation)

7. On what river was Mount Vernon located? (Potomac)

8. Who had military experience? (George Washington)

9. Which army was well trained? (British army)

10. Which army was poorly equipped? (Continental Army)

11. Where was Washington camped in the winter of 1777–1778? (Valley Forge)

12. What did Washington's army begin to do in the spring? (harass the British troops)

13. Whom did Washington strike at unexpectedly? (the enemy, British troops)

14. Who was surrounded at Yorktown? (British army, General Cornwallis)

15. What did Cornwallis have no choice but to do? (surrender)

Is It TRUE or FALSE?

Say TRUE if the sentence is correct. Say FALSE if it is incorrect.

1. A treaty to end the war was signed in Yorktown.

2. George Washington led the Continental Army.

3. The Revolutionary War lasted three years.

4. Washington was a landowner in New York.

5. The Revolutionary War ended in 1776.

6. Washington's plantation was on the banks of the Potomac River.

7. Washington had no military experience.

8. The war against England was very easy for the Americans.

9. The British army was made up of volunteers.

10. The Americans often went without food and clothing.

11. The American army began to harass the British.

12. Washington destroyed the English with a single attack.

13. The Americans had the British surrounded at Yorktown.

14. Washington surrendered to Cornwallis.

Answers

1. False
2. True
3. False
4. False
5. False
6. True
7. False

8. False
9. False
10. True
11. True
12. False
13. True
14. False

Let's Look at Some Important Sentences

Circle the letter of the word or phrase that completes the sentence.

1. A _____ ended the Revolutionary War.

    a. defeat
    b. new attack
    c. treaty
    d. surrenders

2. The _____ War lasted until 1781.

    a. English

    b. Revolutionary

    c. colonial

    d. fighting

3. The commander-in-chief of the _____ was George Washington.

    a. battle

    b. camp

    c. defeat

    d. army

4. Most of the _____ ended in 1781.

    a. fighting

    b. treaty

    c. food

    d. lack of clothing

5. Washington had a _____ called Mount Vernon.

    a. good equipment

    b. plantation

    c. enemy

    d. attack

6. Washington was in the _____ and Indian War.

    a. French

    b. Potomac

    c. Continental

    d. Valley Forge

7. The English were very well _____.

    a. harassed

    b. surrendered

    c. attacked

    d. equipped

8. The Americans lacked _____ and clothing.

    a. food

    b. surviving

    c. volunteers

    d. battles

9. The American army was _____ at Valley Forge.

    a. camped

    b. battling

    c. fighting

    d. surrendered

10. The Americans _____ the British troops.

    a. harassed
    b. surrounding
    c. single attack
    d. unexpectedly

11. In 1781 there was an important _____ at Yorktown.

    a. war
    b. battle
    c. treaty
    d. banks

12. _____ defeat was the end of the Revolutionary War.

    a. Mount Vernon's
    b. Washington's
    c. Cornwallis'
    d. Congress'

Answers

1. c	7. d
2. b	8. a
3. d	9. a
4. a	10. a
5. b	11. b
6. a	12. c

Let's Write the New Words

In the blank, write the word or phrase that completes the sentence. Look at the words in parentheses. They will help you.

1. They were _____ at Yorktown. (beaten, conquered)

2. The _____ of Paris ended the war. (peace document)

3. The English were forced to _____. (give up, yield)

4. The _____ finally ended in 1781. (battle, making war)

5. The British troops were _____. (in a ring, encircled)

6. Washington was a rich _____. (a person who has land)

7. He wanted to strike at the enemy _____. (as a surprise)

8. His _____ was on the Potomac River. (large farm)

9. They wished to _____ the enemy in the morning. (assault, fall upon)

10. Washington already had _____ experience. (referring to an army or soldiers)

11. In the spring they began to _____ them. (torment, annoy)

12. They _____ at Valley Forge. (lived in tents)

13. The British were well trained and _____. (having equipment)

14. The American army was made up of _____. (soldiers serving willingly)

15. The army _____ them unexpectedly. (hits hard)

Answers

1. defeated

2. treaty

3. surrender

4. fighting

5. surrounded

6. landowner

7. unexpectedly

8. plantation

9. attack

10. military

11. harass

12. camped

13. equipped

14. volunteers

15. strikes at

Some Tips About English

■ There are two ways to show *ownership* in English: 1) use an apostrophe before adding s (-'s) or 2) use the preposition *of*. Use an apostrophe before adding s (-'s) with most living things:

John's car   a boy's dog   the people's rights

Use *of* before the word that shows *to whom* or *to what* something belongs:

the roar of the lion   a bouquet of roses   the father of the bride

■ Some important words in this chapter are *irregular verbs*. Their past tense form does not follow the regular pattern. Regular verbs in the past tense end in *–ed*. Irregular verbs make other kinds of changes:

	Regular Verb	*to become*	*to choose*
Present Tense	I want, he wants	I become, he becomes	I choose, he chooses
Past Tense	I wanted, he wanted	I became, he became	I chose, he chose
	to go	*to have*	*to make*
Present Tense	I go, he goes	I have, he has	I make, he makes
Past Tense	I went, he went	I had, he had	I made, he made
	to say	*to take*	*to write*
Present Tense	I say, he says	I take, he takes	I write, he writes
Past Tense	I said, he said	I took, he took	I wrote, he wrote

A New Nation

Colonial Towns

The original 13 colonies had become states in a new nation: the United States of America. The new nation was very large and stretched from the Canadian border in the north to Florida in the south. Americans were mostly from Europe and from many different countries. In addition, there were thousands of African slaves. This meant that there were many cultural differences in the American population.

The towns in the new nation were also different. Boston in the north was the largest of the New England cities. It was not at all similar to Charleston in the south. The population of Boston, like most of New England, was mostly white and of English descent. New York and Philadelphia had a large English population, too, but many Dutch, Germans, Scots, and Irishmen also lived there.

New York was originally a settlement of the Netherlands. It was called New Amsterdam when it was a Dutch colony. In 1613 the Dutch had established a trading post where the town eventually grew. But in 1664 the governor of New Amsterdam, Peter Stuyvesant, surrendered the town to the British after a naval blockade.

Philadelphia was the center of the spirit of American independence. Before and after the American Revolution, it was a place where people met to debate freedom and forms of government. It was in this city that the Continental Congress met, at first, in Carpenter's Hall. Later, the Congress met in Independence Hall. In 1787, delegates from the states met in Philadelphia to write the U.S. Constitution.

The populations of southern cities differed from the populations of northern cities. In the South, cities were made up of both white and black. The white population of towns like Williamsburg, Jamestown, or Charleston was primarily landowners and planters. They often were wealthy and educated and of an aristocratic background. The black population consisted mostly of slaves.

Important Words

Learn the meaning of these new words. Say a sentence using each new word.

stretch = reach, spread, extend	"The mountains stretch a hundred miles from north to south."
border = frontier	"Mexico and the United States share a border in the south."
in addition = also, too	"In addition, you have to wash the dishes."
population = number of people	"The population of Chicago is about four million."
largest (large, larger) = biggest	"Alaska is the largest state."
mostly = principally, for the most part	"The slaves mostly worked on plantations."
countries = nations, lands	"They come from many countries."
descent = ancestry, family background	"My family is of Korean descent."
trading post = a small colonial store	"I buy tools and grain at the trading post."
eventually = in time, later	"Washington eventually became the first president."
blockade = stopping traffic into a harbor by force	"The naval blockade lasted for two weeks."
center = the middle	"Philadelphia was the political center of the colonies."
met = assembled, encountered one another	"The delegates meet in Independence Hall."
later (late, latest) = afterward	"Later she worked as a doctor."
differ = be different, vary	"The North differed greatly from the South."
primarily = fundamentally, mostly	"Many people were primarily planters."

wealthy = rich   "Washington was a wealthy landowner."

educated = learned, schooled   "My mother is a well-educated woman."

aristocratic background = from an upper-class family   "His aristocratic background made him unpopular."

consist of = composed of, made up from   "The committee consists of five members."

Write Your New Words

In the blank of the first sentence, write the missing word. In the second sentence, write the same word from memory.

1. The colonies were now states in a new nation.

The colonies were now _____ in a new nation.

The colonies were now _____ in a new nation.

2. The nation stretched from Canada to Florida.

The nation _____ from Canada to Florida.

The nation _____ from Canada to Florida.

3. Americans were from many different countries.

Americans were from many different _____.

Americans were from many different _____.

4. There were thousands of African slaves.

There were thousands of African _____.

There were thousands of African _____.

5. What is the population of the United States?

What is the _____ of the United States?

What is the _____ of the United States?

6. Boston was the largest of the cities in New England.

Boston was the _____ of the cities in New England.

Boston was the _____ of the cities in New England.

7. Most New Englanders were of English descent.

Most New Englanders were of English _____.

Most New Englanders were of English _____.

8. New York was originally a Dutch settlement.

New York was originally a Dutch _____.

New York was originally a Dutch _____.

9. The Dutch had a trading post there.

The Dutch had a _____ there.

The Dutch had a _____ there.

10. They surrendered the city after a naval blockade.

They surrendered the city after a naval _____.

They surrendered the city after a naval _____.

11. It was the center of the spirit of American independence.

It was the _____ of the spirit of American independence.

It was the _____ of the spirit of American independence.

12. The northern population differed from the southern population.

The northern population _____ from the southern population.

The northern population _____ from the southern population.

13. The southerners were primarily planters.

The southerners were _____ planters.

The southerners were _____ planters.

14. Many of them were wealthy and educated.

Many of them were _____ and _____.

Many of them were _____ and _____.

15. The black population consisted of slaves.

The black _____ consisted of slaves.

The black _____ consisted of slaves.

Some Important Questions and Answers

1. How many original colonies were there? (13)

2. From what continent did most colonists come? (Europe)

3. What city was the center of the spirit of American independence? (Philadelphia)

4. What territory was north of the American colonies? (Canada)

5. What was New York called as a Dutch colony? (New Amsterdam)

6. Who were primarily landowners and planters in the South? (white people)

7. Who worked as servants without freedom? (slaves)

8. Why was the population of America so different? (People came from many places in Europe and Africa.)

9. In what city did the Continental Congress meet? (Philadelphia)

Is It TRUE or FALSE?

Say TRUE if the sentence is correct. Say FALSE if it is incorrect.

1. The original 14 colonies were now states.

2. Many Germans, Dutch, Scots, and Irishmen lived in New York.

3. Philadelphia was originally a Dutch settlement.

4. The Dutch surrendered New Amsterdam after a naval blockade.

5. The new nation stretched from Florida to Canada.

6. There were many differences in the American population.

7. Boston and Charleston were very similar.

8. Jamestown was the center of the spirit of American independence.

9. Many people in New England were of English descent.

10. The Continental Congress met in Williamsburg.

11. The delegates met in Independence Hall.

12. They began to write the new constitution in 1787.

13. Southern cities were made up of both white and black.

14. Most southern landowners were uneducated.

Answers

1.	False	8.	False
2.	True	9.	True
3.	False	10.	False
4.	True	11.	True
5.	True	12.	True
6.	True	13.	True
7.	False	14.	False

Let's Look at Some Important Sentences

Circle the letter of the word or phrase that completes the sentence.

1. Northerners and southerners were _____ from one another.

    a. in addition
    b. different
    c. originally
    d. consisted

2. The colonies had become _____ in a new nation.

    a. similar

    b. states

    c. mostly white

    d. educated

3. The new nation _____ from Canada to Florida.

    a. is wealthy

    b. was largest

    c. population

    d. stretched

4. _____, there were many African slaves.

    a. In addition

    b. Most

    c. In Independence Hall

    d. Planters

5. The _____ of the cities was Boston.

    a. aristocratic

    b. English

    c. largest

    d. similar

6. The population of Boston was _____ white.

    a. too

    b. mostly

    c. a settlement

    d. the British naval blockade

7. New York was originally _____ of the Netherlands.

    a. trading post

    b. a settlement

    c. Dutch

    d. established

8. A town _____ grew there.

    a. eventually

    b. primarily

    c. mostly

    d. differently

9. Many Germans, Scots, and Irishmen _____ there, too.

    a. settlement

    b. descent

    c. consisted of

    d. lived

10. They established a _____ near the river.

    a. trading post

    b. Congress

    c. Carpenter's Hall

    d. revolution

11. The delegates to the convention _____ in Philadelphia.

    a. similar

    b. debates

    c. eventually

    d. met

12. In 1787 they began to write a new _____.

    a. debate

    b. constitution

    c. blockade

    d. convention

13. Americans were immigrants from many _____.

    a. town

    b. borders

    c. trading posts

    d. countries

14. The wealthy landowners were also _____.

    a. planters

    b. northerner

    c. differed

    d. French descent

15. They were _____ and from an aristocratic background.

    a. slaves

    b. both white and black

    c. in the center

    d. educated

Answers

  1. b   **9.** d

  2. b   **10.** a

  3. d   **11.** d

  4. a   **12.** b

  5. c   **13.** d

  6. b   **14.** a

  7. b   **15.** d

  8. a

Let's Write the New Words

In the blank, write the word or phrase that completes the sentence. Look at the words in parentheses. They will help you.

1. The people of Boston were _____ of English descent. (principally, for the most part)

2. The immigrants are from many _____. (nations, lands)

3. The black population _____ slaves. (was composed of, made up from)

4. The nation _____ from Canada to Florida. (reached, spread, extended)

5. The Mexican _____ is in the south. (frontier, boundary)

6. Many landowners were well _____. (learned, schooled)

7. _____, Germans and Irishmen lived in New York. (also, too)

8. Some of the delegates were _____ landowners. (rich)

9. Boston was the _____ city in New England. (biggest)

10. The North and the South _____ greatly. (were different, varied)

11. My new friends are of Italian _____. (ancestry, family background)

12. _____ they began to write a new constitution. (afterward)

13. The delegates _____ in Philadelphia. (assembled, encountered one another)

14. What city was the political _____ of the colonies? (the middle)

15. The British set up a naval _____. (stopping traffic into a harbor by force)

16. The Dutch _____ surrendered the city to the British. (in time, later)

Answers

1. mostly
2. countries
3. consisted of
4. stretched
5. border
6. educated
7. In addition
8. wealthy
9. largest
10. differed
11. descent
12. Later
13. met
14. center
15. blockade
16. eventually

The Flag Is Born

One early American flag was used by American ships from New England. The flag was white and showed a green pine tree in the center. Above it were the words "*An Appeal To Heaven.*"

The Continental Navy had a different flag at that time. The background consisted of 13 red and white stripes. A rattle-snake stretched across the background of stripes. And at the bottom of the flag were the words *"Don't Tread On Me."*

Legend says that Betsy Ross of Philadelphia sewed the first official American flag in 1776. The flag had a background of 13 red and white stripes. In the upper left corner was a field of blue. And in the field of blue was a circle of 13 white stars. The 13 stripes and 13 stars stood for the original 13 colonies.

As the nation grew and more states came into the union, more stars and stripes were added to the flag: one star and one stripe for each new state. In 1818 there were 20 states in the union and, therefore, 20 stars and 20 stripes on the flag. But Congress decided that the number of stripes should remain at 13, and only the number of stars should increase as the union grew.

At the present time, the national flag of the United States of America consists of 13 red and white stripes with a field of blue in the upper left corner. And in the field of blue are 50 white stars—one for each state. The American flag is often called *Old Glory*. In the American national anthem, the flag is called *The Star Spangled Banner*.

Important Words

Learn the meaning of these new words. Say a sentence using each new word.

flag = banner	"The American flag is red, white, and blue."
use = employ, utilize	"This big car uses too much gas."
show = display, demonstrate	"The flag shows a snake in the center."
pine tree = evergreen, fir tree	"A pine tree stood in the center of the garden."
appeal = a request	"He made an appeal for help."
heaven = sky, Elysium	"I believe people go to heaven after death."
background = area in the rear or distance	"The background of the picture is too dark."
stripe = a band, streak, line	"The American flag has 13 stripes."
bottom = the base, lowest point	"She signed her name at the bottom of the letter."
rattlesnake = a poisonous snake with a vibrating tail	"Careful! There's a rattlesnake under that bush!"
legend = a fable, folk story	"There are many legends about this old house."
sew = stitch, attach with needle and thread	"They say Betsy Ross sewed the first flag."
upper = above, higher than something else	"My friends live on an upper floor."
field = space, land	"The stars are on a field of blue."
stood for = represented	"The Declaration of Independence stood for liberty."
increase = become larger	"The states in the Union have increased to 50."
at the present time = now	"At the present time there is no need for new taxes."
glory = splendor, grandeur, fame	"They were proud of the glory of the nation."
spangled = covered, adorned with glitter	"The flag is spangled with 50 stars."

Write Your New Words

In the blank of the first sentence, write the missing word. In the second sentence, write the same word from memory.

1. There are many pine trees in the forest.

There are many _____ in the forest.

There are many _____ in the forest.

2. Do you know *The Star Spangled Banner?*

Do you know *The Star* _____ *Banner?*

Do you know *The Star* _____ *Banner?*

3. American ships used a different flag.

American ships _____ a different flag.

American ships _____ a different flag.

4. There is no glory when you lose.

There is no _____ when you lose.

There is no _____ when you lose.

5. What color is the American flag?

What color is the American _____?

What color is the American _____?

6. What is our population at the present time?

What is our population _____?

What is our population _____?

7. I want to show you something interesting.

I want to _____ you something interesting.

I want to _____ you something interesting.

8. How much did the temperature increase?

How much did the temperature _____?

How much did the temperature _____?

9. I saw a large banner in the background.

I saw a large banner in the _____.

I saw a large banner in the _____.

10. The American flag stood for freedom.

The American flag _____ freedom.

The American flag _____ freedom.

11. There is a stripe down the center of the street.

There is a stripe down the _____ of the street.

There is a stripe down the _____ of the street.

12. We walked through a field of flowers.

    We walked through a _____ of flowers.
    We walked through a _____ of flowers.

13. The document is on an upper shelf.

    The document is on an _____ shelf.
    The document is on an _____ shelf.

14. My name is at the bottom of the list.

    My name is at the _____ of the list.
    My name is at the _____ of the list.

15. Her daughter helped her sew the flag.

    Her daughter helped her _____ the flag.
    Her daughter helped her _____ the flag.

16. Is that story only a legend?

    Is that story only a _____?
    Is that story only a _____?

Some Important Questions and Answers

1. What kind of tree was on an early American flag? (pine tree)

2. What kind of snake was on another early American flag? (rattlesnake)

3. How many stars were on the first official flag? (13)

4. How many stripes were on the first official flag? (13)

5. What color are the stripes on the flag? (red and white)

6. What color are the stars on the flag? (white)

7. What is added to the flag when a new state is added to the Union? (star)

8. What is often called *Old Glory?* (American flag)

9. What is the name of the national anthem? (*The Star Spangled Banner*)

Is It TRUE or FALSE?

Say TRUE if the sentence is correct. Say FALSE if it is incorrect.

1. An early flag was white with a green pine tree on it.

2. Another flag showed a rattlesnake stretched across a field of red and white stripes.

3. Legend says that Betsy Ross sewed the first official American flag.

4. An early American flag had a field of red with 13 stars in it.

5. The American flag has 13 red and 13 white stripes.

6. Until 1818, a new stripe was added to the flag for each new state.

7. At the present time, there are 50 red and white stripes on the flag.

8. Today there are 51 states in the Union.

9. The American flag is sometimes called *Old Glory*.

10. The national anthem is called *The Star Spangled Banner*.

11. At the bottom of the American flag are the words "Don't Tread On Me."

12. The colors of the American flag are red, white, and green.

13. The American flag today has 50 white stars on a field of blue.

Answers

1. True
2. True
3. True
4. False
5. False
6. True
7. False

8. False
9. True
10. True
11. False
12. False
13. True

Let's Look at Some Important Sentences

Circle the letter of the word or phrase that completes the sentence.

1. By 1818 there were 20 states in the _____.

   a. background
   b. field
   c. Union
   d. flag

2. Congress decided there should be only 13 _____ on the flag.

   a. stripes
   b. fields
   c. red stars
   d. blue stars

3. The 13 stripes _____ the original 13 colonies.

    a. consisted of

    b. met

    c. used

    d. stood for

4. The flag showed a green _____ on a field of white.

    a. pine tree

    b. rattlesnake

    c. star

    d. stripe

5. There was more than just one flag _____ during the Revolutionary War.

    a. used

    b. consisted

    c. came into

    d. called

6. There was a pine tree in the _____ of the flag.

    a. stripes

    b. union

    c. corner

    d. center

7. A rattlesnake _____ across the field of stripes.

    a. grew

    b. increased

    c. stretched

    d. was called

8. _____ says that Betsy Ross sewed the first American flag.

    a. Legend

    b. A delegate

    c. Congress

    d. The navy

9. _____ the American flag has 50 stars.

    a. For each state

    b. At the present time

    c. The corner

    d. The number

10. The _____ of the flag consisted of 13 stripes.

    a. center

    b. background

    c. field

    d. stars

11. In the _____ left corner there is a field of blue.

    a. center

    b. red

    c. white

    d. upper

12. There were some words at the _____ of the flag.

    a. bottom

    b. pine tree

    c. rattlesnake

    d. upper

13. The national anthem is called *The Star Spangled* _____.

    a. Flag

    b. Field

    c. Banner

    d. Red, White, and Blue

14. Another name for the American flag is _____.

    a. the Union

    b. the Stripes

    c. Old Glory

    d. An Appeal To Heaven

Answers

1. c	**8.** a
2. a	**9.** b
3. d	**10.** b
4. a	**11.** d
5. a	**12.** a
6. d	**13.** c
7. c	**14.** c

Let's Write the New Words

In the blank, write the word or phrase that completes the sentence. Look at the words in parentheses. They will help you.

1. Don't step on that _____! (a poisonous snake with a vibrating tail)

2. The story of Betsy Ross is mostly a _____. (a fable, a folk story)

3. There are some words at the _____ of the flag. (the base, lowest point)

4. Who _____ the first official flag? (stitched, attached with needle and thread)

5. Our _____ is red, white, and blue. (banner)

60

6. There is a field of blue in an _____ corner. (above, higher than something else)

7. The old flag _____ a pine tree in the center. (displayed, demonstrated)

8. The stars are on a _____ of blue. (space, land)

9. The words on the flag are An _____ To Heaven. (a request)

10. The 13 stripes _____ for the colonies. (represented)

11. The _____ consists of 13 stripes. (area in the rear or distance)

12. The number of white stars _____ to 50. (became larger)

13. How many red and white _____ are on the flag? (bands, streaks, lines)

14. We sometimes call the flag *Old* _____. (splendor, grandeur, fame)

15. Our national anthem is *The Star* _____ *Banner.* (covered, adorned with glitter)

Answers

1. rattlesnake
2. legend
3. bottom
4. sewed
5. flag
6. upper
7. showed
8. field

9. Appeal
10. stood for
11. background
12. increased
13. stripes
14. *Glory*
15. *Spangled*

Some Tips About English

- The English definite article is **the**. It is used with singular or plural nouns when you are speaking about a specific person or thing. The indefinite articles are **a** and **an** and speak about a person or thing in general. They are only used with singular nouns. Use **a** with nouns that begin with a consonant. Use **an** with words that begin with a vowel (a, e, i, o, or u). In the plural, the indefinite article is omitted entirely.

A Specific Person or Thing	A Person or Thing in General
the man	a man
the apple	an apple
the boys	boys
the houses	houses

- In this chapter some of the words used were comparative, and some were superlative. Comparative adjectives and adverbs show a contrast between two persons or things. The first person or thing in the contrast is separated from the second person or thing by the word "than." And "than" follows the comparative adjective or adverb. For example: "My car is newer **than** your car." Most comparatives end in **–er**.

Adjective	Comparative	Sentence
big	bigger	Tom is bigger than Anna.
large	larger	Alaska is larger than Texas.
late	later	She came home later than Jim.

Superlative adjectives and adverbs show the greatest degree of the meaning of the word. Most of these end in **–est**.

Adjective	Superlative	Sentence
big	biggest	They live in the biggest house.
large	largest	The largest ship came from Spain.
late	latest	Maria arrived the latest.

Many long words form their comparative and superlative in another way: They are preceded by the words **more** and **most.**

Adjective	Comparative	Superlative
beautiful	more beautiful	most beautiful
interesting	more interesting	most interesting

There are a few words that form their comparative and superlative forms irregularly. Fortunately, the list is short:

Adjective	Comparative	Superlative
bad	worse	worst
far	farther/further	farthest/furthest
good	better	best
little (amount)	less	least
many	more	most
much	more	most
well	better	best

The Father of Our Country

A New Constitution at Last

With the end of the Revolutionary War, the 13 American colonies had won their liberty. During the struggle for freedom, the people needed a government and a constitution to bring the new states together. The first American constitution was called *the Articles of Confederation*. This constitution was used from 1781 to 1788.

In 1787 there was a constitutional convention in Philadelphia. It was held at Independence Hall. There, the delegates created a new constitution, which was ratified by the states in 1788. The Constitution describes the powers of the American government. These powers are separated into the three branches of government: the Congress, the President of the United States, and the courts. This separation of powers is known as *checks and balances*. It ensures that no single branch of government will become dominant.

The Constitution begins with the Preamble:

> *We the People of the United States, in Order to form a more perfect Union, establish Justice, insure domestic Tranquility, provide for the common defence, promote the general Welfare, and secure the Blessings of Liberty to ourselves and our Posterity, do ordain and establish this Constitution for the United States of America.*

Soon amendments were added to change the Constitution. The first 10 amendments are called the Bill of Rights. Two of these rights are freedom of speech and freedom of religion.

Elections under the new Constitution were held, and George Washington became the first President of the United States. Because of this, he is known as the Father of Our Country.

Important Words

Learn the meaning of these new words. Say a sentence using each new word.

win = gain, secure	"The colonies wanted to win their independence."
liberty = freedom	"Patrick Henry said, 'Give me liberty or give me death.'"
during = in, throughout the time	"He died during the war."
struggle = battle, violent effort	"The struggle for freedom had ended."
together = as one, united	"The states were together in one union."
ratify = accept, approve	"The delegates ratified the Constitution."
describe = tell about	"The Constitution describes our form of government."
powers = authority, control	"Each branch of government has its own powers."
separate = divide, detach	"Church and state are separated."
branch = offshoot, section, group	"There are three branches of government."
court = legal tribunal	"The courts are one branch of government."
ensure = make sure, guarantee	"The Constitution ensures our freedom."
dominant = having the upper hand	"No branch of government shall be dominant."
Preamble = introduction	"The Preamble begins the Constitution."
amendment = change	"The first 10 amendments are the Bill of Rights."
election = choosing by voting	"A presidential election occurs every four years."
rights = guaranteed privileges	"Each citizen has certain rights."
because of = on account of	"Because of these rights, we have freedom of speech."

Write Your New Words

In the blank of the first sentence, write the missing word. In the second sentence, write it from memory.

1. The colonies had finally won their liberty.

   The colonies had finally won their _____.
   The colonies had finally won their _____.

2. Many died during the Revolutionary War.

   Many died _____ the Revolutionary War.
   Many died _____ the Revolutionary War.

3. The struggle for freedom lasted for years.

   The _____ for freedom lasted for years.
   The _____ for freedom lasted for years.

4. The first constitution was used from 1781 to 1788.

   The first _____ was used from 1781 to 1788.
   The first _____ was used from 1781 to 1788.

5. Our Constitution was ratified in 1789.

   Our Constitution was _____ in 1789.
   Our Constitution was _____ in 1789.

6. A convention was held at Independence Hall.

   A convention was held at _____.
   A convention was held at _____.

7. Each branch of government has its own powers.

   Each branch of government has its own _____.
   Each branch of government has its own _____.

8. They believed that church and state should be separate.

   They believed that church and state should be _____.
   They believed that church and state should be _____.

9. There are three branches of government.

   There are three _____ of government.
   There are three _____ of government.

10. The Constitution describes the powers of the government.

The Constitution _____ the powers of the government.

The Constitution _____ the powers of the government.

11. Justice can be found in the courts.

Justice can be found in the _____.

Justice can be found in the _____.

12. The Constitution ensures our liberty.

The Constitution _____ our liberty.

The Constitution _____ our liberty.

13. No branch of government shall be dominant.

No branch of government shall be _____.

No branch of government shall be _____.

14. The first 10 amendments are called the Bill of Rights.

The first 10 amendments are called the _____.

The first 10 amendments are called the _____.

15. The introduction is called the Preamble.

The introduction is called the _____.

The introduction is called the _____.

16. An amendment is a change to the Constitution.

An _____ is a change to the Constitution.

An _____ is a change to the Constitution.

17. We have freedom of religion because of the Bill of Rights.

We have freedom of religion _____ the Bill of Rights

We have freedom of religion _____ the Bill of Rights.

18. The separation of powers is known as checks and balances.

The separation of powers is known as _____.

The separation of powers is known as _____.

Some Important Questions and Answers

1. What was the first American constitution called? (Articles of Confederation)

2. In what city was the constitutional convention held? (Philadelphia)

3. When was the new Constitution ratified? (1788)

4. What are the three branches of government? (Congress, president, courts) (OR legislative, executive, judicial)

5. What is the separation of powers of government called? (checks and balances)

6. Why are there checks and balances? (no branch of government should become dominant)

7. What is the introduction to the Constitution called? (Preamble)

8. What is a change to the Constitution called? (amendment)

9. What do we call the first 10 amendments?) (Bill of Rights)

10. What is one of the rights in the Bill of Rights? (freedom of speech, freedom of religion)

Is It TRUE or FALSE?

Say TRUE if the sentence is correct. Say FALSE if it is incorrect.

1. The colonies lost their liberty with the end of the Revolutionary War.

2. The new states needed a constitution to bring the country together.

3. In 1787 a constitutional convention was held in Boston.

4. The Constitution allows for an official state religion.

5. The first constitution was called the Declaration of Independence.

6. The Constitution ensures that the Congress will be dominant.

7. The new Constitution was ratified in 1789.

8. There are four branches of government.

9. The Declaration of Independence begins with the Preamble.

10. Amendments cannot be added to the Constitution.

11. Americans have the right of freedom of speech and of freedom of religion.

12. The first 10 amendments are called the Bill of Rights.

13. The Constitution can be changed by amendments.

14. The system of checks and balances guarantees the separation of powers.

15. George Washington was the first President of the United States.

16. Benjamin Franklin is known as the Father of Our Country.

Answers

1. False

2. True

3. False

4. False

5. False

6. False

7. True

8. False

9. False

10. False

11. True

12. True

13. True

14. True

15. True

16. False

Let's Look at Some Important Sentences

Circle the letter of the word or phrase that completes the sentence.

1. The 13 American colonies had won their _____.

    a. community
    b. Yorktown
    c. liberty
    d. election

2. The first constitution was called the Articles of _____.

    a. Government
    b. Confederation
    c. Independence
    d. Powers

3. The people needed a _____ to bring the states together.

    a. constitution
    b. article
    c. conventions
    d. struggle

4. The delegates met at _____.

    a. Pennsylvania
    b. Boston
    c. the election
    d. Independence Hall

5. The new Constitution was _____ in 1789.

   a. ratified
   b. separated
   c. described
   d. was known

6. The _____ of government are separated into three branches.

   a. Judicial Branch
   b. Congress
   c. Bill of Rights
   d. powers

7. The _____ introduces the Constitution.

   a. declaration
   b. Articles of Confederation
   c. delegates
   d. Preamble

8. _____ were added to change the Constitution.

   a. Conventions
   b. Amendments
   c. Preamble
   d. Powers

9. The first 10 amendments are known as the _____.

   a. three branches of government
   b. Congress
   c. Constitution
   d. Bill of Rights

10. Americans are guaranteed the _____ .

   a. freedom of speech
   b. new Constitution
   c. their powers
   d. elections

11. The separation of powers is known as _____.

   a. freedom of religion
   b. the legislative branch
   c. checks and balances
   d. separation of church and state

12. The _____ for freedom had finally ended.

   a. elections
   b. power
   c. convention
   d. struggle

13. No branch of government shall be _____.

    a. dominant

    b. free

    c. in the Bill of Rights

    d. separated

14. The Constitution _____ the people's rights.

    a. struggled

    b. described

    c. separated

    d. changed

15. Liberty was won _____ the Revolutionary War.

    a. instead of

    b. because

    c. during

    d. ensured

16. _____ under the new Constitution were held.

    a. Freedom of speech

    b. Elections

    c. The delegates

    d. Checks and balances

Answers

1. c		**9.** d	
2. b		**10.** a	
3. a		**11.** c	
4. d		**12.** d	
5. a		**13.** a	
6. d		**14.** b	
7. d		**15.** c	
8. b		**16.** b	

Let's Write the New Words

In the blank, write the word or phrase that completes the sentence. Look at the words in parentheses. They will help you.

1. Many died _____ the war. (in, throughout the time)

2. We have greater freedom _____ the Bill of Rights. (on account of)

3. The _____ for liberty had finally ended. (battle, violent effort)

4. Citizens are protected by the Bill of _____. (guaranteed privileges)

5. The colonies had _____ their independence. (gained, secured)

6. The battle for _____ was long and hard. (freedom)

7. _____ were held in November. (choosing by voting)

8. The 13 states came _____ as a new nation. (as one, united)

9. The first 10 _____ are very important. (changes to the Constitution)

10. The Constitution was _____ in 1789. (accepted, approved)

11. The _____ introduces the Constitution. (introduction)

12. No branch of government shall be _____. (having the upper hand)

13. The Bill of Rights _____ our freedoms. (tells about)

14. The _____ of government are separated. (authority, control)

15. There are three _____ of government. (offshoots, sections, groups)

16. We believe that church and state should be _____. (divided, detached)

Answers

1. during
2. because of
3. struggle
4. Rights
5. won
6. liberty
7. elections
8. together

9. amendments
10. ratified
11. Preamble
12. dominant
13. describes
14. powers
15. branches
16. separated

The Founding Fathers

The Founding Fathers were the men who guided the states through the Revolutionary War. They were also the delegates to the conventions that produced the Declaration of Independence, the Articles of Confederation, and the Constitution of the United States. They were the early leaders of the new nation.

Some of the most important men at the constitutional convention of 1787 were George Washington, Alexander Hamilton, James Madison, and Benjamin Franklin. John Adams, the new ambassador to Great Britain, was in London. Thomas Jefferson was the American ambassador in Paris. They did not participate in the convention.

These men and many others were well known in the colonies. They were educated and often wealthy men, who wished to serve their nation. Some fought in the war. Some served in the Continental Congress. Others helped to find money and material for the Revolutionary War. One of these patriots, Patrick Henry, is famous for his statement, "Give me liberty or give me death."

George Washington became the first President of the United States and is called the Father of Our Country.

John Adams was Washington's Vice President and later became the second President of the United States.

Alexander Hamilton was the nation's first Secretary of the Treasury.

Thomas Jefferson wrote the Declaration of Independence and later became president.

James Madison helped write the Constitution and later became president.

Benjamin Franklin was America's emissary in Paris during the Revolutionary War.

Important Words

Learn the meaning of these new words. Say a sentence using each new word.

guide = lead, steer	"Washington guided the nation as the first president."
produce = make, write	"James Madison helped produce the Constitution."
early = previous, ahead of this time	"The woman came home early."
leader = conductor, guide	"The Founding Fathers were our first leaders."
ambassador = representative to a foreign land	"Who is our ambassador to France?"
participate in = take part in	"Not everyone participated in the convention."
serve = give service, aid	"Washington served as president for eight years."
material = goods, products	"He found money and material for the war."
patriot = loyal citizen, nationalist	"Patrick Henry was a famous patriot."
death = the end of life	"Washington's death came at the end of the century."
become = get to be, grow to be	"Benjamin Franklin never became president."
first = adjective form of 1	"Who was our first president?"
second = adjective form of 2	"John Adams became the second U.S. President."
secretary = officer in the president's cabinet	"Who is the Secretary of Defense?"
treasury = money storage	"There is no money in the treasury."
emissary = representative to a foreign land	"Franklin was our emissary in France."

Write Your New Words

In the blank of the first sentence, write the missing word. In the second sentence, write the same word from memory.

1. Who guided the country after the war?

Who _____ the country after the war?

Who _____ the country after the war?

2. These men produced several important documents.

These men _____ several important documents.

These men _____ several important documents.

3. Who were our early leaders?

Who were our _____ leaders?

Who were our _____ leaders?

4. The leaders of the nation met in Boston.

The _____ of the nation met in Boston.

The _____ of the nation met in Boston.

5. Adams was the ambassador to England.

Adams was the _____ to England.

Adams was the _____ to England.

6. Jefferson did not participate in the convention.

Jefferson did not _____ the convention.

Jefferson did not _____ the convention.

7. Who served as ambassador to France?

Who _____ as ambassador to France?

Who _____ as ambassador to France?

8. She found the money and material for the war.

She found the money and _____ for the war.

She found the money and _____ for the war.

9. The Founding Fathers were patriots.

The Founding Fathers were _____.

The Founding Fathers were _____.

10. Give me liberty or give me death.

Give me liberty or give me _____.

Give me liberty or give me _____.

11. Washington became the first President.

Washington _____ the first President.

Washington _____ the first President.

12. Who was the first Secretary of the Treasury?

Who was the _____ Secretary of the Treasury?

Who was the _____ Secretary of the Treasury?

13. Adams was the second President.

Adams was the _____ President.

Adams was the _____ President.

14. Can you name the Secretary of Defense?

Can you name the _____ of Defense?

Can you name the _____ of Defense?

15. New taxes will fill the treasury.

New taxes will fill the _____.

New taxes will fill the _____.

16. He was our emissary in Paris.

He was our _____ in Paris.

He was our _____ in Paris.

Some Important Questions and Answers

1. What are America's first leaders called? (Founding Fathers)

2. Who is known as the Father of Our Country? (George Washington)

3. Who said, "Give me liberty or give me death?" (Patrick Henry)

4. Who was the first President of the United States? (George Washington)

5. Who helped to write the Declaration of Independence? (Thomas Jefferson)

6. Who helped to write the Constitution? (James Madison)

Is It TRUE or FALSE?

Say TRUE if the sentence is correct. Say FALSE if it is incorrect.

1. The Founding Fathers are the President's cabinet.

2. The Declaration of Independence is also called the Articles of Confederation.

3. The Founding Fathers were early American leaders.

4. The constitutional convention was in 1791.

5. John Adams was the first American president.

6. In 1787 Jefferson was in Paris.

7. All the Founding Fathers participated in the constitutional convention.

8. Washington was the new ambassador to Great Britain.

9. Patrick Henry was a famous patriot.

10. Alexander Hamilton was the first Secretary of Treasury.

11. Thomas Jefferson never became President.

12. In time James Madison became President.

13. Benjamin Franklin said, "Give me liberty or give me death."

14. Some of the Founding Fathers fought in the Revolutionary War.

15. Franklin was in Paris during the Revolutionary War.

Answers

1. False	**9.** True
2. False	**10.** True
3. True	**11.** False
4. False	**12.** True
5. False	**13.** False
6. True	**14.** True
7. False	**15.** True
8. False	

Let's Look at Some Important Sentences

Circle the letter of the word or phrase that completes the sentence.

1. The _____ Fathers were our first leaders.

    a. American
    b. Constitutional
    c. Founding
    d. Revolutionary

2. These patriots guided the _____ through the war.

    a. states
    b. English
    c. leader
    d. President

3. One convention _____ the Declaration of Independence.

    a. constitution
    b. found
    c. guided
    d. produced

4. The constitutional convention was in _____.

    a. 1781

    b. 1787

    c. 1791

    d. 1797

5. John Adams was the new _____ to Great Britain.

    a. president

    b. delegation

    c. secretary

    d. ambassador

6. Not everyone _____ in the convention.

    a. participated

    b. described

    c. met

    d. was known

7. After the war, _____ was our ambassador in Paris.

    a. Washington

    b. Hamilton

    c. Jefferson

    d. the Secretary of the Treasury

8. Some of the Founding Fathers were _____ and wealthy men.

    a. French

    b. educated

    c. emissaries

    d. not patriots

9. Several of these leaders _____ in the Continental Congress.

    a. participated in

    b. produced

    c. served

    d. became

10. What is Patrick Henry _____ for?

    a. famous

    b. wealthy

    c. educated

    d. patriot

11. Give me liberty or give me _____.

    a. the treasury

    b. a leader

    c. death

    d. money and material

12. Do you know who the _____ President was?

    a. three

    b. first

    c. became

    d. only

13. Franklin served as our _____ in France.

    a. patriot

    b. second

    c. emissary

    d. vice president

14. John Adams became the _____ President of the United States.

    a. second

    b. four

    c. early

    d. changed

15. Alexander Hamilton was the Secretary of the _____.

    a. Treasury

    b. Government

    c. Cabinet

    d. Nation

16. James Madison _____ President later.

    a. guided

    b. became

    c. participated in

    d. vice

Answers

1. c		**9.** c	
2. a		**10.** a	
3. d		**11.** c	
4. b		**12.** b	
5. d		**13.** c	
6. a		**14.** a	
7. c		**15.** a	
8. b		**16.** b	

Let's Write the New Words

In the blank, write the word or phrase that completes the sentence. Look at the words in parentheses. They will help you.

1. Franklin was our _____ in Paris. (representative to a foreign land)

2. The Founding Fathers _____ the nation in the early years. (led, steered)

3. He became the Secretary of the _____. (money storage)

4. The _____ leaders were great patriots. (previous, ahead of this time)

5. Who is the new _____ of Defense? (officer in the president's cabinet)

6. The _____ met in Independence Hall. (conductors, guides)

7. Adams was our _____ President. (adjective form of 2)

8. Madison helped _____ the new Constitution. (make, write)

9. Adams was once the _____ to England. (representative to a foreign land)

10. George Washington was the _____ President. (adjective form of 1)

11. Who _____ the ambassador to France? (got to be, grew to be)

12. Give me liberty or give me _____. (end of life)

13. The delegates were brave _____. (loyal citizens, nationalists)

14. The nation needed money and _____ for the war. (goods, products)

15. Jefferson could not _____ the convention. (take part in)

16. Many patriots _____ in the Continental Congress. (gave service, aided)

Answers

1. emissary [ambassador]
2. guided
3. Treasury
4. early
5. Secretary
6. leaders
7. second
8. produce

9. ambassador [emissary]
10. first
11. became
12. death
13. patriots
14. material
15. participate in
16. served

Some Tips About English

- When you form a question in English, begin with *Do* in the present tense. Begin with *Did* in the past tense:

Statement	Question
He sings well.	Does he sing well?
They have my book.	Do they have my book?
She helped Tom.	Did she help Tom?
The men spoke English.	Did the men speak English?

With the verb *to be*, just begin the sentence with the verb. Do not use *Do*.

Statement	Question
Maria is happy.	Is Maria happy?
The boys were sick.	Were the boys sick?

- Some important words in this chapter are *irregular verbs*. Their past tense form does not follow the regular pattern. Regular verbs in the past tense end in –ed. Irregular verbs make other kinds of changes:

	to fight	to become	to do
Present Tense	I fight; he fights	I become; he becomes	I do; he does
Past Tense	I fought; he fought	I became; he became	I did; he did
	to win	to give	to hold
Present Tense	I win; he wins	I give; he gives	I hold; he holds
Past Tense	I won; he won	I gave; he gave	I held; he held

The First President

George Washington

George Washington was one of the Founding Fathers. He is known as the Father of Our Country, because he was the first president.

He was born in 1732 into a Virginia planter family. His family had wealth and land, and Washington was educated to be an eighteenth century gentleman. But he had interests beyond being a southern gentleman. He studied the military arts and watched as the American colonies began to spread westward. He believed in this expansion into the west. In 1754 he was made a lieutenant colonel and took part in the French and Indian War.

He was a delegate to the Continental Congress, participated as commander-in-chief in the Revolutionary War, and supported the efforts to write a new Constitution.

After the Constitution was ratified, he took his oath of office as the President of the United States on April 30, 1789. The ceremony took place on the balcony of Federal Hall in New York City.

After two terms as president, he retired to his estate, Mount Vernon. He enjoyed only three years there with his wife, Martha. A new capital city was being built, but he would not live to see the work on the new capital completed. On December 14, 1799, Washington died.

Important Words

Learn the meaning of these new words. Say a sentence using each new word.

was born = came into the world by birth	"He was born in Virginia in 1732."
planter = farmer, someone who plants crops	"Washington was a planter like his father."
gentleman = fine and educated man	"Southern gentlemen were often planters."
interests = things that are interesting	"His interests were science and the arts."
beyond = past, in addition to	"New lands were located beyond the mountains."
study = learn	"He had to study science and languages."
military arts = science of war	"Officers were schooled in the military arts."
spread = stretch, extend	"Settlers began to spread into the western territories."
expansion = growth	"This quick expansion made the population grow."
support = uphold	"He supported the Declaration of Independence."
efforts = labors	"Their efforts ended in a new Constitution."
oath = vow, word of honor	"He took the oath of office in 1789.
ceremony = official event, ritual	"The ceremony took place in New York."
term = time in office	"A president's term is four years."
retire = resign from work	"He and Martha retired to Mount Vernon."
enjoy = like, be fond of	"They enjoyed being planters."
capital = city and seat of government	"The new capital was named for Washington."
completed = finished	"The work was completed in two years."

Write Your New Words

In the blank of the first sentence, write the missing word(s). In the second sentence, write the same word(s) from memory.

1. I was born in Mexico.

I _____ in Mexico.

I _____ in Mexico.

2. Many planters were educated.

Many _____ were educated.

Many _____ were educated.

3. Washington was a southern gentleman.

Washington was a southern _____.

Washington was a southern _____.

4. She had many interests.

She had many _____.

She had many _____.

5. What lies beyond the mountains?

What lies _____ the mountains?

What lies _____ the mountains?

6. He studied many subjects.

He _____ many subjects.

He _____ many subjects.

7. They found the military arts interesting.

They found the _____ interesting.

They found the _____ interesting.

8. The colonies spread westward.

The colonies _____ westward.

The colonies _____ westward.

9. Westward expansion was fast.

Westward _____ was fast.

Westward _____ was fast.

10. She supported their goal of freedom.

She _____ their goal of freedom.

She _____ their goal of freedom.

11. I thanked them for their efforts to help.

I thanked them for their _____ to help.

I thanked them for their _____ to help.

12. You have to swear an oath of allegiance to America.

You have to swear an _____ of allegiance to America.

You have to swear an _____ of allegiance to America.

13. The ceremony took place on a balcony.

The _____ took place on a balcony.

The _____ took place on a balcony.

14. Washington served for two terms.

Washington served for two _____.

Washington served for two _____.

15. They retired to Mount Vernon.

They _____ to Mount Vernon.

They _____ to Mount Vernon.

16. He enjoyed his retirement.

He _____ his retirement.

He _____ his retirement.

17. Is New York the capital?

Is New York the _____?

Is New York the _____?

18. The house was completed on time.

The house was _____ on time.

The house was _____ on time.

Important Questions and Answers

1. What do Americans call George Washington? (Father of Our Country)

2. What is Mount Vernon? (Washington's plantation)

3. What war did Washington fight in? (French and Indian War)

4. Who was commander-in-chief of the army in the Revolutionary War? (Washington)

5. Why is Washington the Father of Our Country? (He was the first President.)

6. Why did Washington not see the new capital completed? (He died in 1799.)

Is It TRUE or FALSE?

Say TRUE if the sentence is correct. Say FALSE if it is incorrect.

1. Washington is known as the Father of Our Country.

2. Washington was born in New York in 1732.

3. Washington was one of the Founding Fathers.

4. He was educated to be an eighteenth century gentleman.

5. The American colonies began to spread eastward.

6. Washington was born into a planter family.

7. He believed that expansion into the west was wrong.

8. He was commander-in-chief during the Revolutionary War.

9. He was against the new Constitution.

10. In 1789 he became the first President of the United States.

11. Washington retired to New York.

12. He never saw the new capital completed.

Answers

1. True
2. False
3. True
4. True
5. False
6. True
7. False
8. True
9. False
10. True
11. False
12. True

Let's Look at Some Important Sentences

Circle the letter of the word or phrase that completes the sentence.

1. Washington was a Virginia _____.

   a. judge
   b. planter
   c. businessman
   d. teacher

2. Washington was an eighteenth century _____.

    a. Frenchman

    b. Englishman

    c. businessman

    d. gentleman

3. He had many _____ beyond his plantation.

    a. farms

    b. interests

    c. conventions

    d. delegates

4. He was one of the _____.

    a. Pennsylvania delegates

    b. officials

    c. Founding Fathers

    d. lieutenants

5. Washington was the _____ president.

    a. first

    b. second

    c. third

    d. fifth

6. He studied the _____.

    a. west

    b. military arts

    c. Constitution

    d. French and Indian War

7. He supported westward _____.

    a. expansion

    b. delegates

    c. war

    d. capital

8. And he supported the _____ to write a new Constitution.

    a. efforts

    b. spread

    c. ceremony

    d. new capital

9. He took his _____ of office in 1789.

    a. effort

    b. interests

    c. oath

    d. expansion

10. Washington is known as the _____.

    a. second president
    b. Father of Our Country
    c. New York planter
    d. last commander-in-chief

11. After two _____, he retired to Mount Vernon.

    a. years
    b. wars
    c. centuries
    d. terms

12. Washington _____ in 1799.

    a. died
    b. was born
    c. became president
    d. supported the Constitution

Answers

1. b		**7.** a	
2. d		**8.** a	
3. b		**9.** c	
4. c		**10.** b	
5. a		**11.** d	
6. b		**12.** a	

Let's Write the New Words

In the blank, write the word or phrase that completes the sentence. Look at the words in parentheses. They will help you.

1. He believed in westward _____. (growth)

2. He _____ the new Constitution. (upheld)

3. Settlers began to _____ into the west. (stretch, extend)

4. He knew of their _____ to write a new Constitution. (labors)

5. He was interested in the _____. (science of war)

6. He took the _____ of office in New York. (vow, word of honor)

7. He _____ military science. (learned)

8. The _____ took place in 1789. (official event, ritual)

9. Washington had many _____. (things that are interesting)

10. He served as president for two _____. (times in office)

11. His father was a wealthy _____. (farmer, someone who plants crops)

12. Washington _____ in Virginia. (came into the world by birth)

13. The new _____ was named for Washington. (city and seat of government)

Answers

1. expansion
2. supported
3. spread
4. efforts
5. military arts
6. oath
7. studied

8. ceremony
9. interests
10. terms
11. planter
12. was born
13. capital

The New Capital

Philadelphia had been the seat of national government. But it was decided that a new location and a new capital were needed. In January, 1791, George Washington chose the location of the new capital city. It would be a piece of land in Maryland and located on the Potomac River. And it would be called the District of Columbia.

After Washington's death in 1799, the city was named Washington, D.C. (D.C. = District of Columbia). Although Washington helped in the planning of the capital, he never saw it completed. On June 11, 1800, the seat of government was moved from Philadelphia to the District of Columbia. John Adams was the first President to live in the new capital.

Important Words

seat of government = central location of government

decide = determine, make up one's mind

location = place, site

choose = select, pick out

piece of land = property

planning = preparations, design

move = relocate, transfer

"Philadelphia was the seat of government."

"They decided to move the capital."

"The location of the capital was on the Potomac River."

"Washington chose the location of the new capital."

"The District of Columbia is a piece of land in Maryland."

"Many helped in the planning of the capital."

"In 1800 the capital was moved."

Write Your New Words

In the blank of the first sentence, write the missing word. In the second sentence, write it from memory.

1. The seat of government had to be moved.

The seat of _____ had to be moved.

The seat of _____ had to be moved.

2. It was decided to move the capital.

It was _____ to move the capital.
It was _____ to move the capital.

3. Washington found the new location.

Washington found the new _____.
Washington found the new _____.

4. He chose land on the Potomac River.

He _____ land on the Potomac River.
He _____ land on the Potomac River.

5. The piece of land became the District of Columbia.

The _____ became the District of Columbia.
The _____ became the District of Columbia.

6. He was interested in the planning.

He was interested in the _____.
He was interested in the _____.

7. The capital moved from Philadelphia.

The capital _____ from Philadelphia.
The capital _____ from Philadelphia.

Some Important Questions and Answers

1. What city had been the first seat of American government? (Philadelphia)

2. Who chose the location for the new capital? (Washington)

3. From what state did the land for the capital come? (Maryland)

4. Who was the new capital named for? (George Washington)

5. What does D.C. mean in Washington, D.C.? (District of Columbia)

6. On what river is Washington, D.C. located? (Potomac)

Is It TRUE or FALSE?

Say TRUE if the sentence is correct. Say FALSE if it is incorrect.

1. Philadelphia is the capital of the United States.

2. Washington is in the District of Columbia.

3. John Adams chose the location of the new capital.

4. A piece of land in Maryland became the District of Columbia.

5. The capital was moved from Philadelphia.

6. George Washington helped in planning the new city.

7. George Washington was the first president to live in the new capital.

8. Washington, D.C., became the seat of government in 1800.

9. Washington, D.C., is named for the first President.

Answers

1. False

2. True

3. False

4. True

5. True

6. True

7. False

8. True

9. True

Let's Look at Some Important Sentences

Circle the letter of the word or phrase that completes the sentence.

1. The _____ was moved from Philadelphia.

    a. convention
    b. location
    c. seat of government
    d. nation

2. The new location of the capital was in _____.

    a. the District of Columbia
    b. the western territories
    c. Pennsylvania
    d. Philadelphia

3. George Washington _____ the new location of the capital.

    a. moved
    b. helped
    c. chose
    d. did not move

4. D.C. means _____.

    a. District Courts
    b. District of Columbia
    c. District Convention
    d. District Conferences

5. The new capital city was named _____.

   a. Pennsylvania

   b. Philadelphia

   c. New York

   d. Washington

6. Washington liked a _____ in Maryland for the capital.

   a. city

   b. town

   c. seat of government

   d. piece of land

7. _____ was the first president to live in the new capital.

   a. George Washington

   b. John Adams

   c. Thomas Jefferson

   d. James Madison

8. It was _____ that a new capital was needed.

   a. decided

   b. enjoyed

   c. located

   d. planning

9. Washington helped in the _____ of the capital.

   a. efforts

   b. interests

   c. expansion

   d. planning

10. The capital is located on the _____ River.

   a. Hudson

   b. Mississippi

   c. Potomac

   d. Ohio

Answers

1. c	**6.** d
2. a	**7.** b
3. c	**8.** a
4. b	**9.** d
5. d	**10.** c

Let's Write the New Words

In the blank, write the word or phrase that completes the sentence. Look at the words in parentheses. They will help you.

1. Washington, D.C., became the new _____. (central location of government)

2. Congress _____ to move the capital. (determined, made up their minds)

3. Where was the _____ of the new capital? (place, site)

4. Washington _____ the location of the capital. (selected, picked out)

5. The capital is located on a _____ in Maryland. (property)

6. Washington helped in the _____ of the new capital. (preparations, design)

7. The capital was _____ to the District of Columbia. (relocated, transferred)

Answers

1. seat of government
2. decided
3. location
4. chose

5. piece of land
6. planning
7. moved

The White House

When the plans for the new capital were being made, a special house was designed for the president. Pierre Charles L'Enfant made the original design in 1791. President George Washington supervised the design. When the final plan was adopted, people called the house *the President's House*. Some called it *the President's Palace*. Over the years, the house often was called *the Executive Mansion*.

During the War of 1812 with Great Britain, the British captured Washington and burned the President's Palace. When it was rebuilt, it was painted with fresh, white paint. By the time Theodore Roosevelt became president in 1901, people were calling the house *the White House*.

During Theodore Roosevelt's presidency, the West Wing was added to the house. Later, the West Wing was made larger, and the President's new office was located there: the Oval Office. President William Howard Taft was the first president to work in the Oval Office.

Important Words

plan = scheme, proposal	"He had a plan for the new capital."
special = distinct, uncommon	"The president lives in a special house."
design = drawing, outline	"Washington liked the design of the house."
supervise = oversee, control	"He supervised the work on the house."
palace = castle, royal building	"The king lives in a palace."
mansion = large grand house	"The White House is a mansion."
capture = catch, seize	"The British wanted to capture the capital."
burn = set on fire	"They burned the president's house."

rebuilt = built again   "The house was rebuilt after the war."
paint = coat or brush on color   "They painted the walls white."
add = join, unite   "The West Wing was added later."
oval = elliptical, egg-shaped   "The new office was shaped like an oval."

Write Your New Words

In the blank of the first sentence, write the missing word. In the second sentence, write it from memory.

1. They made a new plan for the house.

They made a new _____ for the house.

They made a new _____ for the house.

2. A special house was designed.

A _____ house was designed.

A _____ house was designed.

3. He liked the new design.

He liked the new _____.

He liked the new _____.

4. Washington supervised the work.

Washington _____ the work.

Washington _____ the work.

5. The house looked like a palace.

The house looked like a _____.

The house looked like a _____.

6. The White House is a mansion.

The White House is a _____.

The White House is a _____.

7. The British captured the city.

The British _____ the city.

The British _____ the city.

8. They burned the capital.

They _____ the capital.

They _____ the capital.

9. The house had to be rebuilt.

The house had to be _____.

The house had to be _____.

10. We painted the walls white.

We _____ the walls white.

We _____ the walls white.

11. A wing was added on the west side.

A wing was _____ on the west side.

A wing was _____ on the west side.

12. The Oval Office is in the West Wing.

The _____ Office is in the West Wing.

The _____ Office is in the West Wing.

Some Important Questions and Answers

1. What did Pierre Charles L'Enfant design? (the White House)

2. Who supervised the design of the President's House? (George Washington)

3. What are other names for the White House? (President's House, President's Palace, Executive Mansion)

4. Who burned the White House in the War of 1812? (British)

5. What wing was added to the White House during Theodore Roosevelt's presidency? (West Wing)

6. What is the president's office in the West Wing called? (Oval Office)

Is It TRUE or FALSE?

Say TRUE if the sentence is correct. Say FALSE if it is incorrect.

1. The President lives in a special house.

2. President Washington supervised the design of the house.

3. The White House was once called *Washington's Palace.*

4. The French burned the President's Palace.

5. Today, the executive mansion is called the *White House.*

6. The West Wing was added when Washington was president.

7. The President's office is called the *Oval Office.*

Answers

1. True
2. True
3. False
4. False

5. True
6. False
7. True

Let's Look at Some Important Sentences

Circle the letter of the word or phrase that completes the sentence.

1. A _____ was made to build a house for the president.

    a. location
    b. plan
    c. capital
    d. nation

2. During the War of _____, the British captured the capital city.

    a. 1776
    b. 1812
    c. 1865
    d. 1899

3. When _____ was president, people were calling the house the *White House*.

    a. George Washington
    b. Benjamin Franklin
    c. George W. Bush
    d. Theodore Roosevelt

4. The original _____ of the White House was made in 1791.

    a. design
    b. rebuilt
    c. difference
    d. mansion

5. The _____ is in the West Wing.

    a. President's Palace
    b. Oval Office
    c. capital
    d. design

6. The British _____ the President's Palace.

    a. liked
    b. planned
    c. burned
    d. rebuilt

7. Washington _____ the design of the president's house.

    a. knew
    b. called
    c. supervised
    d. added

Answers

1. b		**5.** b	
2. b		**6.** c	
3. d		**7.** c	
4. a			

Let's Write the New Words

In the blank, write the word or phrase that completes the sentence. Look at the words in parentheses. They will help you.

1. Washington _____ the work on the house. (oversaw, controlled)

2. The Queen of England lives in a _____. (castle, royal building)

3. The _____ for the house was adopted in 1791. (drawing, outline)

4. The White House is a _____. (large grand house)

5. They wanted a _____ house for the president. (distinct, uncommon)

6. The British _____ the city of Washington. (caught, seized)

7. They made a _____ for the new capital. (scheme, proposal)

8. The president's office is the _____ Office. (elliptical, egg-shaped)

9. The West Wing was _____ later. (joined, united)

10. The walls were _____ white. (coated or brushed on color)

11. The mansion was _____ after the war. (built again)

12. The British _____ the President's Palace. (set on fire)

Answers

1. supervised	**7.** plan
2. palace	**8.** Oval
3. design	**9.** added
4. mansion	**10.** painted
5. special	**11.** rebuilt
6. captured	**12.** burned

Some Tips About English

- The word *build* in this chapter is an *irregular verb*. The past tense form does not follow the regular pattern. Regular verbs in the past tense end in *–ed*. Irregular verbs make other kinds of changes:

	Regular Verbs	*to build*
Present Tense	I enjoy, he enjoys	I build, he builds
Past Tense	I enjoyed, he enjoyed	I built, he built

- English has **two ways** of expressing the present and past tenses. **One way** is the form shown in the preceding examples. In the past tense, you must distinguish between regular and irregular verbs.

	Regular Verbs	*to come*	*to make*
Present Tense	I sign, he signs	I come, he comes	I make, he makes
Past Tense	I signed, he signed	I came, he came	I made, he made

The **other way** to express the present and past tenses is by using the verb *to be* (am, is, are, was, were) and a verb ending in *–ing*. There is no difference between regular and irregular verbs.

	to build	*to come*	*to make*
Present Tense	I am building	I am coming	I am making
	He is building	He is coming	He is making
Past Tense	She was building	She was coming	She was making
	We were building	We were coming	We were making

What is the difference between these two forms of present and past tense? When you use the first type, the meaning is that something is done **often** or **as a habit**. Or it can mean that the action is **completed**. For example:

I work in the city. (I work there **every day**. It is my **habit**.)

She came home at 10 o'clock. (She is home now. The action is **completed**.)

When you use the second type, the meaning is that an action is **incomplete** or **in progress**. For example:

I am working in a factory. (My workday is not **completed**. My work is still **in progress**.)

She was coming home when she suddenly fainted. (She did not arrive home, because she fainted. The action is **incomplete**.)

The Nation Grows

The Louisiana Purchase

In the beginning of the nineteenth century, Americans began to understand that the future of the nation lay in the west. People migrated from the 13 states to begin new lives in the western regions. They farmed there. They hunted and trapped animals. And they began new settlements like the colonists had done 200 years earlier.

President Thomas Jefferson wanted free navigation of the Mississippi River for Americans who lived and worked along the river's banks. But the river and the city of New Orleans were under the control of France. So, in 1803 Jefferson sent Robert Livingston and James Monroe to Paris to negotiate with Napoleon. Their goal was to buy New Orleans. To their surprise, Livingston and Monroe learned that Napoleon was willing to sell the entire Louisiana Territory to the American government. The territory contained 800,000 square miles of land.

A treaty for the purchase of the Louisiana Territory was drawn up. The price was $15,000,000. It was one of the largest land sales in history.

The purchase of the Louisiana Territory was the greatest achievement of Thomas Jefferson's presidency. He sent Lewis and Clark on an expedition into the new territory. They explored the region and wrote descriptions of the land and animals they saw. By the end of their journey, they had arrived at the western coast of the continent—the Pacific Ocean.

Important Words

Learn the meaning of these new words. Say a sentence using each new word.

future = the coming time	"The future is unknown to us."
migrate = move from one place to another	"Some birds migrate south for the winter."
region = area, territory	"The Louisiana Territory was a large region."
farm = plant and harvest crops	"They farmed the land near the river."
hunt = search, look for	"The men were hunting deer and bears."
trap = catch, ensnare	"They trapped a young fox."
navigation = travel by boat	"Free navigation of the river was important."
banks = shoreline of a river	"Their farm was located on the banks of the river."
negotiate = bargain	"Two men were sent to negotiate with Napoleon."
surprise = amazement, wonder	"It was a surprise when he agreed to sell the land."
entire = all	"The government now owned the entire region."
square mile = 1 mile × 1 mile	"The town is located on five square miles of land."
purchase = buy	"It cost millions to purchase the land."
draw up = write, make	"The ambassadors drew up a treaty."
achievement = accomplishment, feat	"It was the greatest achievement of his presidency."
expedition = journey, march	"The expedition took them into unknown territory."
explore = search through new land	"They wanted to explore the other side of the river."

Write Your New Words

In the blank of the first sentence, write the missing word(s). In the second sentence, write the same word(s) from memory.

1. No one knows what the future will be.

No one knows what the _____ will be.

No one knows what the _____ will be.

2. Many people migrated westward.

Many people _____ westward.

Many people _____ westward.

3. They traveled through a beautiful region.

They traveled through a beautiful _____.

They traveled through a beautiful _____.

4. We came here to farm the land.

We came here to _____ the land.

We came here to _____ the land.

5. We like to hunt in winter.

We like to _____ in winter.

We like to _____ in winter.

6. They trapped animals for their fur.

They _____ animals for their fur.

They _____ animals for their fur.

7. He believed in free navigation of the rivers.

He believed in free _____ of the rivers.

He believed in free _____ of the rivers.

8. People lived on the banks of the river.

People lived on the _____ of the river.

People lived on the _____ of the river.

9. They negotiated with Napoleon.

They _____ with Napoleon.

They _____ with Napoleon.

10. To their surprise, he agreed.

   To their _____, he agreed.
   To their _____, he agreed.

11. He sold them the entire territory.

   He sold them the _____ territory.
   He sold them the _____ territory.

12. The region consisted of 800,000 square miles.

   The region consisted of 800,000 _____.
   The region consisted of 800,000 _____.

13. The purchase price was $15,000,000.

   The _____ price was $15,000,000.
   The _____ price was $15,000,000.

14. They drew up a new treaty.

   They _____ a new treaty.
   They _____ a new treaty.

15. It was his greatest achievement.

   It was his greatest _____.
   It was his greatest _____.

16. He sent an expedition westward.

   He sent an _____ westward.
   He sent an _____ westward.

17. They explored the entire region.

   They _____ the entire region.
   They _____ the entire region.

Some Important Questions and Answers

1. Where did Americans migrate in the early nineteenth century? (westward)

2. What country controlled New Orleans? (France)

3. What did Thomas Jefferson want with the Mississippi River? (free navigation)

4. Why did Jefferson send Livingston and Monroe to Paris? (to buy New Orleans)

5. What surprised Livingston and Monroe? (Napoleon wanted to sell the Louisiana Territory.)

6. What was the greatest achievement of Jefferson's presidency? (the purchase of the Louisiana Territory)

7. Who explored the Louisiana Territory? (Lewis and Clark)

Is It TRUE or FALSE?

Say TRUE if the sentence is correct. Say FALSE if it is incorrect.

1. People began to migrate to the east.

2. President Jefferson wanted free navigation of the Mississippi River.

3. Many people farmed in the western regions.

4. Some people hunted and trapped animals.

5. In 1776 Jefferson sent emissaries to France.

6. Livingston and Monroe negotiated with Napoleon.

7. Napoleon was not willing to sell the Louisiana Territory.

8. The price of the territory was $800,000.

9. The Louisiana Purchase was one of the largest land sales in history.

10. The Louisiana Purchase was the greatest achievement of Washington's presidency.

11. Lewis and Clark wrote about the land and the animals they saw.

12. In the beginning of the nineteenth century people believed the future lay in the west.

13. Lewis and Clark finally arrived at the Atlantic Ocean.

14. Before 1803 the city of New Orleans belonged to France.

Answers

1. False

2. True

3. True

4. True

5. False

6. True

7. False

8. False

9. True

10. False

11. True

12. True

13. False

14. True

Let's Look at Some Important Sentences

Circle the letter of the word or phrase that completes the sentence.

1. Many people wanted to _____ land in the west.

   a. learn
   b. farm
   c. negotiate
   d. migrate

2. The _____ of the nation lay in the west.

   a. region
   b. location
   c. navigation
   d. future

3. Many people hunted and _____ animals.

   a. trapped
   b. explored
   c. drew up
   d. arrived

4. They began new lives in the western _____.

   a. colonies
   b. regions
   c. farms
   d. rivers

5. They began new _____ in the west.

   a. regions
   b. purchase
   c. settlements
   d. treaty

6. Jefferson believed in free _____ of the rivers.

   a. territory
   b. negotiations
   c. purchase
   d. navigation

7. In _____ he sent Livingston and Monroe to Paris.

   a. 1800
   b. 1801
   c. 1802
   d. 1803

8. New Orleans was under the _____ of France.

   a. efforts
   b. control
   c. region
   d. negotiation

9. Napoleon agreed to sell the _____ territory.

   a. entire
   b. region
   c. explored
   d. expansion

10. The region contained 800,000 _____ of land.

   a. farms
   b. square miles
   c. hunting and trapping
   d. rivers

11. The _____ of the territory was $15,000,000.

   a. price
   b. sell
   c. treaty
   d. navigation

12. To their _____, Napoleon agreed to sell the entire territory.

   a. achievement
   b. location
   c. free navigation
   d. surprise

13. The Louisiana Purchase was his greatest _____.

   a. negotiation
   b. achievement
   c. expedition
   d. beginning

14. It was the largest land sale in _____.

   a. history
   b. territory
   c. France
   d. New Orleans

15. Lewis and Clark went on an _____ to the new territory.

   a. expedition
   b. navigation
   c. settlement
   d. river

16. Lewis and Clark wrote descriptions of the _____.

    a. treaty

    b. negotiations

    c. land and animals

    d. purchase price

17. They _____ many different regions.

    a. explored

    b. began

    c. helped

    d. purchased

18. Lewis and Clark finally arrived at _____.

    a. the Atlantic Ocean

    b. the Pacific Ocean

    c. New Orleans

    d. Paris

Answers

1. b		**10.** b	
2. d		**11.** a	
3. a		**12.** d	
4. b		**13.** b	
5. c		**14.** a	
6. d		**15.** a	
7. d		**16.** c	
8. b		**17.** a	
9. a		**18.** b	

Let's Write the New Words

In the blank, write the word or phrase that completes the sentence. Look at the words in parentheses. They will help you.

1. They _____ many animals. (caught, ensnared)

2. Jefferson wanted free _____ of the Mississippi. (travel by boat)

3. The men _____ deer and bears. (searched, looked for)

4. Many people lived on the _____ of the river. (shoreline of a river)

5. People came to _____ the land. (plant and harvest crops)

6. Two men _____ with Napoleon. (bargained)

7. The Louisiana Territory was a large _____. (area, territory)

8. To their _____, he agreed to sell the territory. (amazement, wonder)

9. Many people _____ westward. (moved from one place to another)

10. He agreed to sell the _____ territory. (all)

11. They believed that the _____ lay in the west. (the coming time)

12. Lewis and Clark _____ the new land. (searched through new land)

13. Their _____ took them as far as the Pacific. (journey, march)

14. It was the greatest _____ of his presidency. (accomplishment, feat)

15. The ambassadors _____ a treaty. (wrote, made)

16. They _____ the region for $15,000,000. (bought)

17. The territory consisted of 800,000 _____ of land. (1 mile × 1 mile)

Answers

1. trapped

2. navigation

3. hunted

4. banks

5. farm

6. negotiated

7. region

8. surprise

9. migrated

10. entire

11. future

12. explored

13. expedition

14. achievement

15. drew up

16. purchased

17. square miles

Slavery

Slaves were brought to the New World early in American history. By 1650 many ships had transported hundreds of African natives from the African continent to the American colonies. Before the Revolutionary War, slavery existed in all 13 colonies. But from the start of the war until the end of the eighteenth century, slavery was gradually abandoned in the northern states. Because tobacco and cotton farmers in the South needed cheap labor, slavery continued in that region until 1865.

Most slaves worked on plantations. They were permitted to form families, but sometimes slave owners sold off a parent or a child without consideration of the family. There were many slave markets across the South. Planters who needed labor came to these markets to examine the men, women, and children for sale. The planters chose the slaves they wanted and paid for them in the same way that they might purchase a horse or a cow.

In most parts of the South, it was illegal to teach a slave to read and write. Ignorance and harsh punishment were used to control the large population of African slaves.

In some cases, slaves found ways to buy their freedom from their masters. In other cases, slaves simply ran away from the plantation to live free. These free African-Americans often made a new life for themselves in the North.

Important Words

Learn the meaning of these new words. Say a sentence using each new word.

were brought = were shipped	"Many slaves were brought to America."
transport = carry, move	"They were transported by ship."
native = born in a place	"Many native Africans became slaves."
exist = be	"Slavery existed in America for over two centuries."
gradually = slowly, little by little	"They gradually understood the problem."
abandon = quit, give up	"They abandoned slavery after the war."
tobacco = plant for making smoking material	"These planters grow tobacco."
cotton = plant used for making cloth	"Cotton was picked by hand."
labor = work	"Slaves were used as cheap labor."
market = shop, stalls for selling goods	"There were slave markets across the South."
examine = look at carefully	"The planter examined the new slaves."
illegal = against the law	"It was illegal for a slave to read and write."
teach = instruct, educate	"No one would teach them to read and write."
ignorance = having no knowledge	"The slaves were kept in ignorance."
harsh = cruel, severe	"Some masters were harsh with their slaves."
punishment = discipline, beating	"The punishment for a slave was often harsh."
case = example, instance	"In many cases slaves just ran away."
simply = merely, easily	"They simply wanted to be free."

Write Your New Words

In the blank of the first sentence, write the missing word(s). In the second sentence, write the same word(s) from memory.

1. Slaves were brought to America.

Slaves _____ to America.

Slaves _____ to America.

2. Slaves were transported by ship.

Slaves were _____ by ship.

Slaves were _____ by ship.

3. They were native Africans.

They were _____ Africans.

They were _____ Africans.

4. Slavery existed here until 1865.

Slavery _____ here until 1865.

Slavery _____ here until 1865.

5. The North abandoned slavery.

The North _____ slavery.
The North _____ slavery.

6. They grew tobacco.

They grew _____.
They grew _____.

7. Slaves were cheap labor.

Slaves were cheap _____.
Slaves were cheap _____.

8. There were slave markets across the South.

There were slave _____ across the South.
There were slave _____ across the South.

9. He examined the new slave.

He _____ the new slave.
He _____ the new slave.

10. It was illegal for them to read and write.

It was _____ for them to read and write.
It was _____ for them to read and write.

11. They were kept in ignorance.

They were kept in _____.
They were kept in _____.

12. Punishment was often harsh.

_____ was often harsh.
_____ was often harsh.

13. In some cases, slaves simply ran away.

In some _____, slaves simply ran away.
In some _____, slaves simply ran away.

Some Important Questions and Answers

1. When were slaves first brought to America? (early in American history, 1600s)

2. From what continent did slaves come? (Africa)

3. Where was slavery gradually abandoned? (in the North)

4. Who needed cheap labor? (tobacco and cotton farmers)

5. In what year did slavery end? (1865)

6. Where did most slaves work? (on plantations)

7. What was it illegal to teach a slave? (to read and write)

8. How were slaves controlled? (through ignorance and punishment)

Is It TRUE or FALSE?

Say TRUE if the sentence is correct. Say FALSE if it is incorrect.

1. Slaves were brought to the New World in the twentieth century.

2. Before the Revolutionary War, slavery existed in all the colonies.

3. Many slaves worked on plantations.

4. Slave owners never sold off a parent or child of a slave family.

5. Slaves were brought to America from Africa.

6. Planters used slaves as cheap labor.

7. Tobacco and cotton farmers abandoned slavery in 1650.

8. Slavery ended in 1865.

9. Planters bought a slave the same way they might buy a horse.

10. All slaves knew how to read and write.

11. Ignorance and punishment were used to control the slaves.

12. Some slaves were able to buy their freedom.

13. Free African-Americans made a new life for themselves in the North.

14. It was legal to teach a slave to read and write.

15. The North abandoned slavery at the end of the eighteenth century.

Answers

1. False
2. True
3. True
4. False

5. True
6. True
7. False
8. True

9. True

10. False

11. True

12. True

13. True

14. False

15. True

Let's Look at Some Important Sentences

Circle the letter of the word or phrase that completes the sentence.

1. Many ships _____ slaves to the New World.

    a. started

    b. punished

    c. transported

    d. purchased

2. For a long time slavery _____ in all the colonies.

    a. existed

    b. was brought

    c. simply

    d. cheap labor

3. There were already many slaves in America by _____.

    a. 1650

    b. 1800

    c. 1812

    d. 1865

4. _____ farmers needed cheap labor.

    a. Planters

    b. Masters and slaves

    c. Northern

    d. Tobacco and cotton

5. Slavery was _____ abandoned in the North.

    a. never

    b. probably

    c. gradually

    d. in the South

6. Slavery continued in the South until _____.

    a. 1650

    b. 1800

    c. 1812

    d. 1865

7. Sometimes a child would be _____ without its parents.

    a. sold off
    b. transport
    c. punishment
    d. taught to read and write

8. There were many _____ in the South.

    a. locations
    b. slave markets
    c. free slaves
    d. cases

9. It was _____ to teach a slave to read and write.

    a. simply true
    b. punishment
    c. illegal
    d. not very often

10. Some slaves were able to buy their _____ from their masters.

    a. parents
    b. freedom
    c. plantations
    d. education

11. They controlled the slaves with _____ and punishment.

    a. ignorance
    b. slave markets
    c. instruction
    d. illegal education

12. Freed slaves often made a new life for themselves in the _____.

    a. North
    b. South
    c. East
    d. West

13. People came to _____ the slaves at the slave market.

    a. educate
    b. transport
    c. examine
    d. punish

14. They bought a _____ the same way they bought a horse or cow.

    a. farm
    b. slave
    c. planter
    d. master

15. Most slaves worked on _____.

    a. the South

    b. plantations

    c. settlements

    d. the North

16. Slaves were sold off without consideration of their _____.

    a. master

    b. planter

    c. family

    d. purchase price

17. There were many slave markets across the _____.

    a. Africa

    b. ocean

    c. northern colonies

    d. South

18. A slave could not learn to _____.

    a. read and write

    b. plant cotton

    c. plant tobacco

    d. form a family

19. Some slaves _____ from their masters.

    a. purchased

    b. read and wrote

    c. ran away

    d. labored

Answers

1. c		**11.** a
2. a		**12.** a
3. a		**13.** c
4. d		**14.** b
5. c		**15.** b
6. d		**16.** c
7. a		**17.** d
8. b		**18.** a
9. c		**19.** c
10. b		

Let's Write the New Words

In the blank, write the word or phrase that completes the sentence. Look at the words in parentheses. They will help you.

1. You could not _____ them to read and write. (instruct, educate)

2. Slaves were kept in _____. (having no knowledge)

3. The planters came to _____ the slaves. (look at carefully)

4. It was _____ for slaves to read and write. (against the law)

5. Punishment for a slave was often _____. (cruel, severe)

6. The planters visited the slave _____. (shops, stalls for selling goods)

7. Slaves were used as cheap _____. (work)

8. Ignorance and _____ were used to control them. (discipline, beating)

9. Tobacco and _____ farmers needed slaves. (plant used for making cloth)

10. In some _____, slaves bought their freedom. (examples, instances)

11. The North _____ slavery after the Revolutionary War. (quit, gave up)

12. Slavery _____ ended. (slowly, little by little)

13. Slavery _____ in American for more than 200 years. (was)

14. _____ Africans became slaves. (born in Africa)

15. Ships _____ the Africans to America. (carried, moved)

16. Many slaves _____ here before 1650. (were shipped)

17. Some plantations grew _____. (plant for making smoking material)

Answers

1. teach
2. ignorance
3. examine
4. illegal
5. harsh
6. markets
7. labor
8. punishment
9. cotton

10. cases
11. abandoned
12. gradually
13. existed
14. Native
15. transported
16. were brought
17. tobacco

Some Tips About English

- Some important words in this chapter are *irregular verbs*. Their past tense form does not follow the regular pattern. Regular verbs in the past tense end in *–ed*. Irregular verbs make other kinds of changes:

	Regular Verbs	*to draw*	*to teach*
Present Tense	I move, he moves	I draw, he draws	I teach, he teaches
Past Tense	I moved, he moved	I drew, he drew	I taught, he taught

- Sometimes a past tense meaning is expressed in another way: in the present perfect tense. The present perfect tense is formed by the verb *have* and a past participle. Past participles of regular verbs look like the past tense (I have helped, she has worked, we have moved, and so on). But past participles of irregular verbs change in different ways. Look at these examples.

	Regular Verbs	*to draw*
Past Tense	They learned	They drew
Present Perfect Tense	They have learned	They have drawn
	to teach	*to begin*
Past Tense	I taught	I began
Present Perfect Tense	I have taught	I have begun
	to go	*to understand*
Past Tense	We went	We understood
Present Perfect Tense	We have gone	We have understood
	to find	*to speak*
Past Tense	He found	He spoke
Present Perfect Tense	He has found	He has spoken

Use the present perfect tense to mean that **an action began in the past** and **continued to the present.** For example:

"He worked in a factory." = a general statement in the past tense

"He has worked in a factory all his life." = the action began in the past and continued to the present.

You can see a complete list of irregular verbs and past participles in the appendix at the back of this book.

The Nation Dissolves

Connecting East and West

The period after the Louisiana Purchase was a time of important inventions. Robert Fulton was interested in steam power. He is best known for his steamboat, the *Clermont*. The boat's name came from the name of Robert Livingston's estate. Livingston was Fulton's partner.

They finally found a steamboat design that worked successfully. In August, 1807, the first voyage of the *Clermont* took place. The boat and its passengers traveled from New York along the Hudson River to Albany in 32 hours.

Eli Whitney's invention of the cotton gin made cotton plantations profitable. Picking out the green seeds from the cotton by hand was very time-consuming. But Whitney's gin did this automatically and saved many hours of labor. Each decade after 1800 the cotton yield doubled because of this invention.

An invention that was important in uniting the large territory of the United States was the telephone. Alexander Graham Bell, a Scotsman by birth, perfected his idea for the telephone in 1876. By 1884 long-distance service had begun.

Thomas Edison had many inventions. He is well known for the phonograph he invented in 1877. But his greatest achievement was the electric light bulb in 1879.

The railroads quickly spread across the eastern part of the nation. By the middle of the nineteenth century, a large network of rails connected many cities and rural regions.

But the Transcontinental Railroad that connected the east coast with the west coast was the greatest achievement. In 1862 Abraham Lincoln ordered the construction of the railroad. Many immigrants, particularly Chinese, worked to build the railroad. It was completed after the Civil War in 1869.

Important Words

Learn the meaning of these new words. Say a sentence using each new word.

period = time, era	"The period of war was over."
invention = unique new device	"Edison had many inventions."
steam = vapor from boiling water	"Steam power ran the Clermont."
partner = colleague	"She had a new business partner."
successful = reached a goal	"They made a successful voyage in 1807."
take place = happen	"The test took place in Room B."
passenger = traveler	"The boat carried 10 passengers."
cotton gin = cotton and seeds separator	"Whitney invented the cotton gin."
profitable = earning money	"Soon the plantations were profitable again."
time-consuming = using much time	"The work was time-consuming."
automatically = done by a machine	"The seeds were automatically separated from the cotton."
yield = harvest	"The cotton yield this year was good."
double = increase twice in size	"They hope to double the harvest."
perfect = finish, make perfect	"Bell finally perfected his telephone."
long distance = very far	"It's a long distance between Boston and Miami."

network = rail system

rails = long iron bars

rural = of the countryside

construction = building

"The railroad network spread westward."

"Iron rails stretched from coast to coast."

"Even rural towns had a railroad station."

"Construction lasted seven years."

Write Your New Words

In the blank of the first sentence, write the missing word. In the second sentence, write the same word from memory.

1. It was a period of change.

It was a _____ of change.

It was a _____ of change.

2. There were many useful inventions.

There were many useful _____.

There were many useful _____.

3. Steam power made travel easy.

_____ power made travel easy.

_____ power made travel easy.

4. His partner was Livingston.

His _____ was Livingston.

His _____ was Livingston.

5. Edison invented the first successful light bulb.

Edison invented the first _____ light bulb.

Edison invented the first _____ light bulb.

6. The voyage took place on the Hudson River.

The voyage _____ on the Hudson River.

The voyage _____ on the Hudson River.

7. A few passengers got sick.

A few _____ got sick.

A few _____ got sick.

8. The cotton gin helped cotton farmers.

The _____ helped cotton farmers.

The _____ helped cotton farmers.

9. Many plantations were profitable.

Many plantations were _____.

Many plantations were _____.

10. Picking out the seeds was time-consuming.

Picking out the seeds was _____.

Picking out the seeds was _____.

11. All work was done automatically.

All work was done _____.

All work was done _____.

12. What was the cotton yield this year?

What was the cotton _____ this year?

What was the cotton _____ this year?

13. The amount of work doubled.

The amount of work _____.

The amount of work _____.

14. She never perfected the design.

She never _____ the design.

She never _____ the design.

15. It's not a long distance between our homes.

It's not a _____ between our homes.

It's not a _____ between our homes.

16. A rail network is needed here.

A rail _____ is needed here.

A rail _____ is needed here.

17. Chinese laborers laid the rails.

Chinese laborers laid the _____.

Chinese laborers laid the _____.

18. Our farm is in a rural region.

Our farm is in a _____ region.

Our farm is in a _____ region.

19. How long did construction last?

How long did _____ last?

How long did _____ last?

Important Questions and Answers

1. What period was a time of important inventions? (period after the Louisiana Purchase)

2. In what was Robert Fulton interested? (steam power)

3. What did Fulton call his steamboat? (Clermont)

4. Where did the first voyage of the Clermont go? (Albany)

5. What did Eli Whitney invent? (cotton gin)

6. What did the gin do for cotton plantations? (It made them profitable.)

7. What invention helped to unite the territory of the United States? (telephone)

8. Who invented the telephone? (Alexander Graham Bell)

9. Who invented the phonograph? (Thomas Edison)

10. What was Edison's greatest invention? (electric light bulb)

11. Who ordered construction of the Transcontinental Railroad? (Abraham Lincoln)

12. Who laid the rails for this railroad? (many immigrants, Chinese)

Is It TRUE or FALSE?

Say TRUE if the sentence is correct. Say FALSE if it is incorrect.

1. Fulton never found a steamboat design that worked successfully.

2. Fulton's steamboat was named the Clermont.

3. Eli Whitney invented the telephone.

4. Thomas Edison designed the Transcontinental Railroad.

5. Many Chinese immigrants worked on the Transcontinental Railroad.

6. The Transcontinental Railroad was completed after the Civil War.

7. The Clermont was named for Livingston's estate.

8. It took six days to travel from New York to Albany on the Clermont.

9. Long-distance telephone service began by 1884.

10. Alexander Graham Bell invented the telephone.

11. Alexander Graham Bell was an immigrant from Scotland.

12. Whitney's cotton gin saved many hours of labor.

13. Robert Fulton was interested in steam power.

14. George Washington ordered the construction of the Transcontinental Railroad.

15. The telephone helped to unite the territory of the United States.

Answers

1. False
2. True
3. False
4. False
5. True
6. True
7. True
8. False

9. True
10. True
11. True
12. True
13. True
14. False
15. True

Let's Look at Some Important Sentences

Circle the letter of the word or phrase that completes the sentence.

1. Robert Livingston was Fulton's _____.

   a. estate
   b. partner
   c. the *Clermont*
   d. design

2. They found a design that worked _____.

   a. the river
   b. the Hudson River
   c. by the middle of the nineteenth century
   d. successfully

3. The journey from New York to _____ lasted 32 hours.

   a. Albany
   b. Hudson River
   c. Philadelphia
   d. westward

4. Fulton was _____ in steam power.

    a. interested
    b. an immigrant
    c. a Scotsman
    d. passenger

5. The cotton gin made cotton plantations _____.

    a. smaller
    b. profitable
    c. well known
    d. an invention

6. The telephone was an important nineteenth century _____.

    a. railroad
    b. invention
    c. long distance
    d. network

7. _____ invented the cotton gin.

    a. Fulton
    b. Whitney
    c. Bell
    d. Edison

8. The cotton gin _____ the cotton yield.

    a. doubled
    b. perfected
    c. saved
    d. did this automatically

9. Alexander Graham Bell was from _____.

    a. Albany
    b. China
    c. the South
    d. Scotland

10. Edison's greatest achievement was the _____.

    a. electric light bulb
    b. telephone
    c. iron rails
    d. steam power

11. The Transcontinental Railroad _____ the west with the east.

    a. perfected
    b. located
    c. connected
    d. saved

12. A _____ of rails was laid across the land.

    a. network
    b. territory
    c. rural region
    d. river

13. Abraham Lincoln ordered the _____ of the railroad.

    a. location
    b. hours of labor
    c. construction
    d. invention

14. Many Chinese _____ helped built the railroad.

    a. plantations
    b. inventors
    c. immigrants
    d. from Scotland

Answers

1. b		**8.** a
2. d		**9.** d
3. a		**10.** a
4. a		**11.** c
5. b		**12.** a
6. b		**13.** c
7. b		**14.** c

Let's Write the New Words

In the blank, write the word or phrase that completes the sentence. Look at the words in parentheses. They will help you.

1. Cotton plantations were again _____. (earning money)

2. Hand labor was _____. (using much time)

3. Who invented the _____? (cotton and seeds separator)

4. The seeds are _____ separated from the cotton. (done by a machine)

5. The Clermont carried several _____. (travelers)

6. The harvest _____ every year. (increased twice in size)

7. The test of the steamboat _____ on the Hudson. (happened)

8. Bell _____ the telephone in 1876. (finished, made perfect)

9. The design for the boat worked _____. (reached a goal)

117

10. _____ power ran the Clermont. (vapor from boiling water)

11. A _____ of rails spread across the country. (rail system)

12. Many _____ appeared in the nineteenth century. (unique new devices)

13. This was an important _____ for inventors. (time, era)

14. Railroads brought products to _____ regions. (of the countryside)

Answers

1. profitable

2. time-consuming

3. cotton gin

4. automatically

5. passengers

6. doubled

7. took place

8. perfected

9. successfully

10. Steam

11. network

12. inventions

13. period

14. rural

The Civil War

Abraham Lincoln was elected president in November, 1860. He was the first Republican president and was inaugurated in March, 1861. Lincoln said that *government cannot endure permanently half slave, half free. . . .* Abolitionists supported Lincoln in his belief that slavery should end. But the threats to abolish slavery brought the nation to crisis.

The southern states, where most slaves lived, threatened to secede from the Union. They wanted to protect their right to hold slaves. As the crisis worsened, the southern states seceded one by one: First South Carolina; soon after Mississippi, Florida, Alabama, Georgia, Louisiana, and Texas; and finally Virginia, Arkansas, Tennessee, and North Carolina. These 11 states became the Confederate States of America. Their flag was known as the *Stars and Bars*.

Lincoln believed these 11 states had no right to leave the Union. The Union had to be preserved, and Lincoln would fight to do so. And so the War Between the States—the Civil War—began. During the war, Lincoln issued the *Emancipation Proclamation*, which freed the slaves in the southern states. But they would not be free until the war was over.

Many soldiers died on both sides as the war continued until 1865. In January of that year, Congress approved the Thirteenth Amendment to the Constitution, which abolished slavery throughout the country. Finally, on April 9, 1865,

Robert E. Lee, a general of the Confederate Army, surrendered to Ulysses S. Grant, a general of the Union Army, and the war was over.

Tragically, just five days later, Lincoln was assassinated at Ford's Theater by John Wilkes Booth. Booth was an actor who had supported the South in the war.

Important Words

Learn the meaning of these new words. Say a sentence using each new word

inaugurate = admit to office in a ceremony	"Lincoln was inaugurated in 1861."
permanently = forever	"Slavery cannot remain permanently in the nation."
abolitionist = someone who wants to stop something	"Abolitionists were against slavery."
support = hold up, help	"We supported his new ideas."
belief = idea, something someone believes	"Her belief in freedom was strong."
threat = warning, menacing statement	"Their threats did not frighten her."
threaten = make threats	"The South threatened to leave the Union."
crisis = time of great danger	"The nation found itself in crisis."
secede = leave, abandon	"South Carolina was the first to secede."
worsen = become worse	"The patient's health began to worsen."
preserve = keep safe	"Lincoln wanted to preserve the United States."
until = up to the time	"They were not free until the end of the war."
approve = adopt, accept	"Congress approved the amendment."
throughout = in every region	"Every slave throughout the land was free."
tragically = sadly	"Tragically, many soldiers died in the war."
assassinate = kill	"John Wilkes Booth assassinated Lincoln."

Write Your New Words

In the blank of the first sentence, write the missing word. In the second sentence, write the same word from memory.

1. When is the president inaugurated?

   When is the president _____?

   When is the president _____?

2. The Union must remain permanently together.

   The Union must remain _____ together.

   The Union must remain _____ together.

3. Abolitionists hated slavery.

   _____ hated slavery.

   _____ hated slavery.

4. Many supported Lincoln's ideas.

   Many _____ Lincoln's ideas.

   Many _____ Lincoln's ideas.

5. His belief in freedom was strong.

His _____ in freedom was strong.

His _____ in freedom was strong.

6. He made a threat against me.

He made a _____ against me.

He made a _____ against me.

7. The South threatened war.

The South _____ war.

The South _____ war.

8. It was a time of crisis.

It was a time of _____.

It was a time of _____.

9. Which state was first to secede?

Which state was first to _____?

Which state was first to _____?

10. The situation began to worsen.

The situation began to _____.

The situation began to _____.

11. Lincoln preserved the Union.

Lincoln _____ the Union.

Lincoln _____ the Union.

12. The war lasted until 1865.

The war lasted _____ 1865.

The war lasted _____ 1865.

13. When was the amendment approved?

When was the amendment _____?

When was the amendment _____?

14. Slavery had ended throughout the land.

Slavery had ended _____ the land.

Slavery had ended _____ the land.

15. Tragically, a civil war began.

_____, a civil war began.

_____, a civil war began.

16. Booth assassinated Lincoln.

Booth _____ Lincoln.

Booth _____ Lincoln.

Important Questions and Answers

1. Who was the first Republican president? (Abraham Lincoln)

2. What did Lincoln believe about slavery? (It should end.)

3. What brought the nation to crisis? (threats to abolish slavery)

4. In what region did most slaves live? (South)

5. What did the southern states threaten to do? (secede from the Union)

6. What state was the first to secede? (South Carolina)

7. What did the 11 seceded states call themselves? (Confederate States of America)

8. What did Lincoln want to preserve? (the Union)

9. What document freed the slaves in the South? (Emancipation Proclamation)

10. What year did the Civil War end? (1865)

11. What southern general surrendered to Ulysses S. Grant? (Robert E. Lee)

12. What happened on April 14, 1865? (Booth killed Lincoln)

13. Where was Lincoln assassinated? (in Ford's Theater)

Is It TRUE or FALSE?

Say TRUE if the sentence is correct. Say FALSE if it is incorrect.

1. Most slaves lived in the North.

2. New York was the first state to secede from the Union.

3. Lincoln was elected president in November, 1860.

4. Lincoln was the first Republican president.

5. Lincoln believed in slavery.

6. Abolitionists were people who wanted to end slavery.

7. Eleven southern states seceded from the Union.

8. The southern states were called the Southern States of America.

9. Lincoln would fight to preserve the Union.

10. Lincoln issued the Emancipation Proclamation to free the slaves.

11. No one died during the Civil War.

12. The Civil War ended in 1776.

13. The Thirteenth Amendment abolished slavery.

14. General Grant surrendered to General Lee to end the Civil War.

15. An actor named Booth assassinated Lincoln.

Answers

1. False
2. False
3. True
4. True
5. False
6. True
7. True
8. False

9. True
10. True
11. False
12. False
13. True
14. False
15. True

Let's Look at Some Important Sentences

Circle the letter of the word or phrase that completes the sentence.

1. Lincoln was elected president in _____.

   a. 1859
   b. 1860
   c. 1861
   d. 1865

2. Lincoln was inaugurated in March, _____.

   a. 1859
   b. 1860
   c. 1861
   d. 1865

3. People who were against slavery were called _____.

    a. Americans

    b. southerners

    c. northerners

    d. abolitionists

4. Most slaves lived in the _____.

    a. North

    b. South

    c. East

    d. West

5. In 1860 the southern states began to _____.

    a. support

    b. secede

    c. protect

    d. elect

6. There were _____ Confederate States.

    a. nine

    b. ten

    c. eleven

    d. fifteen

7. The southern flag was known as the _____.

    a. Stars and Bars

    b. Stars and Stripes

    c. Red Banner

    d. Red, White, and Blue

8. Lincoln wanted to _____ the Union.

    a. elect

    b. fight

    c. free

    d. preserve

9. The War Between the States is also called the _____.

    a. Civil War

    b. War of 1812

    c. Revolutionary War

    d. French and Indian War

10. The Emancipation Proclamation _____ the slaves in the South.

    a. supported

    b. freed

    c. located

    d. protected

11. The _____ Amendment made slavery illegal.

    a. Tenth

    b. Eleventh

    c. Twelfth

    d. Thirteenth

12. Robert E. Lee was a _____.

    a. southern general

    b. Lincoln supporter

    c. abolitionist

    d. Union general

13. The Civil War ended in _____.

    a. 1861

    b. 1862

    c. 1864

    d. 1865

14. Lincoln was _____ in Ford's Theater.

    a. protected

    b. assassinated

    c. surrendered

    d. elected

15. The president was killed by _____.

    a. Robert E. Lee

    b. Ulysses S. Grant

    c. John Wilkes Booth

    d. an angry crowd

16. Abraham Lincoln _____ the Union and freed the slaves.

    a. fought

    b. saved

    c. seceded

    d. surrendered

Answers

1. b		**9.** a	
2. c		**10.** b	
3. d		**11.** d	
4. b		**12.** a	
5. b		**13.** d	
6. c		**14.** b	
7. a		**15.** c	
8. d		**16.** b	

Let's Write the New Words

In the blank, write the word or phrase that completes the sentence. Look at the words in parentheses. They will help you.

1. Georgia _____ to leave the Union. (made threats)

2. They supported his _____ in freedom. (idea, something someone believes)

3. It was a time of great _____. (time of great danger)

4. Which states _____ from the Union? (left, abandoned)

5. He made _____ against me. (warnings, menacing statements)

6. Everyone _____ the decision. (held up, helped)

7. The situation began to _____. (become worse)

8. There were many _____ in the North. (people who want to stop something)

9. Lincoln _____ the Union. (kept safe)

10. The war did not end _____ 1865. (up to the time)

11. Slavery was _____ ended. (forever)

12. The nation _____ of the decision. (adopted, accepted)

13. Lincoln was _____ in 1861. (admitted to office in a ceremony)

14. Who _____ the president? (killed)

15. _____, the states seceded from the Union. (sadly)

16. Slaves _____ the nation were now free. (in every region)

Answers

1. threatened
2. belief
3. crisis
4. seceded
5. threats
6. supported
7. worsen
8. abolitionists

9. preserved
10. until
11. permanently
12. approved
13. inaugurated
14. assassinated
15. Tragically
16. throughout

Some Tips About English

- Using English adverbs is easy. Most adverbs are formed by adding –ly to an adjective.

adjective	adverb
slow	slowly
careful	carefully
easy	easily

- Adjectives describe a noun. Adverbs describe the action of a verb.

adjective	adverb
a slow train	The train moved slowly.
a careful answer	He answered carefully.
the easy test	She passed the test easily.

- The word *fast* is both an adjective and an adverb.

adjective	adverb
a fast car	He drives fast.

The adverb *fast* is often replaced by the adverb *quickly*.

- You have to be careful with the word *good*. Its adverb form is *well*.

adjective	adverb
a good speech	She speaks well.
the good runner	He runs well.

But there is one more problem with *well*. It can be an adjective when it means *healthy*. Compare these sentences:

John is *good*. (an adjective that says that John is *NOT BAD*)

John is *well*. (an adjective that says that John is NOT SICK)

Immigration

America is a nation of immigrants. Some of us have been here for generations. Others are newcomers. Except for the Native Americans, we all came to this new land as immigrants. The earliest to come to the New World were the English, Dutch, French, and Spanish.

In the nineteenth century, thousands of Irish left their homeland, which was experiencing a potato famine that caused great suffering to the Irish people. By 1850 about 960,000 people in the United States had been born in Ireland.

From 1848 until the Civil War more than a million Germans came to start a new life in America. Many chose to live in cities like New York, Chicago, Cincinnati, or Milwaukee. Others settled on farms in places like Iowa and Illinois. During that same period thousands of German Jews and Frenchmen also arrived here.

The construction of the Transcontinental Railroad stimulated Chinese immigration. Many men came here to work and to send money back to their families in China. When the railroad was finished, a large number of Chinese decided to stay here.

Until 1870 there had been little Italian immigration. But as Italy suffered from overcrowding and low wages, Italians began to leave their homeland. By 1900 nearly 700,000 Italians had settled in America.

Since the middle of the nineteenth century until the present day, millions of immigrants from nearly every country in the world have come here to work and to build new lives as Americans.

Important Words

Learn the meaning of these new words. Say a sentence using each new word.

generation = all people born about the same time	"Their generation is old-fashioned."
newcomer = new arrival	"The newcomers lived in New York."
except for = excluding	"Except for Native Americans, we are all immigrants."
suffer = undergo pain, tolerate	"The dog suffered from the heat."
famine = starvation	"Many Irish died during the famine."
stimulate = arouse	"Immigration stimulated population growth."
overcrowding = excess population	"They left Italy because of overcrowding."
wages = pay, salary	"She wanted better wages."

Write Your New Words

In the blank of the first sentence, write the missing word. In the second sentence, write the same word from memory.

1. Each generation has its problems.

Each _____ has its problems.

Each _____ has its problems.

2. We greeted the newcomers.

We greeted the _____.

We greeted the _____.

3. Except for her, everyone is sick.

_____ her, everyone is sick.

_____ her, everyone is sick.

4. People were suffering in Europe.

People were _____ in Europe.

People were _____ in Europe.

5. The potato famine killed thousands.

The potato _____ killed thousands.

The potato _____ killed thousands.

6. Poverty stimulated immigration.

Poverty _____ immigration.

Poverty _____ immigration.

7. Overcrowding was the problem.

_____ was the problem.

_____ was the problem.

8. She did not accept low wages.

She did not accept low _____.

She did not accept low _____.

Important Questions and Answers

1. What country is a nation of immigrants? (United States)

2. Who came to the New World the earliest? (English, Dutch, French, Spanish)

3. Why did thousands of people leave Ireland? (There was a potato famine.)

4. What nationality settled in Chicago, Cincinnati, and Milwaukee? (Germans)

5. What stimulated Chinese immigration? (construction of the Transcontinental Railroad)

6. Who immigrated to America because of overcrowding and low wages? (Italians)

7. How many countries have immigrants come from? (nearly all countries)

8. What people lived in America before the Europeans came? (Native Americans)

Is It TRUE or FALSE?

Say TRUE if the sentence is correct. Say FALSE if it is incorrect.

1. Italy is a nation of immigrants.

2. Many Irish came to America in the nineteenth century.

3. There was a terrible potato famine in France.

4. Thousands of Germans came to America during the Revolutionary War.

5. German Jews and Frenchmen immigrated in the middle of the nineteenth century.

6. Railroad construction stimulated Chinese immigration.

7. Before 1870 there had been little Italian immigration.

8. The original Americans are the Native Americans.

Answers

1. False

2. True

3. False

4. False

5. True

6. True

7. True

8. True

Let's Look at Some Important Sentences

Circle the letter of the word or phrase that completes the sentence.

1. From 1848 until the _____ many Germans came to America.

   a. War of 1812
   b. Revolution
   c. nineteenth century
   d. Civil War

2. The English, _____, French, and Spanish came to America early.

   a. Chinese
   b. Dutch
   c. Italians
   d. German Jews

3. Many Chinese came here to work on the _____.

    a. river
    b. railroad
    c. coast
    d. highways

4. Many German _____ also came to America.

    a. Frenchmen
    b. Spanish
    c. Jews
    d. in 1848

5. America is a nation of _____.

    a. Irish
    b. Germans
    c. Irish and Germans
    d. immigrants

6. Construction of the _____ brought new immigrants to America.

    a. Transcontinental Railroad
    b. Civil War
    c. New York and Chicago
    d. New World

7. Some Germans settled on _____.

    a. farms
    b. the railroad
    c. low wages
    d. construction

8. _____ was a problem in Italy.

    a. Frenchmen
    b. Overcrowding
    c. The homeland
    d. A generation

9. Some Americans have been here for _____.

    a. Native Americans
    b. generations
    c. Iowa and Illinois
    d. construction

10. Millions of immigrants have come here from nearly every _____ in the world.

    a. country
    b. immigration
    c. farm
    d. century

Answers

1. d		**6.** a	
2. b		**7.** a	
3. b		**8.** b	
4. c		**9.** b	
5. d		**10.** a	

Let's Write the New Words

In the blank, write the word or phrase that completes the sentence. Look at the words in parentheses. They will help you.

1. Many _____ from the war. (underwent pain, tolerated)

2. There was a great potato _____ in Ireland. (starvation)

3. _____ Native Americans, we are all immigrants. (excluding)

4. Overcrowding _____ immigration to America. (aroused)

5. _____ were arriving from everywhere. (new arrivals)

6. One of the problems was _____. (excess population)

7. I am the first _____ to live here. (all people born about the same time)

8. They left Italy because of low _____. (pay, salary)

Answers

1. suffered

2. famine

3. Except for

4. stimulated

5. Newcomers

6. overcrowding

7. generation

8. wages

The Statue of Liberty

The Statue of Liberty stands on a pedestal on Liberty Island in New York Harbor. It is one of the first things that immigrants to this country see when they arrive. It is a symbol of America and freedom. And it serves as an inspiration for all who seek liberty.

It was a gift from the people of France to celebrate America's 100th birthday. The statue symbolized the friendship and support France had given to this nation during the Revolutionary War.

The sculptor, Bartholdi, was commissioned to design the statue in 1876. It is made of copper plates, which were laid over a framework designed by Alexandre Eiffel. Eiffel was the designer for the Eiffel Tower in Paris.

The Statue of Liberty was finally erected 10 years late. On October 28, 1886, it was officially dedicated before a crowd of thousands of spectators.

Important Words

Learn the meaning of these new words. Say a sentence using each new word.

pedestal = base, stand   "The statue was put on a pedestal."

symbol = sign, something representing something else   "The eagle is an American symbol."

serve as = act as   "Washington served as president for eight years."

inspiration = influence, arousal   "The flag was the inspiration for *The Star Spangled Banner.*"

seek = look for, search   "He is seeking help with his problems."

celebrate = mark with a festival   "We celebrated her birthday last Friday."

symbolize = represent something else   "The statue symbolizes liberty."

sculptor = artist who works in stone and metal   "The sculptor made a statue out of stone."

commission = payment for a task   "He received a commission to paint a picture."

copper = reddish metal   "Copper plates cover the statue."

framework = scaffold, skeleton   "The framework was made of steel."

erect = build   "The statue was erected in four months."

dedicate = officially put into service   "It wasn't dedicated until 10 years later."

Write Your New Words

In the blank of the first sentence, write the missing word. In the second sentence, write it from memory.

1. The statue is on a pedestal.

The statue is on a _____.

The statue in on a _____.

2. The flag is a symbol of the nation.

The flag is a _____ of the nation.

The flag is a _____ of the nation.

3. The statue serves as a symbol of freedom.

The statue _____ a symbol of freedom.

The statue _____ a symbol of freedom.

4. My wife is my inspiration.

My wife is my _____.

My wife is my _____.

5. They seek a better life in America.

They _____ a better life in America.

They _____ a better life in America.

6. We always celebrate the Fourth of July.

We always _____ the Fourth of July.

We always _____ the Fourth of July.

7. The stars on the flag symbolize the states.

The stars on the flag _____ the states.

The stars on the flag _____ the states.

8. Bartholdi was a sculptor.

Bartholdi was a _____ .

Bartholdi was a _____ .

9. Her commission was $1,000.

Her _____ was $1,000.

Her _____ was $1,000.

10. The skin of the statue was made of copper.

The skin of the statue was made of _____ .

The skin of the statue was made of _____ .

11. Eiffel designed the framework.

Eiffel designed the _____ .

Eiffel designed the _____ .

12. The statue was erected in the harbor.

The statue was _____ in the harbor.

The statue was _____ in the harbor.

13. The mayor dedicated the statue.

The mayor _____ the statue.

The mayor _____ the statue.

Important Questions and Answers

1. From what nation was the Statue of Liberty a gift? (France)

2. From what kind of metal was the statue made? (copper)

3. What does the Statue of Liberty stand on? (pedestal)

4. What is one of the first things immigrants see when they arrive in New York harbor? (Statue of Liberty)

5. What was the statue supposed to celebrate? (100th birthday of America)

6. Who was commissioned to design the statue? (Bartholdi)

7. What did Eiffel design? (framework of the statue)

8. What year was the statue dedicated? (1886)

9. What is the name of the island where the statue stands? (Liberty Island)

Is It TRUE or FALSE?

Say TRUE if the sentence is correct. Say FALSE if it is incorrect.

1. The Statue of Liberty stands in Boston Harbor.

2. The Statue of Liberty is a symbol of freedom and America.

3. The statue was a gift from the English people.

4. The statue symbolizes the friendship of France during the Revolutionary War.

5. A German immigrant was commissioned to design the statue.

6. The skin of the statue is made of wooden plates.

7. Alexandre Eiffel designed the framework of the statue.

8. The Statue of Liberty was dedicated one year late.

9. The Statue of Liberty is located on Liberty Island.

Answers

1. False
2. True
3. False
4. True
5. False

6. False
7. True
8. False
9. True

Let's Look at Some Important Sentences

Circle the letter of the word or phrase that completes the sentence.

1. The Statue of _____ is located in New York Harbor.

   a. New York
   b. Paris
   c. Freedom
   d. Liberty

2. The statue serves as an _____ for all who seek liberty.

    a. inspiration
    b. immigrant
    c. celebration
    d. design

3. The statue is made of _____ plates.

    a. copper
    b. steel
    c. round
    d. wooden

4. The Statue of Liberty stands on a _____.

    a. support
    b. tower
    c. pedestal
    d. symbol

5. Bartholdi was commissioned to design the statue in _____.

    a. 1776
    b. 1866
    c. 1876
    d. 1896

6. The statue was a _____ from the people of France.

    a. celebration
    b. gift
    c. tower
    d. dedication

7. The _____ was designed by Alexandre Eiffel.

    a. island
    b. pedestal
    c. statue
    d. framework

8. _____ was America's friend and supporter during the Revolutionary War.

    a. France
    b. England
    c. Germany
    d. Great Britain

9. The Statue of Liberty was erected _____ years late.

    a. ten
    b. eight
    c. five
    d. two

10. The statue was _____ before a crowd of thousands.

    a. dedicated

    b. celebrate

    c. seen

    d. in the harbor

11. The statue celebrated America's 100th _____.

    a. year

    b. century

    c. birthday

    d. island

12. The Statue of Liberty is located on Liberty _____.

    a. Street

    b. Harbor

    c. Tower

    d. Island

Answers

1. d		**7.** d	
2. a		**8.** a	
3. a		**9.** a	
4. c		**10.** a	
5. c		**11.** c	
6. b		**12.** d	

Let's Write the New Words

In the blank, write the word or phrase that completes the sentence. Look at the words in parentheses. They will help you.

1. Bartholdi was a _____. (artist who works in stone and metal)

2. The statue _____ liberty. (represents something else)

3. The designer received a large _____. (payment for a task)

4. They _____ their first anniversary. (mark with a festival)

5. The plates on the statue are made of _____. (reddish metal)

6. Some immigrants _____ liberty. (look for, search)

7. Eiffel designed the _____ of the statue. (scaffold, skeleton)

8. The flag was the _____ for the national anthem. (influence, arousal)

9. The statue was _____ in 1886. (built)

10. It was _____ before a large crowd of people. (officially put into service)

11. The flag is an American _____. (sign, something representing something else)

12. The statue stands on a _____. (base, stand)

Answers

1. sculptor

2. symbolizes

3. commission

4. celebrated

5. copper

6. seek

7. framework

8. inspiration

9. erected

10. dedicated

11. symbol

12. pedestal

The Spanish-American War

America went to war with Spain in 1898. There were three major causes for this war:

- The sinking of the U. S. battleship *Maine*
- The Cuban struggle for independence
- American imperialism and the desire for global influence

The war lasted only four months, from April 25 until August 12. Most of the fighting took place in the Philippines and in Cuba. Theodore Roosevelt led a cavalry unit called the Rough Riders in the Cuban campaign. Admiral Dewey was victorious over the Spanish navy in the battle of Manila Bay in the Philippines.

When the war finally ended, the United States had become a global power. Spain's defeat was the end of her colonial empire. And Spain's former colonies were now possessions of the United States: Puerto Rico, Guam, and the Philippines.

Not all Americans agreed with America's annexation of the Philippines. Mark Twain, a famous writer of the time, criticized the government for this action.

Important Words

Learn the meaning of these new words. Say a sentence using each new word.

major = great, important	"It was a major defeat for Spain."
cause = reason	"There were three causes for the war."
sinking = destroying a ship and making it sink	"The sinking of the *Maine* shocked America."
imperialism = belief in a growing empire	"Some in America believed in imperialism."
global = worldwide	"Pollution is a global problem."
cavalry = soldiers on horseback	"The cavalry attacked the enemy."
campaign = waging war	"The Cuban campaign lasted four months."
former = previous, earlier	"Guam was a former colony of Spain."
possession = something owned	"The colonies became American possessions."
annexation = take possession, add	"Many did not like the annexation of the Philippines."
criticize = judge, find fault with	"Mark Twain criticized the government."

Write Your New Words

In the blank of the first sentence, write the missing word. In the second sentence, write the same word from memory.

1. A major battle took place for San Juan Hill.

   A _____ battle took place for San Juan Hill.
   A _____ battle took place for San Juan Hill.

2. One of the causes was American imperialism.

   One of the _____ was American imperialism.
   One of the _____ was American imperialism.

3. The sinking of the *Maine* shocked America.

   The _____ of the *Maine* shocked America.
   The _____ of the *Maine* shocked America.

4. Not everyone approved of imperialism.

   Not everyone approved of _____.
   Not everyone approved of _____.

5. America became a global power.

   America became a _____ power.
   America became a _____ power.

6. The cavalry attacked San Juan Hill.

   The _____ attacked San Juan Hill.
   The _____ attacked San Juan Hill.

7. The Cuban campaign took many lives.

   The Cuban _____ took many lives.
   The Cuban _____ took many lives.

8. Puerto Rico is a former Spanish colony.

   Puerto Rico is a _____ Spanish colony.
   Puerto Rico is a _____ Spanish colony.

9. The colonies became American possessions.

   The colonies became American _____.
   The colonies became American _____.

10. The annexation of the Philippines caused new problems.

The _____ of the Philippines caused new problems.

The _____ of the Philippines caused new problems.

11. Many Americans criticized the government.

Many Americans _____ the government.

Many Americans _____ the government.

Important Questions and Answers

1. With what country did America go to war in 1898? (Spain)

2. What happened to the battleship *Maine*? (It sank after an explosion.)

3. How long did the Spanish-American War last? (four months)

4. What future president led the Rough Riders? (Theodore Roosevelt)

5. What had the United States become when the war ended? (a global power)

6. Who was victorious in the battle of Manila Bay? (Admiral Dewey)

7. What Spanish colonies became American possessions? (Puerto Rico, Guam, Philippines)

8. How did some Americans feel about the annexation of the Philippines? (They criticized the government for this action.)

Is It TRUE or FALSE?

Say TRUE if the sentence is correct. Say FALSE if it is incorrect.

1. All Americans agreed with the annexation of the Philippines.

2. The former Spanish colonies became American possessions.

3. The United States annexed Japan.

4. The Mexican struggle for independence was a cause for the war.

5. Admiral Dewey defeated the Spanish navy in Manila Bay.

6. The sinking of the *Maine* was one cause for the war.

7. Theodore Roosevelt was an admiral in the navy.

8. The Spanish-American War lasted four years.

9. With the end of the war America became a global power.

10. Mark Twain criticized American imperialism.

Answers

1. False		**6.** True	
2. True		**7.** False	
3. False		**8.** False	
4. False		**9.** True	
5. True		**10.** True	

Let's Look at Some Important Sentences

Circle the letter of the word or phrase that completes the sentence.

1. The United States had become a _____ power.

    a. American
    b. global
    c. European
    d. Spanish

2. Spain's defeat was the end of her colonial _____.

    a. empire
    b. imperialism
    c. navy
    d. victory

3. He was _____ over the Spanish navy in Manila Bay.

    a. located
    b. official
    c. global
    d. victorious

4. America had a desire for global _____.

    a. cavalry
    b. annexation
    c. influence
    d. war

5. Not everyone liked American _____.

    a. imperialism
    b. possession
    c. admirals
    d. battleships

6. The _____ of the *Maine* was a cause for the war.

    a. possession
    b. sinking
    c. struggle
    d. battleship

7. Spain's _____ colonies were now American possessions.

   a. former
   b. empire
   c. independent
   d. colonial

8. The _____ was called the Rough Riders.

   a. navy
   b. global
   c. cavalry
   d. Cuban

9. Puerto Rico, Guam, and _____ became American possessions.

   a. Spain
   b. the Philippines
   c. Florida
   d. global power

10. Mark Twain criticized the _____ of the Philippines.

   a. power
   b. empire
   c. sinking
   d. annexation

Answers

1. b
2. a
3. d
4. c
5. a

6. b
7. a
8. c
9. b
10. d

Let's Write the New Words

In the blank, write the word or phrase that completes the sentence. Look at the words in parentheses. They will help you.

1. America became a _____ power. (worldwide)

2. Theodore Roosevelt led the _____ unit. (soldiers on horseback)

3. American _____ was fully accepted. (belief in a growing empire)

4. The Cuban _____ lasted four months. (waging war)

5. Their _____ colonies now belonged to America. (previous, earlier)

6. The _____ of the *Maine* was the worst news. (destroying a ship and making it sink)

7. Guam and Puerto Rico became American _____. (something owned)

8. There were three _____ for the war. (reasons)

9. Some Americans _____ the government. (judged, found fault with)

10. Cuban independence was a _____ cause of the war. (great, important)

Answers

1. global

2. cavalry

3. imperialism

4. campaign

5. former

6. sinking

7. possessions

8. causes

9. criticized

10. major

Some Tips About English

- English plurals are quite easy. They are formed by adding *-s* or *–es* to a noun. Look at these examples:

Singular	Plural	Singular	Plural
boy	boys	lunch	lunches
house	houses	box	boxes
window	windows	kiss	kisses
book	books	sandwich	sandwiches

There are a few irregular plural forms.

Singular	Plural	Singular	Plural
child	children	mouse	mice
foot	feet	person	people
goose	geese	deer	deer
knife	knives	leaf	leaves
man	men	ox	oxen
tooth	teeth	woman	women
wife	wives	wolf	wolves

- The words *seek* and *sink* in this chapter are *irregular verbs*. Their past and present perfect tense forms do not follow the regular pattern.

	Regular Verbs	to seek	to sink
Present Tense	He helps	He seeks	He sinks
Past Tense	He helped	He sought	He sank
Present Perfect Tense	He has helped	He has sought	He has sunk

The Executive Branch

The American government is made up of three branches: the Executive Branch, the Legislative Branch, and the Judicial Branch. The Executive Branch makes certain that the laws of the land are obeyed.

The President heads this branch. He is assisted by the Vice President, who also serves as the President of the Senate. He also replaces the President if the President is unable to do his job.

The President is helped by his Cabinet. The Cabinet members head the various departments of the government:

Department of State

Department of the Treasury

Department of Defense

Department of Justice

Department of the Interior

Department of Agriculture

Department of Commerce

Department of Labor

Department of Health and Human Services

Department of Housing and Urban Development

Department of Transportation

Department of Energy

Department of Education

Department of Veterans Affairs

Department of Homeland Security

The boss of the employees of these departments and of other agencies of government is the President of the United States.

The President is the head of state. He meets foreign dignitaries and arranges treaties, although all treaties must be approved by Congress. The President is also the Commander-in-Chief of all the armed forces. He can send troops overseas to deal with a problem. But only Congress can declare war.

When Congress makes a new law, they send it to the President in the form of a bill. If the President signs the bill, it becomes law. If he does not approve the bill, it is called a *veto*.

If the President dies, the Vice President becomes president. If the Vice President also dies, the Speaker of the House of Representatives becomes President. Then the following order of succession is used:

President Pro Tempore of the Senate

Secretary of State

Secretary of the Treasury

Secretary of Defense

Attorney General

The remaining members of the Cabinet

Important Words

Learn the meaning of these new words. Say a sentence using each new word.

obey = comply with, yield to   "The child does not obey his parents."

head = leader, highest official   "Who is the head of Homeland Security?"

replace = take the place of   "The vice president could replace the president."

department = division, branch   "The Cabinet consists of various departments."

head of state = nation's leader   "The president is our head of state."

dignitary = high official from a foreign land   "We greeted dignitaries from Africa."

armed forces = army, navy, marines   "U.S. armed forces have bases around the world."

overseas = in foreign lands   "Some soldiers are serving overseas."

bill = proposed law   "The president vetoed the bill."

succession = following in order   "Do you know the order of succession?"

Write Your New Words

In the blank of the first sentence, write the missing word. In the second sentence, write the same word from memory.

1. You must obey the law.

You must _____ the law.

You must _____ the law.

2. The President is head of the Executive Branch.

The President is _____ of the Executive Branch.

The President is _____ of the Executive Branch.

3. I replaced the broken window.

I _____ the broken window.

I _____ the broken window.

4. The attorney general heads the Justice Department.

The attorney general heads the Justice _____.

The attorney general heads the Justice _____.

5. The heads of state met in Rome.

The _____ met in Rome.

The _____ met in Rome.

6. Dignitaries from around the world began to arrive.

_____ from around the world began to arrive.

_____ from around the world began to arrive.

7. Did you serve in the armed forces?

   Did you serve in the _____?

   Did you serve in the _____?

8. My brother was sent overseas.

   My brother was sent _____.

   My brother was sent _____.

9. Congress sent the bill to the President.

   Congress sent the _____ to the President.

   Congress sent the _____ to the President.

10. What is the order of succession for the presidency?

    What is the order of _____ for the presidency?

    What is the order of _____ for the presidency?

Important Questions and Answers

1. What branch of government makes certain that laws are obeyed? (Executive Branch)

2. Who is the head of the Executive Branch? (president)

3. Who is the President of the United States now? (George W. Bush)

4. Who is the Vice President of the United States now? (Dick Cheney)

5. What does the Cabinet do? (helps the President)

6. What do the members of the Cabinet head? (departments of government)

7. Who is President of the Senate? (vice president)

8. What is it called when the President does not sign a bill into law? (veto)

9. Who is Commander-in-Chief of the armed forces? (president)

10. What branch of government can declare war? (Congress, Legislative Branch)

11. Who becomes President if the President dies? (vice president)

12. Who is the head of state of the United States? (president)

13. Who is the boss of all government employees? (president)

Is it TRUE or FALSE?

Say TRUE if the sentence is correct. Say FALSE if it is incorrect.

1. The Executive Branch makes the laws of the land.

2. The Vice President is the head of the Executive Branch.

3. The Vice President is the President of the Senate.

4. The President signs a bill to make it a law.

5. The Executive Branch makes certain that laws are obeyed.

6. The President is helped by his Cabinet.

7. The President is the boss of all government employees.

8. The attorney general becomes President if the President dies.

9. If the President does not sign a bill, it is called a veto.

10. Cabinet members head the departments of government.

11. The President is the Commander-in-Chief of the armed forces.

12. Only the President can declare war.

13. The President of the United States is Dick Cheney.

Answers

1. False

2. False

3. True

4. True

5. True

6. True

7. True

8. False

9. True

10. True

11. True

12. False

13. False

Let's Look at Some Important Sentences

1. A bill does not become law if it is _____.

   a. signed
   b. vetoed
   c. made by Congress
   d. needed

2. The President is the Commander-in-Chief of the _____.

   a. Congress
   b. Executive Branch
   c. armed forces
   d. Cabinet

3. The _____ is the President of the Senate.

   a. Vice President
   b. President
   c. Speaker of the House
   d. attorney general

4. The President is the head of the _____ Branch.

   a. Legislative
   b. Cabinet
   c. department
   d. Executive

5. Only Congress can _____.

   a. veto bills
   b. sign bills into law
   c. head the Cabinet
   d. declare war

6. Cabinet members head the various _____ of government.

   a. departments
   b. branches
   c. armed forces
   d. officers

7. The President greets foreign _____.

   a. laws
   b. dignitaries
   c. armies
   d. tourists

8. The President can send troops _____ to deal with problems.

   a. from foreign lands
   b. to the navy
   c. overseas
   d. from the Executive Branch

9. The President is our _____.

   a. Secretary of State
   b. Executive Branch
   c. Judicial Branch
   d. head of state

10. The order in which people become President if the President dies is called the order of _____.

    a. succession

    b. presidency

    c. Congress

    d. Speaker of the House

11. The government consists of three _____.

    a. departments

    b. branches

    c. representatives

    d. employees

12. The _____ replaces the President if the President is unable to do his job.

    a. attorney general

    b. Legislative Branch

    c. Cabinet

    d. Vice President

13. _____ is the President of the United States.

    a. Ronald Reagan

    b. George W. Bush

    c. Bill Clinton

    d. Al Gore

Answers

1. b		**8.** c	
2. c		**9.** d	
3. a		**10.** a	
4. d		**11.** b	
5. d		**12.** d	
6. a		**13.** b	
7. b			

Let's Write the New Words

In the blank, write the word or phrase that completes the sentence. Look at the words in parentheses. They will help you.

1. What is the order of _____? (following in order)

2. The President is our _____. (nation's leader)

3. If a _____ is vetoed, it cannot become law. (proposed law)

4. The _____ of Defense is part of the Cabinet. (division, branch)

5. The President sent troops _____. (to foreign lands)

6. The Vice President _____ the President if the President cannot do his job. (takes the place of)

7. The President commands the _____. (army, navy, marines)

8. Who is the _____ of the Executive Branch? (leader, highest official)

9. Many _____ visited the capital. (high officials from foreign lands)

10. Everyone must _____ the law. (comply with, yield to)

Answers

1. succession

2. head of state

3. bill

4. Department

5. overseas

6. replaces

7. armed forces

8. head

9. dignitaries

10. obey

The Presidents and Vice Presidents of the United States

There have been 43 Presidents of the United States. Some of them served with one vice president. Others had a different vice president for each term. And if a vice president became president after the death of a president, he often had no vice president during his term. Here is a list of all the presidents and their vice presidents.

	President	Vice President	Years in Office
1	George Washington	John Adams	1789–1797
2	John Adams	Thomas Jefferson	1797–1801
3	Thomas Jefferson	Aaron Burr/George Clinton	1801–1809
4	James Madison	George Clinton/Elbridge Gerry	1809–1817
5	James Monroe	Daniel D. Tompkins	1817–1825
6	John Quincy Adams	John C. Calhoun	1825–1829
7	Andrew Jackson	John C. Calhoun/Martin Van Buren	1829–1837
8	Martin Van Buren	Richard M. Johnson	1837–1841
9	William Henry Harrison	John Tyler	1841
10	John Tyler	None	1841–1845
11	James K. Polk	George M. Dallas	1845–1849
12	Zachary Taylor	Millard Fillmore	1849–1850
13	Millard Fillmore	None	1850–1853
14	Franklin Pierce	William R. King	1853–1857
15	James Buchanan	John C. Breckinridge	1857–1861
16	Abraham Lincoln	Hannibal Hamlin/Andrew Johnson	1861–1865
17	Andrew Johnson	None	1865–1869

	President	Vice President	Years in Office
18	Ulysses S. Grant	Schuyler Colfax/Henry Wilson	1869–1877
19	Rutherford B. Hayes	William A. Wheeler	1877–1881
20	James Garfield	Chester A. Arthur	1881
21	Chester A. Arthur	None	1881–1885
22	Grover Cleveland	Thomas A. Hendricks	1885–1889
23	Benjamin Harrison	Levi P. Morton	1889–1893
24	Grover Cleveland	Adlai E. Stevenson	1893–1897
25	William McKinley	Garret A. Hobart/ Theodore Roosevelt	1897–1901
26	Theodore Roosevelt	Charles W. Fairbanks	1901–1909
27	William H. Taft	James S. Sherman	1909–1913
28	Woodrow Wilson	Thomas R. Marshall	1913–1921
29	Warren G. Harding	Calvin Coolidge	1921–1923
30	Calvin Coolidge	Charles G. Dawes	1923–1929
31	Herbert C. Hoover	Charles Curtis	1929–1933
32	Franklin D. Roosevelt	John N. Garner/Henry A. Wallace/ Harry S. Truman	1933–1945
33	Harry S. Truman	Alben Barkley	1945–1953
34	Dwight D. Eisenhower	Richard M. Nixon	1953–1961
35	John F. Kennedy	Lyndon B. Johnson	1961–1963
36	Lyndon B. Johnson	Hubert H. Humphrey	1963–1969
37	Richard M. Nixon	Spiro T. Agnew/Gerald R. Ford	1969–1974
38	Gerald R. Ford	Nelson A. Rockefeller	1974–1977
39	Jimmy Carter	Walter F. Mondale	1977–1981
40	Ronald W. Reagan	George H.W. Bush	1981–1989
41	George Herbert Walker Bush	Dan Quayle	1989–1993
42	William J. Clinton	Albert Gore Jr.	1993–2001
43	George Walker Bush	Richard B. Cheney	2001–

George Washington, the first President, did not belong to a political party. John Adams, who became the second President, belonged to the Federalist Party. He was the only member of that party to become President. Following John Adams, presidents were elected from the Democratic-Republican Party. John Quincy Adams was the last president from that party. And Presidents Harrison, Tyler, Taylor, and Fillmore were Whigs. All other presidents up to the present time came from the Democrat or the Republican Party.

In order to become president, a citizen must be at least 35 years old and have been born in the United States. Foreign-born citizens cannot become president. At the present time, a citizen may serve only two terms as president. Before the Constitution was amended, Franklin D. Roosevelt was elected President four times.

Several presidents were *war presidents* and led the nation during dangerous times:

- James Madison—the War of 1812 with Great Britain
- James K. Polk—the Mexican-American War
- Abraham Lincoln—the Civil War
- William McKinley—the Spanish-American War
- Woodrow Wilson—World War I
- Franklin D. Roosevelt and Harry S. Truman—World War II against Germany, Italy, and Japan
- Harry S. Truman and Dwight Eisenhower—the Korean Conflict
- John F. Kennedy, Lyndon Johnson, and Richard Nixon—the Vietnam War
- George Herbert Walker Bush—Desert Storm (Iraq War)
- George W. Bush—Iraqi Freedom (Iraq War)

Herbert Hoover was President when the *stock market crash* occurred in 1929. The Great Depression followed, and Hoover and Franklin D. Roosevelt struggled to heal the American economy.

President Kennedy led the nation during the Cuban Missile Crisis. Richard Nixon was in office when Americans first landed on the moon on July 20, 1969. And Presidents Reagan and George Herbert Walker Bush watched as the Cold War gradually came to an end and the Berlin Wall finally came down.

Through good times and bad times, America's presidents have led the nation to become one of the most powerful countries of all time and the oldest democracy on the planet.

Important Words

Learn the meaning of these new words. Say a sentence using each new word.

belong to = be a member of an organization	"He belongs to the Republican Party."
party = political organization	"There are two major parties in the United States."
present time = now	"Who is president at the present time?"
dangerous = harmful, risky, perilous	"War time is a dangerous time."
conflict = struggle, clash	"The Korean Conflict followed World War II."
crash = violent downfall, failure	"What year was the stock market crash?"
depression = low economic state	"The depression lasted until World War II."
heal = make better, improve health	"It was hard to heal the economy."
missile = rocket	"The U.S.S.R. placed missiles on the island of Cuba."
crisis = dangerous moment	"The crisis ended peacefully."
gradually = slowly	"The Cold War gradually came to an end."
planet = satellite of the Sun, Earth	"We live on planet Earth."

Write Your New Words

In the blank of the first sentence, write the missing word. In the second sentence, write the same word from memory.

1. She belongs to our party.

She _____ our party.

She _____ our party.

2. There are two major parties in America.

There are two major _____ in America.

There are two major _____ in America.

3. Who is President at the present time?

Who is President at the _____?

Who is President at the _____?

4. He led the country in a dangerous time.

He led the country in a _____ time.

He led the country in a _____ time.

5. Truman was President during the Korean Conflict.

Truman was president during the Korean _____.

Truman was President during the Korean _____.

6. The stock market crash occurred in 1929.

The stock market _____ occurred in 1929.

The stock market _____ occurred in 1929.

7. The Great Depression lasted until the war.

The Great _____ lasted until the war.

The Great _____ lasted until the war.

8. Roosevelt tried to heal the economy.

Roosevelt tried to _____ the economy.

Roosevelt tried to _____ the economy.

9. When was the Cuban Missile Crisis?

When was the Cuban _____ Crisis?

When was the Cuban _____ Crisis?

10. The attack at Pearl Harbor was a time of crisis.

The attack at Pearl Harbor was a time of _____.

The attack at Pearl Harbor was a time of _____.

11. The Cold War gradually ended.

The Cold War _____ ended.

The Cold War _____ ended.

12. We live on planet Earth.

We live on _____ Earth.

We live on _____ Earth.

Important Questions and Answers

1. What are the names of the two major American political parties? (Democrat and Republican)

2. Who was president during World War II? (Franklin Roosevelt and Harry Truman)

3. In what year was the stock market crash? (1929)

4. What followed the stock market crash? (Great Depression)

5. What happened on July 20, 1969? (Americans landed on the moon.)

6. Who tried to heal the American economy? (Herbert Hoover and Franklin Roosevelt)

7. What crisis occurred during Kennedy's presidency? (Cuban Missile Crisis)

8. What war was going on when Nixon became president? (Vietnam)

9. What country has the oldest democracy on the planet? (U.S.A.)

10. What wall came down at the end of the Cold War? (Berlin Wall)

11. What party did George Washington belong to? (none)

12. Who is George W. Bush's vice president? (Dick Cheney)

13. Who was president during the War of 1812? (James Madison)

14. Whose father was President during Desert Storm, the first Iraq War? (George W. Bush's father, George Herbert Walker Bush)

15. Who was president when the stock market crash occurred? (Herbert Hoover)

16. Who was president during the Great Depression? (Herbert Hoover and Franklin Roosevelt)

Is It TRUE or FALSE?

Say TRUE if the sentence is correct. Say FALSE if it is incorrect.

1. Richard Nixon was Kennedy's vice president.

2. The stock market crash of 1929 occurred during Hoover's presidency.

3. Harry S. Truman was president during the Korean Conflict.

4. Eisenhower's presidency ended in 1961.

5. The Great Depression followed the Spanish-American War.

6. Lyndon Johnson was president during the Vietnam War.

7. John Adams wanted to heal the American economy after the stock market crash.

8. Americans landed on the moon on July 4, 1959.

9. The Cuban Missile Crisis occurred during Eisenhower's presidency.

10. France has the oldest democracy on the planet.

11. As the Cold War ended, the Berlin Wall came down.

12. Calvin Coolidge was a war president.

13. George W. Bush was president during the second Iraqi War.

14. Dick Cheney is President of the United States.

15. Franklin D. Roosevelt was elected President four times.

16. Citizens can be elected President for only two terms.

17. In order to become President, a citizen has to be at least 35 years old.

18. Foreign-born citizens can become President.

Answers

1.	False	10.	False
2.	True	11.	True
3.	True	12.	False
4.	True	13.	True
5.	False	14.	False
6.	True	15.	True
7.	False	16.	True
8.	False	17.	True
9.	False	18.	False

Let's Look at Some Important Sentences

Circle the letter of the word or phrase that completes the sentence.

1. The first President was _____.

    a. Thomas Jefferson
    b. George Washington
    c. Abraham Lincoln
    d. Bill Clinton

2. There was only one President from the _____ Party.

    a. Republican
    b. Democrat
    c. Federalist
    d. Socialist

3. Presidents during wartime are called _____ presidents.

    a. war
    b. peaceful
    c. dignitaries
    d. vice

4. Every President since Lincoln was either a _____ or a Republican.

    a. Whig
    b. American citizen
    c. foreign-born citizen
    d. Democrat

5. _____ presidents were born outside the United States.

    a. No
    b. Two
    c. Three
    d. Five

6. _____ was President during World War II.

    a. John Adams
    b. William McKinley
    c. Richard Nixon
    d. Franklin D. Roosevelt

7. The Vice President of the United States is _____.

    a. Al Gore
    b. Jimmy Carter
    c. Dick Cheney
    d. Gerald Ford

8. You must be at least _____ years old to become President.

    a. 21
    b. 25
    c. 30
    d. 35

9. Lincoln was president during _____.

    a. the Civil War
    b. the Revolution
    c. World War I
    d. the Korean Conflict

10. _____ was President during the Vietnam War.

    a. Lyndon Johnson
    b. Harry S. Truman
    c. Woodrow Wilson
    d. George Herbert Walker Bush

11. President Kennedy led the nation during _____.

    a. World War I
    b. the Spanish-American War
    c. the Iraq War
    d. the Cuban Missile Crisis

12. The United States has the oldest _____ in the world.

    a. democracy
    b. president
    c. vice president
    d. Cabinet

13. During George Herbert Walker Bush's presidency _____ ended.

    a. the Cold War
    b. World War II
    c. the Great Depression
    d. the stock market crash

14. During Richard Nixon's administration, Americans landed _____.

    a. in Canada
    b. in Vietnam
    c. at the Berlin Wall
    d. on the moon

15. The United States has become one of the most _____ nations in history.

    a. powerful
    b. Republican
    c. Federalist
    d. gradual

16. There are _____ major political parties in the United States.

    a. two
    b. three
    c. five
    d. seven

Answers

1.	b	9.	a
2.	c	10.	a
3.	a	11.	d
4.	d	12.	a
5.	a	13.	a
6.	d	14.	d
7.	c	15.	a
8.	d	16.	a

Let's Write the New Words

In the blank, write the word or phrase that completes the sentence. Look at the words in parentheses. They will help you.

1. The _____ began in 1929. (low economic state)

2. Roosevelt tried to _____ the economy. (make better, improve health)

3. The stock market _____ was a shock. (violent downfall, failure)

4. The depression was an economic _____. (dangerous moment)

5. The Korean _____ followed World War II. (struggle, clash)

6. He led the nation in _____ times. (harmful, risky, perilous)

7. Soviet _____ were in Cuba. (rockets)

8. The war _____ came to an end. (slowly)

9. Who is Vice President at the _____? (now)

10. There are two major political _____ in the United States. (political organizations)

11. We are the most powerful nation on the _____. (satellite of the Sun, Earth)

12. Does she _____ the Democrat Party? (is a member of an organization)

Answers

1.	depression	7.	missiles
2.	heal	8.	gradually
3.	crash	9.	present time
4.	crisis	10.	parties
5.	Conflict	11.	planet
6.	dangerous	12.	belong to

Some Tips About English

There are three ways to express the future tense in English. Each one of these ways is used in a particular manner.

- Use *shall* or *will* followed by a verb. This form of the future tense is used to say that **an action will be completed** in the future.
    - I shall sing a song for you.
    - He will borrow our car.
    - They will visit us tomorrow.
- Use *shall* or *will* followed by *be* and a verb ending in *–ing*. This form of the future tense says that **the action is in progress** or **incomplete** in the future.
    - We shall be cleaning the kitchen.
    - Will you be watching the game?
    - She will be reading a book.
- Use *be going to* followed by a verb. This form of the future tense means that this is **the intended action** and **will be completed** in the future.
    - I am going to buy a new car tomorrow.
    - Are they going to spend the night here?
    - We are going to vacation in Mexico.

Traditionally, *shall* is used with the first person singular or plural pronouns (I, we). *Will* is used with the other pronouns. But in casual speech, most Americans use *will* for all pronouns.

Patriotism

The Pledge of Allegiance

The Pledge of Allegiance is a statement that Americans make to show that they are loyal citizens and believe in the principles of democracy and liberty. It is often stated in some American classrooms at the beginning of the school day. Some organizations begin their meetings with *The Pledge*. When you say *The Pledge*, you should face the flag and then speak. Most people put their right hands on their hearts. The words are simple and easily understood.

I pledge allegiance to the Flag of the United States of America, and to the Republic, for which it stands, one nation, under God, indivisible, with liberty and justice for all.

School children learn *The Pledge* starting with their first day in school. By the time they are adults, they have memorized the words.

Because the Constitution requires that church and state be separate, some citizens believe the words *under God* should be omitted from *The Pledge*.

A Baptist minister named Francis Bellamy wrote the original Pledge in August 1892. His words are slightly different from the ones spoken today. This is the original:

I pledge allegiance to my Flag and to the Republic, for which it stands, one nation, indivisible, with liberty and justice for all.

Important Words

Learn the meaning of these new words. Say a sentence using each new word.

pledge = promise	"I pledged $50 to help his family."
allegiance = loyalty, faithfulness	"My allegiance is to the United States of America."
statement = something said in words	"His statement was simple but clear."
loyal = true, faithful	"She is a loyal American."
principle = basic truth or rule	"I believe in the principles of democracy."
face = look at	"Everyone faced the flag."
stand for = represent	"The flag stands for the Republic."
indivisible = cannot be divided	"The nation is forever indivisible."
memorize = put in your memory	"I want to memorize *The Pledge of Allegiance*."
require = demand, need	"My landlord required payment today."
omit = leave out	"He omitted a few words from his speech."
slightly = a little bit	"The original version is slightly different."

Write Your New Words

In the blank of the first sentence, write the missing word(s). In the second sentence, write the same word(s) from memory.

1. Do you know *The Pledge of Allegiance?*

Do you know *The* _____ *of Allegiance?*

Do you know *The* _____ *of Allegiance?*

2. His allegiance is to America.

His _____ is to America.

His _____ is to America.

3. The police wrote down my statement.

The police wrote down my _____.

The police wrote down my _____.

4. She is a loyal citizen.

She is a _____ citizen.

She is a _____ citizen.

5. We understand the principles of democracy.

We understand the _____ of democracy.

We understand the _____ of democracy.

6. Please face the flag.

Please _____ the flag.

Please _____ the flag.

7. What does America stand for?

What does America _____?

What does America _____?

8. Our nation is indivisible.

Our nation is _____.

Our nation is _____.

9. Do I have to memorize The Preamble?

Do I have to _____ The Preamble?

Do I have to _____ The Preamble?

10. Do you require anything else?

Do you _____ anything else?

Do you _____ anything else?

11. Don't omit anything from the original.

Don't _____ anything from the original.

Don't _____ anything from the original.

12. She speaks English slightly better than I do.

She speaks English _____ better than I do.

She speaks English _____ better than I do.

Important Questions and Answers

1. What kind of statement is *The Pledge of Allegiance?* (a statement of loyalty to America)

2. Where do people face when they say *The Pledge?* (They face the flag.)

3. Where is *The Pledge* often said? (at the beginning of some meetings and in some classrooms)

4. What does the American flag stand for? (the Republic, the Union)

5. When do children start learning *The Pledge?* (the first day of school)

6. What principles are mentioned in *The Pledge?* (liberty and justice for all)

7. Why have many adults memorized *The Pledge?* (They have said it many times since childhood.)

8. Who wrote the original *Pledge of Allegiance?* (Francis Bellamy, a Baptist minister)

9. Why do some citizens want to omit the words "under God?" (It is a matter of separation of church and state.)

10. What document requires the separation of church and state? (Constitution)

Is It TRUE or FALSE?

Say TRUE if the sentence is correct. Say FALSE if it is incorrect.

1. People usually face the flag when they say *The Pledge of Allegiance.*

2. The flag stands for the American Constitution.

3. When you say *The Pledge,* you are showing your loyalty to America.

4. The original *Pledge of Allegiance* was written by Congress.

5. An indivisible nation is one that cannot be divided.

6. Everyone believes the words "under God" should stay in *The Pledge.*

7. *The Pledge* reminds us of the principles of liberty and justice for all.

8. Children learn *The Pledge* when they go to high school.

9. Sometimes meetings are started with *The Pledge of Allegiance.*

10. *The Pledge* we say today is the same as the original.

11. The Constitution says that church and state must be separated.

12. Most Americans have memorized *The Pledge* by the time they are adults.

Answers

1. True

2. False

3. True

4. False

5. True

6. False

7. True

8. False

9. True

10. False

11. True

12. True

Let's Look at Some Important Sentences

Circle the letter of the word or phrase that completes the sentence.

1. Some _____ begin their meetings with *The Pledge of Allegiance.*

    a. foreigners

    b. ministers

    c. organizations

    d. tests

2. You should _____ the flag when you say *The Pledge.*

    a. face

    b. find

    c. hold

    d. borrow

3. When you say *The Pledge,* it means you are a _____ American.

    a. new

    b. child

    c. adult

    d. loyal

4. A Baptist _____ wrote the original *Pledge of Allegiance.*

    a. senator

    b. school boy

    c. organizer

    d. minister

5. The *Pledge of Allegiance* states a belief in liberty and _____.

    a. elections

    b. justice for all

    c. indivisible

    d. church and state

6. Some school children say *The Pledge* in their _____.

   a. homes
   b. classrooms
   c. free time
   d. play

7. The words of *The Pledge* are _____ to understand.

   a. meetings
   b. democracy
   c. simple
   d. principles

8. Saying *The Pledge* means you believe in _____.

   a. democracy
   b. the original version
   c. American citizens
   d. Congress

9. The flag stands for _____.

   a. *The Pledge*
   b. the American Republic
   c. God
   d. the government

10. The Constitution requires _____ of church and state.

   a. loyalty
   b. liberty
   c. separation
   d. a statement

11. _____ wrote the original *Pledge of Allegiance*.

   a. Francis Bellamy
   b. Congress
   c. Betsy Ross
   d. The schools

12. A nation that cannot be divided is _____.

   a. separated
   b. indivisible
   c. a democracy
   d. justice for all

13. Many adults have _____ *The Pledge*.

   a. stated
   b. understood
   c. omitted
   d. memorized

14. Some citizens believe the words _____ should be omitted from *The Pledge*.

    a. under God

    b. one nation

    c. to the Republic

    d. my Flag

Answers

1. c

2. a

3. d

4. d

5. b

6. b

7. c

8. a

9. b

10. c

11. a

12. b

13. d

14. a

Let's Write the New Words

In the blank, write the word or phrase that completes the sentence. Look at the words in parentheses. They will help you.

1. We are one _____ nation. (cannot be divided)

2. Most people _____ *The Pledge of Allegiance.* (put in their memory)

3. America _____ liberty and justice for all. (represents)

4. What does the Constitution _____? (demand, need)

5. I turned to _____ the flag. (look at)

6. Some want to _____ the words under God. (leave out)

7. We believe in the _____ of democracy. (basic truths or rules)

8. The new version is _____ different. (a little bit)

9. We are _____ to the United States. (true, faithful)

10. *The Pledge* is a simple _____ of loyalty. (something said in words)

11. I give my _____ to my new country. (loyalty, faithfulness)

12. I want to learn *The _____ of Allegiance.* (promise)

Answers

1. indivisible
2. memorize
3. stands for
4. require
5. face
6. omit

7. principles
8. slightly
9. loyal
10. statement
11. allegiance
12. Pledge

Old Glory

Old Glory is the nickname of the American flag. The first American flag is said to have been sewn by Betsy Ross. It was first used in 1777. The flag had 13 stars and 13 stripes. As the number of states increased, so, too, the number of stars and stripes increased on the flag. In 1818 Congress decided that the number of stars would continue to increase, but the number of stripes would be fixed at 13.

During the Civil War, there were 34 stars on the flag. Even after the South seceded from the Union, President Lincoln retained the 34 stars on the flag.

There are now 50 stars on the American flag. The 49th star was added on July 4, 1959, after Alaska was admitted to the Union. The 50th star was added on July 4, 1960, after Hawaii entered the Union.

At a time of national mourning, the flag is flown at half-staff. First, the flag is raised to the top of the flagpole. Then it is lowered to half-staff. Before the flag is taken down for the day, it is again raised to the top of the flagpole. Then it is lowered to the ground. The flag can be flown upside-down as a distress signal.

Many people cover their hearts with their right hands when the flag passes by in a parade. Men usually remove their hats as a sign of respect.

Important Words

Learn the meaning of these new words. Say a sentence using each new word.

nickname = pet name, special name	"The flag's nickname is *Old Glory*."
is said = people say	"This hill is said to be the site of a great battle."
fixed = made permanent	"The number of stripes is fixed at thirteen."
retain = keep	"I retained the bills you sent me."
admit to = allow in	"Another state was admitted to the Union."
enter = come in	"When did Hawaii enter the Union?"
mourning = time of grieving after a death	"A period of mourning followed his death."
half-staff = halfway up the pole	"The flag flew at half-staff."
top = highest point	"There is a large bird at the top of the tree."
flagpole = pole from which the flag flies	"There is a flagpole in front of the school."
lower = bring down	"We lower the flag at sundown."
upside-down = up is down, down is up	"The picture is hanging upside-down."
distress = great trouble	"The nation was in a time of distress."
parade = ceremonious procession or march	"The parade went down Main Street."

Write Your New Words

In the blank of the first sentence, write the missing word(s). In the second sentence, write it from memory.

1. Does the flag have a nickname?

   Does the flag have a _____?
   Does the flag have a _____?

2. It is said that Betsy Ross sewed the first flag.

   It _____ that Betsy Ross sewed the first flag.
   It _____ that Betsy Ross sewed the first flag.

3. The price is fixed at 10 dollars.

   The price is _____ at 10 dollars.
   The price is _____ at 10 dollars.

4. Lincoln retained all the stars on the flag.

   Lincoln _____ all the stars on the flag.
   Lincoln _____ all the stars on the flag.

5. When was Alaska admitted to the Union?

   When was Alaska _____ the Union?
   When was Alaska _____ the Union?

6. Hawaii entered the Union in 1960.

   Hawaii _____ the Union in 1960.
   Hawaii _____ the Union in 1960.

7. The nation was in mourning.

   The nation was in _____.
   The nation was in _____.

8. Why is the flag flying at half-staff?

   Why is the flag flying at _____?
   Why is the flag flying at _____?

9. Raise the flag to the top of the pole.

   Raise the flag to the _____ of the pole.
   Raise the flag to the _____ of the pole.

10. There is a flagpole in the park.

    There is a _____ in the park.
    There is a _____ in the park.

11. It is time to lower the flag.

    It is time to _____ the flag.
    It is time to _____ the flag.

12. Why is the flag flying upside-down?

    Why is the flag flying _____?
    Why is the flag flying _____?

13. That is a signal of distress.

    That is a signal of _____.
    That is a signal of _____.

14. There are many flags in the parade.

    There are many flags in the _____.
    There are many flags in the _____.

Important Questions and Answers

1. How many stars were on the flag during the Civil War? (34)

2. At what number did Congress fix the number of stripes on the flag? (13)

3. When was the Betsy Ross flag first used? (1777)

4. How many stars are on the American flag now? (50)

5. What state was admitted to the Union in 1959? (Alaska)

6. What was the last state to enter the Union? (Hawaii)

7. How is the flag flown during a time of mourning? (at half-staff)

8. Who is said to have sewn the first American flag? (Betsy Ross)

9. What do many people cover when the flag passes by? (their hearts)

10. What do men usually remove as a sign of respect? (their hats)

11. What does it mean if the flag is flying upside-down? (distress signal)

12. What do the white stars on the flag stand for? (the states)

Is It TRUE or FALSE?

Say TRUE if the sentence is correct. Say FALSE if it is incorrect.

1. Until 1959 the stars and stripes increased as new states were added to the Union.

2. Congress fixed the number of stars at 50 in 1818.

3. President Lincoln retained the 34 stars on the flag during the Civil War.

4. The nickname of the American flag is *Old Glory*.

5. Many people cover their hearts when the flag passes by.

6. Some people say that Betsy Ross sewed the first flag.

7. Men usually remove their hats as a sign of respect for the flag.

8. There are 13 stripes on the flag.

9. The last state to enter the Union was Hawaii.

10. The flag is flown half-staff during a parade.

11. The flag flying upside-down is a distress signal.

12. The 49th state was Virginia.

13. There are 50 states in the Union.

14. There are 50 stars on the American flag.

Answers

1. False
2. False
3. True
4. True
5. True
6. True
7. True

8. True
9. True
10. False
11. True
12. False
13. True
14. True

Let's Look at Some Important Sentences

Circle the letter of the word or phrase that completes the sentence.

1. Congress decided that the number of stripes would be _____ at 13.

   a. entered
   b. admitted
   c. fixed
   d. lowered

2. The Betsy Ross flag was first used in _____.

    a. 1777

    b. 1789

    c. 1818

    d. 1861

3. Even though the South _____, Lincoln retained 34 stars on the flag.

    a. seceded

    b. won the war

    c. began the Civil War

    d. returned

4. *Old Glory* is a _____.

    a. number of states

    b. nickname

    c. foreign flag

    d. parade

5. There are now _____ states in the Union.

    a. 34

    b. 49

    c. 50

    d. 55

6. In the past there were more than 13 _____ on the flag.

    a. colors

    b. fields of blue

    c. states

    d. stripes

7. People often cover their _____ when the flag passes by.

    a. heads

    b. hearts

    c. parades

    d. stripes

8. The 50th star was added to the flag in _____.

    a. 1861

    b. 1929

    c. 1950

    d. 1960

9. In a time of _____ the flag is flown at half-staff.

    a. parades

    b. mourning

    c. war

    d. respect

10. Men remove their hats as a sign of _____ for the flag.

   a. respect
   b. parade
   c. mourning
   d. increase

11. Flying the flag upside-down is a _____ signal.

   a. distress
   b. mourning
   c. fixed
   d. flagpole

12. _____ became a state in 1959.

   a. New York
   b. Maine
   c. California
   d. Alaska

13. There are never more than _____ stripes on the flag.

   a. 10
   b. 13
   c. 20
   d. 50

Answers

   1. c
   2. a
   3. a
   4. b
   5. c
   6. b
   7. d

   8. b
   9. b
   10. a
   11. a
   12. d
   13. b

Let's Write the New Words

In the blank, write the word or phrase that completes the sentence. Look at the words in parentheses. They will help you.

1. We _____ the flag at sundown. (bring down)

2. Is there a _____ in the park? (pole from which the flag flies)

3. Why is the flag _____? (up is down, down is up)

4. There is an eagle on the _____ of the flagpole. (highest point)

5. Is that a _____ signal? (great trouble)

6. Lower all flags to _____. (halfway up the pole)

7. The flag led the _____. (ceremonious procession or march)

8. After his death, the nation was in _____. (time of grieving after a death)

9. What is the flag's _____? (pet name, special name)

10. Our state _____ the Union many years ago. (came in)

11. It _____ that Betsy Ross sewed the first flag. (people say)

12. When was Alaska _____ to the Union? (allowed in)

13. The number of stripes is _____ at 13. (made permanent)

14. Lincoln _____ all the stars on the flag. (kept)

Answers

1. lower
2. flagpole
3. upside-down
4. top
5. distress
6. half-staff
7. parade

8. mourning
9. nickname
10. entered
11. is said
12. admitted
13. fixed
14. retained

Some Tips About English

It is very common to use *contractions* in English. A contraction is a combination of two words with an apostrophe placed where letters are omitted.

Look at the contractions in the following chart, which are a combination of a **pronoun** and a **verb:**

Pronoun	am	are	is	has	have	will	would
I	I'm				I've	I'll	I'd
you		you're			you've	you'll	you'd
he			he's	he's		he'll	he'd
she			she's	she's		she'll	she'd
it			it's	it's			
we		we're			we've	we'll	we'd
they		they're			they've	they'll	they'd
who			who's	who's		who'll	who'd

Other contractions are formed by combining a **verb** with the word **NOT**:

Verb	With NOT	Contraction
are	are not	aren't
can	cannot	can't
could	could not	couldn't
did	did not	didn't
do	do not	don't
has	has not	hasn't
have	have not	haven't
is	is not	isn't
must	must not	mustn't
need	need not	needn't
should	should not	shouldn't
was	was not	wasn't
were	were not	weren't
will	will not	won't
would	would not	wouldn't

A Land of Laws

The Legislative Branch of Government

The Legislative Branch of our government makes the laws. Our national legislature is called the Congress. It is made up of two chambers: the Senate and the House of Representatives. The members of Congress are elected by the voters of each state.

The number of representatives from a state to the House of Representatives is based upon population. Therefore, each state has a different number of representatives in the House. The total number of representatives in the House is 435. In order to be a member of the House of Representatives, (1) you have to be a resident of the state you represent; (2) you have to be at least 25 years old; and (3) you have to have been a U.S. citizen for at least seven years. The term for a representative is two years.

A senator's term is six years. Each state has two senators in the Senate, which has a total of 100 members. In order to be elected to the Senate, (1) you have to be a resident of the state you represent; (2) you have to be at least 30 years old; and (3) you have to have been a U.S. citizen for at least nine years.

Congress has the responsibility of raising revenue, declaring war, and making the nation's laws. Congress advises and consents on important executive and judicial appointments and on treaties arranged by the president. The powers and responsibilities of Congress are spelled out in the Constitution. The Constitution provides the system of *checks and balances*, which safeguards majority rule and minority rights and the separation of the national and state governments.

Congress meets in the Capitol Building in Washington, D.C.

Important Words

Learn the meaning of these new words. Say a sentence using each new word.

legislature = elected officials who make laws	"Our national legislature meets in the Capitol."
chamber = assembly of officials	"Congress is made up of two chambers."
voter = a person who votes	"The voters have elected a new senator."
represent = to act on behalf of	"Ms. Brown will represent us in Congress."
responsibility = accountability, burden	"Congress has the responsibility of making laws."
raise (money) = find, arrange for	"We have to raise more money."
revenue = income	"Most revenue comes from taxes."
advise = give an opinion, recommend	"Congress advises the president on some issues."
consent = agree to	"The Senate did not consent to the idea."
appointment = selection for an office or service	"The president made a new appointment to the court."
arrange = plan, settle on	"The treaty is arranged but must still be approved by Congress."
spelled out = clearly written	"The people's rights are spelled out in the Constitution."
provide = prepare, supply	"The Constitution provides us with certain rights."
safeguard = ensure, protect, keep safe	"The new law safeguards civil rights."
majority = the greater number of people in agreement	"A majority voted for the new law."
minority = the smaller number of people in agreement	"A minority was against the war."

Write Your New Words

In the blank of the first sentence, write the missing word. In the second sentence, write it from memory.

1. The state legislature meets in the capital.

The state _____ meets in the capital.
The state _____ meets in the capital.

2. Congress is divided into two chambers.

Congress is divided into two _____.
Congress is divided into two _____.

3. The voters elected a new president.

The _____ elected a new president.
The _____ elected a new president.

4. Who represents us in Congress?

Who _____ us in Congress?
Who _____ us in Congress?

5. Being a senator is a great responsibility.

Being a senator is a great _____.
Being a senator is a great _____.

6. They must raise money for the highway project.

They must _____ money for the highway project.
They must _____ money for the highway project.

7. Most revenue comes from taxes.

Most _____ comes from taxes.
Most _____ comes from taxes.

8. The lawyer advised me to remain silent.

The lawyer _____ me to remain silent.
The lawyer _____ me to remain silent.

9. Congress consented to the plan.

Congress _____ to the plan.
Congress _____ to the plan.

10. His appointment as a judge was approved.

His _____ as a judge was approved.

His _____ as a judge was approved.

11. We arranged a meeting with the senators.

We _____ a meeting with the senators.

We _____ a meeting with the senators.

12. Our rights are spelled out in the Constitution.

Our rights are _____ in the Constitution.

Our rights are _____ in the Constitution.

13. It provides for checks and balances.

It _____ for checks and balances.

It _____ for checks and balances.

14. The amendments safeguard our rights.

The amendments _____ our rights.

The amendments _____ our rights.

15. I believe in majority rule.

I believe in _____ rule.

I believe in _____ rule.

16. Minority rights must be protected.

_____ rights must be protected.

_____ rights must be protected.

Important Questions and Answers

1. What is our national legislature called? (Congress)

2. How many chambers make up Congress? (two)

3. Which branch of government makes our laws? (Legislative Branch)

4. How many members are there in the House of Representatives? (435)

5. How many members are there in the Senate? (100)

6. How is the number of representatives from a state determined? (by population)

7. How many senators does each state have? (two)

8. How old must you be to be a representative? (25)

9. How old must you be to be a senator? (30)

10. How long is a senator's term? (six years)

11. How long is a representative's term? (two years)

12. How long must you have been a U.S. citizen to become a senator? (nine years)

13. How long must you have been a U.S. citizen to become a representative? (seven years)

14. What branch of government can declare war? (Congress, Legislative Branch)

15. Where is the system of checks and balances provided? (in the Constitution)

16. In what building does Congress meet? (Capitol)

17. Where is the Capitol located? (in Washington, D.C.)

Is It TRUE or FALSE?

Say TRUE if the sentence is correct. Say FALSE if it is incorrect.

1. The Executive Branch makes our laws.

2. Congress is made up of two chambers.

3. The two chambers of Congress are the Senate and the House of Representatives.

4. The number of senators is determined by population.

5. You do not have to be a U.S. citizen to become a senator.

6. Representatives must live in the state that they represent.

7. A senator must be at least 21 years old.

8. A system of checks and balances protect majority rule and minority rights.

9. There are 435 members of the Senate.

10. Each state has the same number of senators.

11. A representative's term is for two years.

12. Congress has the responsibility of raising revenue.

13. Only the president can declare war.

14. The Capitol Building is in Washington, D.C.

15. The Congress advises and consents on treaties.

16. A senator's term is for four years.

17. There are 100 members in the Senate.

Answers

1. False
2. True
3. True
4. False
5. False
6. True
7. False
8. True
9. False

10. True
11. True
12. True
13. False
14. True
15. True
16. False
17. True

Let's Look at Some Important Sentences

Circle the letter of the word or phrase that completes the sentence.

1. The number of representatives in the House is based upon _____.

   a. voters
   b. population
   c. the Senate
   d. the Congress

2. A senator has to be a resident of the _____ he or she represents.

   a. state
   b. country
   c. nation
   d. city

3. You have to be a citizen for _____ years to become a representative.

   a. five
   b. six
   c. seven
   d. eight

4. The _____ Branch makes the country's laws.

   a. Executive
   b. Judicial
   c. Congress
   d. Legislative

5. The Congress is made up of two _____.

    a. chambers

    b. legislatures

    c. Senates

    d. representatives

6. Congress has the responsibility of raising _____.

    a. an army

    b. the flag

    c. crops

    d. revenue

7. You have to be _____ years old to become a senator.

    a. 21

    b. 25

    c. 30

    d. 35

8. The members of Congress are elected by the voters of each _____.

    a. capital

    b. chamber

    c. state

    d. branch

9. There are _____ members in the Senate.

    a. 100

    b. 125

    c. 250

    d. 435

10. Each state has _____ number of representatives in the House.

    a. a different

    b. the same

    c. twice the

    d. an equal

11. Congress meets in the _____.

    a. White House

    b. two chambers

    c. court

    d. Capitol

12. The Constitution provides a system of _____.

    a. checks and balances

    b. two parties

    c. two branches of government

    d. representation

13. The Constitution safeguards _____ rule.

    a. executive

    b. judicial

    c. majority

    d. presidential

14. The powers of Congress are _____ in the Constitution.

    a. spelled out

    b. law

    c. representatives

    d. senators

15. There are _____ members of the House of Representatives.

    a. 100

    b. 250

    c. 375

    d. 435

Answers

1. b		**9.** a	
2. a		**10.** a	
3. c		**11.** d	
4. d		**12.** a	
5. a		**13.** c	
6. d		**14.** a	
7. c		**15.** d	
8. c			

Let's Write the New Words

In the blank, write the word or phrase that completes the sentence. Look at the words in parentheses. They will help you.

1. Her _____ to the court was approved. (selection for an office or service)

2. Congress did not _____ to the plan. (agree to)

3. The President _____ the treaty signing for Monday. (planned, settled on)

4. The Cabinet _____ the President. (gives an opinion, recommends)

5. Our rights are _____ in the Constitution. (clearly written)

6. Congress gets _____ from taxes. (income)

7. The Constitution _____ the rules for government. (prepares, supplies)

8. It is Congress' job to _____ revenue. (find, arrange for money)

9. These laws _____ our rights. (ensure, protect, keep safe)

10. What is the _____ of Congress? (accountability, burden)

11. A _____ wanted a change in the law. (the greater number of people in agreement)

12. Who _____ us in the Senate? (acts on our behalf)

13. A _____ protested against the new tax. (the smaller number of people in agreement)

14. The _____ elected a new mayor. (persons who vote)

15. The state _____ meets in the capital. (elected officials who make laws)

16. Congress is made up of two _____. (assemblies of officials)

Answers

1. appointment
2. consent
3. arranged
4. advises
5. spelled out
6. revenue
7. provides
8. raise

9. safeguard
10. responsibility
11. majority
12. represents
13. minority
14. voters
15. legislature
16. chambers

Bills and Laws

A bill, which is an idea for a new law, can be introduced in either the House of Representatives or in the Senate. For example, if a bill is introduced in the House, it is presented in written form to all the members of the House. Then it is assigned to a House committee, which studies the bill and listens to experts who are interested in the bill. If the committee does not like the bill, they can put it aside. This is called *tabling* the bill. If they like the bill, it is released and returned to the House for voting. It passes if the vote is a simple majority (218 votes out of 435).

Now the bill is sent to the Senate for consideration. In the Senate, the bill is also assigned to a committee. And that committee can either table or release the bill. If it is released and returned to the Senate, it is debated and eventually voted on. It passes if the vote is a simple majority (51 votes out of 100).

The President's role in the law-making process is one of approval. If he approves of a bill, he signs it, and it becomes law. If he disapproves of the bill, he does not sign it and returns it to the Congress sometimes with his recommendations for change. He has 10 days to do this. But he can ignore the bill, which is called a *pocket veto*, and after 10 days it becomes law.

Dr. Martin Luther King, Jr., was a leader of the Civil Rights Movement of the 1950s and 1960s. The peaceful demonstrations and protests that he led pressured Congress to enact the Voting Rights Act of 1965, which outlawed voting tests and poll taxes. These tests and taxes were a form of discrimination designed to limit an African-American's right to vote.

On April 4, 1968, Dr. King was assassinated in Memphis, Tennessee.

Important New Words

introduce = bring in, make known	"A senator introduced the bill."
present = show, give	"The bill was presented to the House."
assign = transfer to, appoint to	"The bill was assigned to a committee."
expert = skilled person, authority	"Experts gave their opinion about the law."
table = stop an action, avoid	"They tabled the bill."
release = set free, send on	"The bill will be released tomorrow."
pass = win the vote	"The bill passed with a simple majority."
consideration = examination, evaluation	"The bill is in the Senate for consideration."
role = part, participation	"The role of Congress is to make laws."
law-making = creating laws	"Congress is a law-making body."
process = method, procedure	"The legal process is sometimes long."
recommendation = statement that something is favorable	"They studied the president's recommendations."
ignore = leave unnoticed, disregard	"If he ignores the bill, it's a pocket veto."
demonstration = public exhibition, mass meeting	"There were many civil rights demonstrations in the sixties."
pressure = moral force	"The protests put pressure on the government."
enact = put into law	"The Voting Rights Law was enacted in 1965."
outlaw = forbid, make illegal	"The Constitution outlaws slavery."
poll tax = money paid in order to vote	"Some southern states had a poll tax."
discrimination = unfair treatment	"Dr. King fought racial discrimination."
limit = hinder, hold back	"The states cannot limit a citizen's right to vote."

Write Your New Words

In the blank of the first sentence, write the missing word(s). In the second sentence, write the same word(s) from memory.

1. The bill was introduced by Senator Brown.

The bill was _____ by Senator Brown.

The bill was _____ by Senator Brown.

2. It was presented in written form.

It was _____ in written form.

It was _____ in written form.

3. The bill was assigned to a committee.

The bill was _____ to a committee.

The bill was _____ to a committee.

4. The Senate questioned several experts.

The Senate questioned several _____.

The Senate questioned several _____.

5. The committee tabled action on the bill.

The committee _____ action on the bill.

The committee _____ action on the bill.

6. When it was released, it went to the Senate.

When it was _____, it went to the Senate.

When it was _____, it went to the Senate.

7. It passed with a simple majority.

It _____ with a simple majority.

It _____ with a simple majority.

8. The bill went to a committee for consideration.

The bill went to a committee for _____.

The bill went to a committee for _____.

9. What role does the President play?

What _____ does the President play?

What _____ does the President play?

10. Congress is a law-making body.

Congress is a _____ body.

Congress is a _____ body.

11. The legal process can be slow.

The legal _____ can be slow.

The legal _____ can be slow.

12. His recommendation for changes was studied.

His _____ for changes was studied.

His _____ for changes was studied.

13. The President ignored the bill.

The President _____ the bill.

The President _____ the bill.

14. There was a demonstration near the Capitol.

There was a _____ near the Capitol.

There was a _____ near the Capitol.

15. They put pressure on Congress.

They put _____ on Congress.

They put _____ on Congress.

16. The law was enacted last year.

The law was _____ last year.

The law was _____ last year.

17. The Constitution outlaws slavery.

The Constitution _____ slavery.

The Constitution _____ slavery.

18. A poll tax is illegal.

A _____ is illegal.

A _____ is illegal.

19. Dr. King fought discrimination.

Dr. King fought _____.

Dr. King fought _____.

20. No one can limit your right to vote.

No one can _____ your right to vote.

No one can _____ your right to vote.

Important Questions and Answers

1. What is a bill? (an idea for a new law)

2. What can a committee do if they do not like a bill? (table it)

3. What does a committee do with a bill? (study it, listen to experts)

4. Where does a House Bill go if it passes in the House? (to the Senate)

5. How many votes is a simple majority in the House? (218)

6. How many votes is a simple majority in the Senate? (51)

7. What happens to a bill that is released by a Senate committee? (It is debated and voted on in the Senate.)

8. What is the President's role in the law-making process? (approval of laws)

9. What is it called when the President does not sign a bill into law? (veto)

10. What is it called when the President ignores a bill for more than 10 days? (pocket veto)

11. What important law was enacted in 1965? (Voting Rights Act)

12. Who was an important Civil Rights leader of the 1960s? (Dr. Martin Luther King, Jr.)

13. What did the Voting Rights Act outlaw? (poll tax, voting tests)

14. How did Dr. King die? (He was assassinated.)

Is It TRUE or FALSE?

Say TRUE if the sentence is correct. Say FALSE if it is incorrect.

1. If a House committee does not like a bill, the committee can table it.

2. A simple majority in the House is 51 votes.

3. A bill is an idea for a new law.

4. Committees listen to the President's ideas for a bill.

5. A bill can be introduced in either the House of Representatives or the Senate.

6. If a bill passes in the House and the Senate, it is sent to Congress.

7. The President approves new laws.

8. If the President signs a bill, it becomes law.

9. If the President ignores a bill, it is called tabling.

10. Only the Senate can make a pocket veto.

11. Dr. Martin Luther King, Jr., was a leader of the Civil Rights Movement.

12. Demonstrations and protests pressured Congress to enact the Voting Rights Act.

13. Poll taxes and voting tests are used in all states.

14. The Constitution outlaws new bills.

15. Dr. Martin Luther King, Jr., was assassinated in Memphis in 1968.

16. A bill can pass in the House or in the Senate by a simple majority.

Answers

1. True
2. False
3. True
4. False
5. True
6. False
7. True
8. True
9. False
10. False
11. True
12. True
13. False
14. False
15. True
16. True

Let's Look at Some Important Sentences

Circle the letter of the word or phrase that completes the sentence.

1. If a committee puts aside a bill, the bill is _____.

   a. law
   b. illegal
   c. tabled
   d. enacted

2. A _____ is introduced in the House of Representatives in written form.

   a. bill
   b. veto
   c. presidential recommendation
   d. senator

3. Bills are studied in _____.

   a. committees
   b. the Capitol
   c. the White House
   d. the law

4. A bill can pass in the House with a _____.

   a. veto
   b. pocket veto
   c. recommendation
   d. simple majority

5. When a bill is released from a Senate committee, it goes to the Senate for _____.

   a. a majority
   b. debate
   c. recommendations
   d. 10 days

6. A simple majority in the Senate is _____ votes.

    a. 35

    b. 51

    c. 275

    d. 435

7. Committees listen to the advice of _____.

    a. experts

    b. the Vice President

    c. the Senate

    d. the Judicial Branch

8. After a bill passes in the House and Senate, it is sent to _____.

    a. Washington, D.C.

    b. Congress

    c. a committee

    d. the President

9. If the President _____ a bill, it becomes law.

    a. vetoes

    b. recommends

    c. votes for

    d. signs

10. A *pocket veto* is when the President _____ a bill.

    a. likes

    b. signs

    c. changes

    d. ignores

11. The Voting Rights Act outlawed voting tests and the _____.

    a. poll tax

    b. demonstrations

    c. Civil Rights Movement

    d. President's role

12. _____ was a leader of the Civil Rights Movement.

    a. George W. Bush

    b. A senator from the South

    c. Dr. Martin Luther King, Jr.

    d. Thomas Jefferson

13. There were peaceful _____ against discrimination.

    a. demonstrations

    b. experts

    c. recommendations

    d. bills

14. Poll taxes _____ an African-American's right to vote.

    a. released

    b. protested

    c. limited

    d. tabled

15. Dr. Martin Luther King, Jr., was _____ in 1968.

    a. assassinated

    b. approved

    c. protested

    d. pressured

Answers

1. c		**9.** d	
2. a		**10.** d	
3. a		**11.** a	
4. d		**12.** c	
5. b		**13.** a	
6. b		**14.** c	
7. a		**15.** a	
8. d			

Let's Write the New Words

In the blank, write the word or phrase that completes the sentence. Look at the words in parentheses. They will help you.

1. His _____ was to change the law. (statement that something is favorable)

2. It is a pocket veto if the president _____ the bill. (leaves unnoticed, disregards)

3. There is a special _____ for making a new law. (method, procedure)

4. There was a _____ in the capital. (public exhibition, mass meeting)

5. Congress is the _____ body. (creating laws)

6. The protests put _____ on Congress. (moral force)

7. What is the President's _____ in making laws? (part, participation)

8. When was this law _____? (put into law)

9. The bill is in the Senate for _____. (examination, evaluation)

10. Slavery has been _____ for more than a century. (forbidden, made illegal)

11. The bill _____ the House and Senate. (won the vote)

12. There no longer is a _____. (money paid in order to vote)

13. The committee _____ the bill. (set free, sent on)

14. Dr. King fought racial _____. (unfair treatment)

15. The committee _____ the bill. (stopped an action, avoided)

16. The members question several _____. (skilled persons, authorities)

17. The bill was _____ to a committee. (transferred to, appointed to)

18. No one can _____ our rights. (hinder, hold back)

19. The bill was _____ in the Senate. (brought in, made known)

20. The bill was _____ to the House. (shown, given)

Answers

1. recommendation
2. ignores
3. process
4. demonstration
5. law-making
6. pressure
7. role
8. enacted
9. consideration
10. outlawed

11. passed
12. poll tax
13. released
14. discrimination
15. tabled
16. experts
17. assigned
18. limit
19. introduced
20. presented

Some Tips About English

■ It is common to express certain sentences in the *passive voice*. The passive voice is simply a structure where the subject of the sentence is placed at the **end of the sentence** in a **passive position**. It is easy to change from the *active voice* to the *passive voice*. Look at these examples:

Active Voice	Passive Voice
Congress enacts the laws.	The laws are enacted **by Congress.**
A senator introduces the bill.	The bill is introduced **by a senator.**
The House raises revenue.	Revenue is raised **by the House.**

- If the active voice sentence is in the past tense, the verb *is* or *are* in the passive sentence is stated in the past tense—*was* or *were*.

Active Voice	Passive Voice
The soldier used the gun.	The gun was used **by the soldier.**
The Senate wrote a new bill.	A new bill was written **by the Senate.**
The president signed the letters.	The letters were signed **by the president.**

The active voice sentences and the passive voice sentences provide the same meaning. It is only the structure that is different.

- The passive voice structure can be used even when the subject of the sentence is omitted.

Passive Voice—Subject Omitted
Revenue was raised for the war.
The White House was set on fire and nearly destroyed.
The Constitution is seldom changed.

The structure of the passive voice is always a form of **to be** (am, are, is, was, were, and so on) and a past participle. And that structure can be used in any tense by putting **to be** in the appropriate tense. Look at these examples:

Present Tense:	Laws are enacted by Congress.
Past Tense:	Laws **were** enacted by Congress.
Present Perfect Tense:	Laws **have been** enacted by Congress.
Past Perfect Tense:	Laws **had been** enacted by Congress.
Future Tense:	Laws **will be** enacted by Congress.

Voting and Elections

In order to vote in an election, you must be a registered voter. You can register at many places in your state. Many county and state offices provide registration services. Even groups, such as the League of Women Voters, sponsor registration programs.

After you are registered, you can vote in local, county, state, and federal elections. Federal elections are held on the Tuesday after the first Monday in November. During much of our history, most Americans were farmers. Therefore, November was chosen as election month, because it came after harvest season. And Tuesday was selected, because it avoided Monday, the first and very busy business day of the week.

In presidential elections each state has electors allotted to it based upon population. When you vote for a presidential candidate in your state, you are voting for the state's electors for that candidate. The candidate who wins the state's popular vote wins all the state's electors. On the Monday following the second Wednesday of December, each state's electors meet in their state capital and cast their electoral votes for the winning presidential and vice presidential candidates. This is called the Electoral College.

At noon on January 20, the President and Vice President are sworn into office.

Important Words

Learn the meaning of these new words. Say a sentence using each new word.

in order to = for the purpose of	"You must be a citizen in order to vote."
register = sign up	"You can register to vote at the state Department of Motor Vehicles."
league = club, organization	"What baseball teams are in the National League?"
sponsor = promote, arrange	"They sponsor a debate before the election."
therefore = for that reason	"Therefore, you must register if you want to vote."
season = time of year, spring, summer, fall, winter	"What season do you like best?"
avoid = keep away from, evade	"In the morning you should avoid the freeway."
business = commerce, trade	"Business is good at holiday time."
Elector = someone who elects	"How many electors does your state have?"
allot = distribute, assign	"Each state is allotted a specific number of electors."
candidate = nominee, office-seeker	"Her party selected her as their candidate."
popular = from the people at large	"He won the popular vote."
cast a vote = vote	"The electors cast their votes in the capital."
college = assembly, gathering	"How does the Electoral College work?"
swear into office = take an oath	"The President was sworn into office at noon."

Write Your New Words

In the blank of the first sentence, write the missing word(s). In the second sentence, write the same word(s) from memory.

1. In order to vote, you must register.

_____ vote, you must register.

_____ vote, you must register.

2. I registered to vote at a county office.

I _____ to vote at a county office.

I _____ to vote at a county office.

3. What is the League of Women Voters?

What is the _____ of Women Voters?

What is the _____ of Women Voters?

4. They sponsor a voter registration.

They _____ a voter registration.

They _____ a voter registration.

5. Therefore, our candidate wins the election.

_____, our candidate wins the election.

_____, our candidate wins the election.

6. The election comes after harvest season.

The election comes after harvest _____.

The election comes after harvest _____.

7. I would like to avoid the traffic.

I would like to _____ the traffic.

I would like to _____ the traffic.

8. Business will be better tomorrow.

_____ will be better tomorrow.

_____ will be better tomorrow.

9. How many electors does each state have?

How many _____ does each state have?

How many _____ does each state have?

10. They allotted some money for the project.

They _____ some money for the project.

They _____ some money for the project.

11. Our candidate lost the election.

Our _____ lost the election.

Our _____ lost the election.

12. Did she win the popular vote?

Did she win the _____ vote?

Did she win the _____ vote?

13. I cast my vote early.

I _____ early.

I _____ early.

14. The Electoral College meets in the capital.

The Electoral _____ meets in the capital.

The Electoral _____ meets in the capital.

15. They were sworn into office on January 20.

They were _____ on January 20.

They were _____ on January 20.

Important Questions and Answers

1. What organization sponsors voter registration? (League of Women Voters)

2. What must you do in order to vote? (register)

3. Where can you register to vote? (at county and state offices)

4. On what day is a federal election held? (the Tuesday after the first Monday in November)

5. What does a November election avoid? (harvest season)

6. What occupation did Americans have during much of our history? (farmers)

7. What day of the week is a busy business day? (Monday)

8. What is the number of state electors based upon? (population)

9. Who wins the state's electors? (the candidate who wins the state's popular vote)

10. When are the President and Vice President sworn into office? (at noon on January 20)

11. Where do a state's electors vote for the president? (in the capital)

12. What does the League of Women Voters sponsor? (voter registration)

13. In what month are federal elections held? (November)

14. In what month do electors cast their electoral votes? (December)

Is It TRUE or FALSE?

Say TRUE if the sentence is correct. Say FALSE if it is incorrect.

1. You have to register in Washington, D.C., if you wish to vote.

2. Groups, such as the League of Women Voters, sponsor voter registration.

3. After you are registered to vote, you can only vote in local elections.

4. The Electoral College casts its votes for the presidential candidate that has won the popular vote of a state.

5. Many county and state offices provide voter registration services.

6. Federal elections are held in March.

7. Monday is considered a very busy business day.

8. The number of state electors is based upon population.

9. Federal elections are held on the Tuesday after the first Monday in November.

10. The presidential candidate who wins the state's popular vote wins all the state's electors.

11. The President and Vice President are sworn into office at noon on May 1.

12. Electors cast their votes in the state capital.

13. During much of our history, most Americans were farmers.

14. Voting in the Electoral College takes place in December.

Answers

1. False

2. True

3. False

4. True

5. True

6. False

7. True

8. True

9. True

10. True

11. False

12. True

13. True

14. True

Let's Look at Some Important Sentences

Circle the letter of the word or phrase that completes the sentence.

1. If you are _____ to vote, you can vote in local, county, state, and federal elections.

    a. chosen

    b. a candidate

    c. an American

    d. registered

2. Federal elections are held in _____.

    a. November

    b. December

    c. January

    d. March

3. Each state has _____ allotted to it based upon population.

    a. electors

    b. candidates

    c. voters

    d. a college

4. The _____ of Women Voters often sponsors registration programs.

    a. State

    b. League

    c. Capital

    d. Electoral College

5. You can register to vote in county and _____ offices.

    a. capital

    b. state

    c. business

    d. electoral

6. The candidate who wins the state's _____ vote wins the state's electors.

    a. local

    b. seasonal

    c. county

    d. popular

7. Federal elections are held on the _____ after the first Monday in November.

    a. Tuesday

    b. Wednesday

    c. Thursday

    d. Friday

8. November was chosen as election month in order to avoid _____ .

    a. December

    b. harvest season

    c. the Electoral College

    d. local elections

9. The President and Vice President are sworn into office at noon on _____.

    a. January 20

    b. December 15

    c. the Tuesday after the second Monday of November

    d. May 1

10. If a candidate wins the state's popular vote, he or she wins the state's _____.

    a. local election

    b. electors

    c. League of Women Voters

    d. vice presidential candidate

11. The Electoral _____ is the gathering where the electors cast their votes.

    a. election

    b. vote

    c. College

    d. business office

12. During our history, many Americans were _____.

    a. from western states

    b. registered

    c. candidates

    d. farmers

13. Electors _____ their votes on the Monday following the second Wednesday of December.

    a. cast

    b. call for

    c. avoid

    d. register

Answers

1. d	**8.** b
2. a	**9.** a
3. a	**10.** b
4. b	**11.** c
5. b	**12.** d
6. d	**13.** a
7. a	

Let's Write the New Words

In the blank, write the word or phrase that completes the sentence. Look at the words in parentheses. They will help you.

1. When is harvest _____? (time of year, spring, summer, fall, winter)

2. _____, only registered citizens can vote. (for that reason)

3. We _____ busy days like Monday. (keep away from, evade)

4. Their club _____ voter registration programs. (promotes, arranges)

5. Monday is a busy _____ day. (commerce, trade)

6. The _____ of Women Voters provides that service. (club, organization)

7. The number of _____ is based upon population. (someone who elects)

8. Fifty new voters were _____ today. (signed up)

9. Each state is _____ a specific number of electors. (distributed, assigned)

10. You must be registered _____ vote. (for the purpose of)

11. Their presidential _____ won all the electors. (nominee, office-seeker)

12. Who won the _____ vote in the state? (from the people at large)

13. They are _____ at noon. (take an oath)

14. The Electoral _____ meets in the capital. (assembly, gathering)

15. We _____ for the best candidate. (voted)

Answers

1. season
2. Therefore
3. avoid
4. sponsors
5. business
6. League
7. electors
8. registered

9. allotted
10. in order to
11. candidate
12. popular
13. sworn into office
14. College
15. cast our votes

Amendments and the Bill of Rights

The United States Constitution can be changed. A change is called an *amendment*. To the present day there have been 27 amendments.

Some later amendments made earlier amendments invalid. For example, the Twenty-first Amendment repealed the Eighteenth Amendment, which made the production and sale of alcohol illegal in the United States. The Eighteenth Amendment was also known as *Prohibition*.

The first 10 amendments are the Bill of Rights. They are the important constitutional guarantees of the rights of citizens and the states. These include the following:

- Freedom of religion, speech, press, assembly, and petition of the government
- The right to bear arms
- Soldiers will not be housed in private homes
- No unreasonable search or seizure
- The right to due process of law
- The right of a speedy and public trial
- The right to trial by jury
- No cruel or unusual punishment
- Other rights not listed in the Constitution are retained by the people
- Powers not delegated to the federal government are reserved to the states

Amendment XIII abolished slavery:

Neither slavery nor involuntary servitude, except as a punishment for crime whereof the party shall have been duly convicted, shall exist within the United States, or any place subject to their jurisdiction.

Amendment XIX gave women the right to vote:

The right of citizens of the United States to vote shall not be denied or abridged by the United States or by any State on account of sex.

Important Words

Learn the meaning of these new words. Say a sentence using each new word.

invalid = no longer in force	"The Eighteenth Amendment is now invalid."
repeal = revoke a law	"Prohibition was repealed in 1933."
sale = selling	"For more than a decade the sale of alcohol was illegal."
alcohol = spirits, whiskey	"You must be an adult to buy alcohol."
guarantee = promise of security	"The Constitution guarantees our rights."
include = make a part of, enclose	"Free speech is included in the Bill of Rights."
press = media that produce newspapers and magazines	"Freedom of the press is guaranteed in the Constitution."
assembly = gathering	"A peaceful assembly of people stood in front of the courthouse."
petition = formal request or application	"We have the right to petition our government."
bear arms = carry weapons	"Who has the right to bear arms?"
unreasonable = irrational, unjustified	"An unreasonable search of your home is outlawed."

seizure = taking, confiscation   "Seizure of private property is not allowed."

due process = appropriate method   "Everyone has the right of due process of the law."

cruel = severe, without pity   "His punishment was very cruel."

reserve = set aside, keep as one's own   "Certain powers are reserved for the states."

Write Your New Words

In the blank of the first sentence, write the missing word(s). In the second sentence, write the same word(s) from memory.

1. That amendment is no longer valid.

That amendment is no longer _____.

That amendment is no longer _____.

2. It is possible to repeal a bad law.

It is possible to _____ a bad law.

It is possible to _____ a bad law.

3. The sale of alcohol was illegal.

The _____ of alcohol was illegal.

The _____ of alcohol was illegal.

4. She's too young to drink alcohol.

She's too young to drink _____.

She's too young to drink _____.

5. Freedom of religion is guaranteed.

Freedom of religion is _____.

Freedom of religion is _____.

6. Our rights include freedom of speech.

Our rights _____ freedom of speech.

Our rights _____ freedom of speech.

7. The press has certain rights.

The _____ has certain rights.

The _____ has certain rights.

8. We have the right of peaceful assembly.

We have the right of peaceful _____.

We have the right of peaceful _____.

9. The people petitioned the governor.

The people _____ the governor.

The people _____ the governor.

10. Citizens have the right to bear arms.

Citizens have the right to _____.

Citizens have the right to _____.

11. Unreasonable search is not allowed.

_____ search is not allowed.

_____ search is not allowed.

12. Is the seizure of my property legal?

Is the _____ of my property legal?

Is the _____ of my property legal?

13. We have the right of due process of the law.

We have the right of _____ of the law.

We have the right of _____ of the law.

14. Did he receive cruel treatment?

Did he receive _____ treatment?

Did he receive _____ treatment?

15. These powers are reserved for the states.

These powers are _____ for the states.

These powers are _____ for the states.

Important Questions and Answers

1. What are the first 10 amendments called? (Bill of Rights)

2. How can you change the Constitution? (with an amendment)

3. How many amendments have there been? (27)

4. What is it called when one amendment makes another amendment invalid? (repealing the amendment)

5. What was the Eighteenth Amendment known as? (Prohibition)

6. What did the Eighteenth Amendment prohibit? (sale of alcohol)

7. What does the First Amendment guarantee? (freedom of religion, speech, press, assembly, petition of the government)

8. Who has the right to bear arms? (all citizens)

9. Who retains the rights not listed in the Constitution? (the people)

10. To whom are the powers that are not delegated to the federal government reserved? (the states)

11. Which amendment abolished slavery? (13)

12. Which amendment gave women the right to vote? (19)

13. Who has the right to a speedy and public trial? (all citizens)

Is It TRUE or FALSE?

Say TRUE if the sentence is correct. Say FALSE if it is incorrect.

1. The Bill of Rights guarantees the rights of citizens and the states.

2. The U.S. Constitution can never be changed.

3. The Eighteenth Amendment was also known as the Bill of Rights.

4. There have been 27 amendments to the Constitution.

5. An amendment is a change to the Constitution.

6. Freedom of religion and speech are guaranteed in the Constitution.

7. Having a good job is in the Bill of Rights.

8. The Twenty-seventh Amendment gave women the right to vote.

9. According to the Constitution, soldiers cannot be housed in private homes.

10. Rights not listed in the Constitution are illegal.

11. The Thirteenth Amendment abolished slavery.

12. The police can search a citizen's home at any time.

13. An amendment is repealed when a new amendment makes an old amendment invalid.

14. The Bill of Rights is the first 10 amendments to the Constitution.

Answers

1. True	8. False
2. False	9. True
3. False	10. False
4. True	11. True
5. True	12. False
6. True	13. True
7. False	14. True

Let's Look at Some Important Sentences

Circle the letter of the word or phrase that completes the sentence.

1. The first _____ amendments are the Bill of Rights.

   a. five
   b. ten
   c. fifteen
   d. eighteen

2. There have been _____ amendments to the Constitution.

   a. 27
   b. 10
   c. 18
   d. 5

3. A change to the Constitution is called an _____.

   a. bill
   b. amendment
   c. petition
   d. right

4. Citizens are protected from _____ search or seizure.

   a. local
   b. private
   c. unreasonable
   d. speedy

5. The powers that the federal government does not have are reserved to the _____.

   a. states
   b. Congress
   c. Executive Branch
   d. due process of law

6. The Eighteenth Amendment is also known as _____.

   a. the right to bear arms
   b. Constitution
   c. illegal
   d. Prohibition

7. Freedom of the press is _____ in the Bill of Rights.

   a. a public trial
   b. guaranteed
   c. a change
   d. punishment

8. Amendment XIII abolished _____.

   a. alcohol
   b. slavery
   c. the right to vote
   d. the right to bear arms

9. A later amendment can _____ an earlier amendment.

   a. reserve
   b. prohibit
   c. allow
   d. repeal

10. The Nineteenth Amendment gave women _____.

   a. the right to bear arms
   b. the right to trial by jury
   c. the right to vote
   d. the right to petition the government

Answers

1. b	6. d
2. a	7. b
3. b	8. b
4. c	9. d
5. a	10. c

Let's Write the New Words

In the blank, write the word or phrase that completes the sentence. Look at the words in parentheses. They will help you.

1. We have the right of peaceful _____. (gathering)

2. The workers decided to _____ the government. (make a formal request or application)

3. Freedom of the _____ is also guaranteed. (media that produce newspapers and magazines)

4. What freedoms are _____ in the Bill of Rights? (made a part of, enclosed)

5. Americans have the right to _____. (carry weapons)

6. The Constitution _____ our rights. (promises security)

7. We are protected from _____ searches. (irrational, unjustified)

8. You must be an adult to buy _____. (spirits, whiskey)

9. _____ of private property is illegal. (Taking, Confiscation)

10. Prohibition ended the _____ of alcohol. (selling)

11. We have the right of _____ of the law. (appropriate method)

12. In what year was Prohibition _____? (revoked a law)

13. _____ punishment is not allowed. (Severe, Without pity)

14. Amendment XXI made Amendment XVIII _____. (no longer in force)

15. Certain powers are _____ to the states. (set aside, kept as their own)

Answers

1. assembly

2. petition

3. press

4. included

5. bear arms

6. guarantees

7. unreasonable

8. alcohol

9. Seizure

10. sale

11. due process

12. repealed

13. Cruel

14. invalid

15. reserved

Some Tips About English

■ The *past perfect tense* is identical to the *present perfect tense* except that the verb **have** is in the past tense—**had.** It is used to say that **an action began in the past** and **it ended in the past**. Some examples:

Present Perfect Tense	Past Perfect Tense
I have never voted until now.	I had never voted in my youth.
He has come to dinner tonight.	He had come to dinner every Sunday.
We have finally sold the car.	We had sold the car by the end of winter.

■ Some important words in this chapter are *irregular verbs*. Their past tense and participial forms do not follow the regular pattern.

	Regular Verb	bear arms	swear him in
Present Tense	I avoid	I bear arms	I swear him in
Past Tense	I avoided	I bore arms	I swore him in
Present Perfect	I have avoided	I have born arms	I have sworn him in
Past Perfect	I had avoided	I had born arms	I had sworn him in
Future	I will avoid	I will bear arms	I will swear him in

Justice for All

Judicial Branch

The Judicial Branch of Government is made up of the courts. State courts deal with cases that involve individual state laws. Federal courts deal with cases that involve federal laws.

There are three levels to the court system—whether state or federal. They are (1) district or circuit courts; (2) courts of appeal; and (3) supreme courts.

The Supreme Court of the federal government is the highest court in the land. It hears cases that have come up through the other two levels of courts. It is the Supreme Court's responsibility to decide whether laws are constitutional, what the meaning of laws is, and how laws should be applied.

The Supreme Court is made up of nine justices, and each of them serves on the court for life. The current Chief Justice of the United States is William H. Rehnquist. The other eight Associate Justices are as follows:

John Paul Stevens	Antonin Scalia
David H. Souter	Ruth Bader Ginsburg
Sandra Day O'Connor	Anthony M. Kennedy
Clarence Thomas	Stephen G. Breyer

All justices are appointed by the President of the United States and approved by the Senate.

District or circuit courts are trial courts. Appellate courts hear appeals regarding a case that has been tried in the district or circuit court. And the Supreme Court is where a final appeal can be made.

Note: The information given in this chapter regarding the individual Justices and their titles is subject to change, as the current Chief Justice might be retiring. Please double-check the information before taking your citizenship test.

Important Words

Learn the meaning of these new words. Say a sentence using each new word.

deal with = consider, treat	"Appellate courts deal with appeals."
involve = be about, comprise	"Some cases involve civil rights."
level = part, category	"The court system has three levels."
highest (high, higher) = uppermost, having the greatest authority	"The highest court is the Supreme Court."
apply = use	"Not all laws are applied fairly."
Chief Justice = head judge	"Rehnquist is the Chief Justice of the United States."
Associate Justice = partner judge	"There are eight Associate Justices."
regarding = about	"They hear cases regarding federal laws."
final = last	"They made their final appeal in the Supreme Court."

Write Your New Words

In the blank of the first sentence, write the missing word. In the second sentence, write it from memory.

1. What court deals with appeals?

    What court _____ appeals?
    What court _____ appeals?

2. This case involves civil rights.

    This case _____ civil rights.
    This case _____ civil rights.

3. There are three levels in the court system.

    There are three _____ in the court system.
    There are three _____ in the court system.

4. What is the highest court in the land?

    What is the _____ court in the land?
    What is the _____ court in the land?

5. They judge whether laws are applied fairly.

    They judge whether laws are _____ fairly.
    They judge whether laws are _____ fairly.

6. Who is the Chief Justice?

    Who is the _____?
    Who is the _____?

7. Antonin Scalia is an Associate Judge.

    Antonin Scalia is an _____.
    Antonin Scalia is an _____.

8. They heard a case regarding freedom of speech.

    They heard a case _____ freedom of speech.
    They heard a case _____ freedom of speech.

9. You make a final appeal before the Supreme Court.

    You make a _____ appeal before the Supreme Court.
    You make a _____ appeal before the Supreme Court.

Important Questions and Answers

1. Which courts deal with state laws? (state courts)

2. How many levels are there in the court system? (3)

3. Which court is the highest in the land? (Supreme Court)

4. Which branch of government is made up of the courts? (Judicial Branch)

5. Which courts deal with federal laws? (federal courts)

6. What are the three levels of courts? (district or circuit court, court of appeals, and supreme court)

7. Which court decides whether laws are constitutional? (Supreme Court)

8. Who is the Chief Justice of the United States? (William H. Rehnquist)

9. How many Associate Justices are there? (8)

10. Who appoints the justices of the Supreme Court? (the President)

11. Who approves the appointment of the justices? (Senate)

12. In what court are appeals made? (appellate court)

Is It TRUE or FALSE?

Say TRUE if the sentence is correct. Say FALSE if it is incorrect.

1. There are four levels to the court system.

2. The Supreme Court decides whether laws are constitutional.

3. The Judicial Branch of government is made up of the courts.

4. Federal courts deal with state laws.

5. The Chief Justice of the Supreme Court is Sandra Day O'Conner.

6. There are nine justices on the Supreme Court.

7. There are eight Chief Justices on the Supreme Court.

8. Courts are either district courts, courts of appeal, or state courts.

9. Justices of the Supreme Court are appointed by the President.

10. Appellate courts hear appeals.

11. State courts deal with cases regarding state law.

Answers

1. False
2. True
3. True
4. False
5. False
6. True

7. False
8. False
9. True
10. True
11. True

Let's Look at Some Important Sentences

Circle the letter of the word or phrase that completes the sentence.

1. The Supreme Court is made up of _____ justices.

   a. 8
   b. 9
   c. 12
   d. 15

2. The _____ Justice is William H. Rehnquist.

   a. Associate
   b. State
   c. Federal
   d. Chief

3. The Judicial Branch of government is made up of the _____.

   a. courts
   b. judges
   c. justices
   d. Supreme Court

4. There are _____ levels to the court system.

   a. 2
   b. 3
   c. 4
   d. 6

5. _____ courts deal with cases regarding state law.

   a. State
   b. Local
   c. Federal
   d. Supreme

6. Appeals are heard in the _____ court.

    a. state

    b. appellate

    c. federal

    d. national

7. There are nine _____ Justices on the Supreme Court.

    a. Federal

    b. State

    c. Associate

    d. Supreme

8. The Supreme Court decides whether laws are _____.

    a. constitutional

    b. federal

    c. local

    d. in the Supreme Court

9. All justices are appointed by the _____.

    a. states

    b. President

    c. Chief Justice

    d. House of Representatives

10. The Supreme Court is where a _____ appeal can be made.

    a. final

    b. unfair

    c. level

    d. state

11. Justices of the Supreme Court serve for _____.

    a. two terms

    b. life

    c. five years

    d. ten years

Answers

1. b	**7.** c
2. d	**8.** a
3. a	**9.** b
4. b	**10.** a
5. a	**11.** b
6. b	

Let's Write the New Words

In the blank, write the word or phrase that completes the sentence. Look at the words in parentheses. They will help you.

1. The _____ is William H. Rehnquist. (head judge)

2. Laws must be _____ fairly. (used)

3. There are eight _____ on the Supreme Court. (partner judges)

4. What is the _____ court in the land? (uppermost, having the greatest authority)

5. They hear a case _____ civil rights. (about)

6. There are three _____ to the court system. (parts, categories)

7. A _____ appeal is made in the Supreme Court. (last)

8. State courts _____ state laws. (consider, treat)

9. Some cases _____ the Constitution. (are about, comprise)

Answers

1. Chief Justice
2. applied
3. Associate Justices
4. highest
5. regarding
6. levels
7. final
8. deal with
9. involve

Capital Cities

The capital of the 50 states of the United States of America is Washington, D.C. But each of the 50 states also has a capital city.

State	Capital City
Alabama	Montgomery
Alaska	Juneau
Arizona	Phoenix
Arkansas	Little Rock
California	Sacramento
Colorado	Denver
Connecticut	Hartford
Delaware	Dover
Florida	Tallahassee

State	Capital City
Georgia	Atlanta
Hawaii	Honolulu
Idaho	Boise
Illinois	Springfield
Indiana	Indianapolis
Iowa	Des Moines
Kansas	Topeka
Kentucky	Frankfort
Louisiana	Baton Rouge
Maine	Augusta
Maryland	Annapolis
Massachusetts	Boston
Michigan	Lansing
Minnesota	St. Paul
Mississippi	Jackson
Missouri	Jefferson City
Montana	Helena
Nebraska	Lincoln
Nevada	Carson City
New Hampshire	Concord
New Jersey	Trenton
New Mexico	Santa Fe
New York	Albany
North Carolina	Raleigh
North Dakota	Bismarck
Ohio	Columbus
Oklahoma	Oklahoma City
Oregon	Salem
Pennsylvania	Harrisburg
Rhode Island	Providence
South Carolina	Columbia
South Dakota	Pierre
Tennessee	Nashville

(continued)

State	Capital City
Texas	Austin
Utah	Salt Lake City
Vermont	Montpelier
Virginia	Richmond
Washington	Olympia
West Virginia	Charleston
Wisconsin	Madison
Wyoming	Cheyenne

Sometimes people think that the biggest city in the state is the capital city. But that is not always true. For example, New York City is not the capital of New York. The capital is Albany. Los Angeles is not the capital of California. The capital is Sacramento. Detroit is not the capital of Michigan. The capital is Lansing. And the capital of Illinois is not Chicago; it is Springfield.

Do you know the capital of your state? Can you locate it on a map?

Writing Capitals and States

In the blank of the first phrase, write the missing capital or state. In the second phrase, write it from memory.

1. Washington, D. C.

_____, D. C.

_____, D. C.

2. Albany, New York

Albany, _____

Albany, _____

3. Juneau, Alaska

_____, Alaska

_____, Alaska

4. Austin, Texas

Austin, _____

Austin, _____

5. Lansing, Michigan

_____, Michigan

_____, Michigan

6. Write the capital of your state in the first blank. Write the name of your state in the second blank.

_____

_____

Important Questions and Answers

1. What is the capital of the United States? (Washington, D.C.)

2. What do the letters D.C. stand for? (District of Columbia)

3. What state do you live in? (Learn the name of your state.)

4. What is the capital of your state? (Learn the name of the capital of your state.)

5. How many state capitals are there in the United States? (50)

Is It TRUE or FALSE?

Say TRUE if the sentence is correct. Say FALSE if it is incorrect.

1. The capital of Washington State is Washington, D.C.

2. The capital of Illinois is Chicago.

3. The capital of California is Sacramento.

4. New York City is the capital of New York State.

5. Washington, D.C., is the nation's capital.

Answers

1. False

2. False

3. True

4. False

5. True

Let's Look at Some Important Sentences

Circle the letter of the word or phrase that completes the sentence.

1. The _____ of the state is located in the state capital.

   a. biggest city
   b. government
   c. judicial branch
   d. population

2. Each _____ has a capital city.

   a. state

   b. region

   c. senator

   d. representative

3. The states of the Union have a total of _____ capital cities.

   a. 40

   b. 50

   c. 75

   d. 100

4. Some people believe that Los Angeles is the capital of _____.

   a. Nevada

   b. Arizona

   c. New Jersey

   d. California

5. The _____ city is not always the capital city.

   a. biggest

   b. highest

   c. local

   d. federal

Answers

1. b

2. a

3. b

4. d

5. a

Some Tips About English

It is common to express certain sentences in the *passive voice*. As you saw in Chapter Thirteen, the passive voice is simply a structure in which the subject of the sentence is placed at the **end of the sentence** in a **passive position.** It is easy to change from the *active voice* to the *passive voice*. Look at these examples:

Active Voice	*Passive Voice*
The president appoints a judge.	A judge is appointed by **the president.**
They approve the appointment.	The appointment is approved **by them.**

If the active voice sentence is in the past tense, the verb *is* or *are* is stated in the past tense—*was* or *were*.

Active Voice	*Passive Voice*
The president appointed judges.	Judges were appointed **by the president.**
They approved the appointment.	The appointment was approved **by them.**

The active voice sentences and the passive voice sentences provide the same meaning. It is only the structure that is different.

- The passive voice structure can be used even when the subject of the sentence is omitted.

Passive Voice—Subject Omitted

Judges were appointed.
The appointment was approved.
The laws are applied fairly.

- The structure of the passive voice is always a form of **to be** (am, are, is, was, were, and so on) and a past participle. And that structure can be used in any tense by putting **to be** in the appropriate tense. Look at these examples:

Present Tense:	The laws **are** applied fairly.
Past Tense:	The laws **were** applied fairly.
Present Perfect Tense:	The laws **have been** applied fairly.
Past Perfect Tense:	The laws **had been** applied fairly.
Future Tense:	The laws **will be** applied fairly.

A Great Nation

Mayors and Governors

The mayor is the chief executive officer of a city or town. He or she is elected by the citizens of the city or town. The mayor works with the City Council to provide services for the community. The City Council is the elected legislative body of the city.

Many cities provide services like these:

- Building Department to oversee new construction
- Traffic Department to provide traffic signals and safe streets
- Transportation to provide buses, trains, and subways
- Library
- Streets and Sanitation to maintain streets and sewers
- Education
- Police and Fire Departments
- Corrections to maintain prisons

Do you know the name of the mayor of your town?

The governor is the chief executive officer of a state. He or she is elected by the citizens of the state. The governor's office and the state legislature are located in the capital city. They provide statewide services similar to those provided in the cities. Do you know the name of the governor of your state?

Important Words

Learn the meaning of these new words. Say a sentence using each new word.

body = official group, organization	"The City Council is a legislative body."
services = work performed for the benefit of others	"What services does the city provide?"
oversee = manage, control	"What department oversees new construction?"
traffic = movement of cars and trucks on a street	"Traffic is slow today."
transportation = movement of cargo or passengers by vehicle	"What form of transportation do you use?"
library = collection of books	"The new library is on Main Street."
sanitation = hygiene, maintaining cleanliness	"Good sanitation means good health."
maintain = keep	"Maintaining good streets is a big job."
sewer = underground drain	"The rainwater flowed into the sewer."
education = schools and learning	"Education is an important part of life."
fire department = service for extinguishing fires	"The fire department fought the blaze."
corrections = prison system	"The department of corrections is on the first floor."
prison = jail	"They built a new prison."
statewide = across the whole state	"Statewide elections were held in November."

Write Your New Words

In the blank of the first sentence, write the missing word. In the second sentence, write it from memory.

1. The Senate is a legislative body.

   The Senate is a legislative _____.
   The Senate is a legislative _____.

2. The city provides many services.

   The city provides many _____.
   The city provides many _____.

3. Which department oversees the prisons?

   Which department _____ the prisons?
   Which department _____ the prisons?

4. We need new traffic signals.

   We need new _____ signals.
   We need new _____ signals.

5. There is regular transportation into the city.

   There is regular _____ into the city.
   There is regular _____ into the city.

6. Do you have a library card?

   Do you have a _____ card?
   Do you have a _____ card?

7. She works for the sanitation department.

   She works for the _____ department.
   She works for the _____ department.

8. Who maintains the streets?

   Who _____ the streets?
   Who _____ the streets?

9. This sewer is not draining.

   This _____ is not draining.
   This _____ is not draining.

10. She has a good education.

She has a good _____.

She has a good _____.

11. Quick! Call the fire department!

Quick! Call the _____!

Quick! Call the _____!

12. He works as a corrections officer.

He works as a _____ officer.

He works as a _____ officer.

13. Her brother is in prison.

Her brother is in _____.

Her brother is in _____.

14. They provide statewide services.

They provide _____ services.

They provide _____ services.

Important Questions and Answers

1. Who is the chief executive officer of a city? (mayor)

2. Who is the chief executive officer of a state? (governor)

3. What is the legislative body of a city called? (City Council)

4. What city department provides buses, trains, and subways? (transportation)

5. Who elects the mayor? (citizens of the city or town)

6. Who elects the governor? (citizens of the state)

7. Where is the governor's office located? (state capital)

8. What does the department of corrections maintain? (prisons)

9. Where can you get books? (library)

10. Who is the mayor of your city? (Learn the name of your mayor.)

11. Who is the governor of your state? (Learn the name of your governor.)

Is It TRUE or FALSE?

Say TRUE if the sentence is correct. Say FALSE if it is incorrect.

1. The mayor is the chief executive officer of a state.

2. The City Council is elected by the citizens of a city.

3. The Building Department oversees the construction of new buildings.

4. Cities cannot provide services to the community.

5. The governor's office is in the capital city.

6. Streets and Sanitation maintains the streets and sewers.

7. The governor is the head of the City Council.

Answers

1. False
2. True
3. True
4. False

5. True
6. True
7. False

Let's Look at Some Important Sentences

Circle the letter of the word or phrase that completes the sentence.

1. The City Council is the _____ body of a city.

   a. local
   b. statewide
   c. legislative
   d. corrections

2. The _____ is the chief executive officer of a city.

   a. mayor
   b. governor
   c. president
   d. senator

3. The City Council is elected by the _____ of the city.

   a. citizens
   b. mayor
   c. statewide election
   d. Building Department

4. The governor is the chief executive officer of a _____.

   a. state
   b. city
   c. department
   d. town

5. The mayor and City Council provide services to the _____.

   a. state
   b. community
   c. fire department
   d. police department

6. The state legislature is located in the _____.

   a. department of corrections
   b. town
   c. City Council
   d. capital

7. Buses and subways are part of the _____ Department.

   a. Library
   b. Education
   c. Transportation
   d. Corrections

8. The _____ Department oversees new construction.

   a. Streets and Sanitation
   b. Building
   c. Education
   d. Police

Answers

1. c
2. a
3. a
4. a

5. b
6. d
7. c
8. b

Let's Write the New Words

In the blank, write the word or phrase that completes the sentence. Look at the words in parentheses. They will help you.

1. Where is the new _____? (collection of books)

2. The _____ department cleans the sewers. (hygiene, maintaining cleanliness)

3. _____ between New York and Boston is good. (movement of cargo or passengers by vehicle)

4. The streets must also be _____ in winter. (kept in good condition)

5. The _____ are kept clean. (underground drains)

6. Our city has a good _____ plan. (schools and learning)

7. The _____ is moving well now. (movement of cars and trucks on a street)

8. A good _____ is important. (service for extinguishing fires)

9. What department _____ the prisons? (manages, controls)

10. The department of _____ needs money. (prison system)

11. Our city provides many _____. (work performed for the benefit of others)

12. I was never in _____. (jail)

13. What is the legislative _____ of a city called (official group, organization)

14. _____ elections were held. (across the whole state)

Answers

1. library
2. sanitation
3. Transportation
4. maintained
5. sewers
6. education
7. traffic

8. fire department
9. oversees
10. corrections
11. services
12. prison
13. body
14. Statewide

The Star Spangled Banner

The Star Spangled Banner is the national anthem of our country. It was originally written as a poem by Francis Scott Key. He wrote the poem after watching the British bombardment of Fort McHenry near Baltimore during the War of 1812. He was so inspired by the American victory that he had to describe the battle for other patriots.

The poem was sung to the tune of a well-known British song *To Anacreon in Heaven*. The song grew in popularity, and by the time of the Civil War, it was as popular as *Hail Columbia* or *Yankee Doodle*.

But *The Star Spangled Banner* did not become the nation's anthem until 1931 when Congress officially adopted it.

Do you know the words to our national anthem?

O' say can you see, by the dawn's early light,
What so proudly we hail'd at the twilight's last gleaming,
Whose broad stripes and bright stars through the perilous fight
O'er the ramparts we watch'd were so gallantly streaming?

And the rocket's red glare, the bomb bursting in air,
Gave proof through the night that our flag was still there.
O say does that star-spangled banner yet wave
O'er the land of the free and the home of the brave?

Important Words

Learn the meaning of these new words. Say a sentence using each new word.

bombardment = attack with cannons	"The bombardment of the city began in the morning."
inspired = moved, made emotional	"The victory inspired him to write the poem."
tune = song	"This is a happy tune."
popularity = approval by many people	"Her popularity helped her win the election."
dawn = sunrise	"I never get up before dawn."
proudly = with pride and honor	"He proudly showed me his diploma."
hail (hail'd → hailed) = greet, salute	"The crowd hailed the returning soldiers."
twilight = faint light at dawn or dusk	"The sky is beautiful at twilight."
gleaming = shining	"The stars were gleaming brightly."
perilous = dangerous	"It was a perilous time for the nation."
o'er (o'er → over) = above	"The flag flew over the fort."
rampart = embankment around a fort	"The soldiers were running towards the ramparts."
watch'd (watch'd → watched) = looked at, observed	"He watched the rockets explode."
gallantly = bravely, courageously	"He served gallantly in the war."
streaming = flowing	"Banners were streaming down from the buildings."
glare = strong light	"The glare of the sun almost blinded me."
bursting = exploding	"Bombs were bursting all around us."
proof = evidence, convincing fact	"He needed proof to believe her story."
wave = fly, flutter	"A flag is waving over the entrance to the museum."
brave = courageous	"The brave soldier was called a hero."

Write Your New Words

In the blank of the first sentence, write the missing word(s). In the second sentence, write the same word(s) from memory.

1. The bombardment began at dawn.

The _____ began at dawn.

The _____ began at dawn.

2. He was inspired to write the poem.

He was _____ to write the poem.

He was _____ to write the poem.

3. Do you know this tune?

Do you know this _____?

Do you know this _____?

4. Her popularity grew with every day.

Her _____ grew with every day.

Her _____ grew with every day.

5. The sky at dawn was gray.

The sky at _____ was gray.

The sky at _____ was gray.

6. They proudly saluted the flag.

They _____ saluted the flag.

They _____ saluted the flag.

7. The people hailed the hero.

The people _____ the hero.

The people _____ the hero.

8. The city was quiet at twilight.

The city was quiet at _____.

The city was quiet at _____.

9. The gleaming diamonds were beautiful.

The _____ diamonds were beautiful.

The _____ diamonds were beautiful.

10. The voyage to America was perilous.

The voyage to America was _____.

The voyage to America was _____.

11. The flag flew over the fort.

The flag flew _____ the fort.

The flag flew _____ the fort.

12. They attacked the ramparts.

They attacked the _____.

They attacked the _____.

13. He watched the start of the battle.

He _____ the start of the battle.

He _____ the start of the battle.

14. The soldiers fought gallantly.

The soldiers fought _____.

The soldiers fought _____.

15. Tears are streaming down her face.

Tears are _____ down her face.

Tears are _____ down her face.

16. I turned away from the bright glare.

I turned away from the bright _____.

I turned away from the bright _____.

17. Bombs were bursting all around.

Bombs were _____ all around.

Bombs were _____ all around.

18. You need proof of citizenship.

You need _____ of citizenship.

You need _____ of citizenship.

19. The flag waved overhead.

The flag _____ overhead.

The flag _____ overhead.

20. They are brave men and women.

They are _____ men and women.

They are _____ men and women.

Some Questions and Answers

1. What is the name of our national anthem? *(The Star Spangled Banner)*

2. Who wrote the words to the national anthem? (Francis Scott Key)

3. What inspired him to write the poem? (American victory at Fort McHenry)

4. What did the British bombard? (Fort McHenry)

5. What tune is the national anthem? (a British song/*To Anacreon in Heaven*)

6. What happened to the song by the Civil War? (It grew in popularity.)

7. What does Francis Scott Key call America in the national anthem? (the land of the free and the home of the brave)

Is It TRUE or FALSE?

Say TRUE if the sentence is correct. Say FALSE if it is incorrect.

1. By the Civil War *The Star Spangled Banner* was as popular as *Yankee Doodle.*

2. Key's poem was sung to the tune of a British song.

3. Our national anthem is *Hail Columbia.*

4. The words to the national anthem were written by Francis Scott Key.

5. *The Star Spangled Banner* became the national anthem during the Civil War.

6. Key wrote the poem during the Revolutionary War.

7. Key watched the British bombardment of New York.

8. America had no official national anthem until 1931.

Answers

1. True
2. True
3. False
4. True

5. False
6. False
7. False
8. True

Let's Look at Some Important Sentences

Circle the letter of the word or phrase that completes the sentence.

1. Key wrote *The Star Spangled Banner* as a _____.

   a. tune
   b. flag
   c. poem
   d. national anthem

2. He was watching the British bombardment of _____.

   a. Fort McHenry
   b. Washington, D.C.
   c. the Civil War
   d. the flag

3. *The Star Spangled Banner* is the _____ of the country.

   a. British song
   b. first poem
   c. popular song
   d. national anthem

4. Key was _____ by the American victory at Fort McHenry.

   a. inspired

   b. writing a poem

   c. watching

   d. singing

5. At one time, *The Star Spangled Banner* was as _____ as *Yankee Doodle*.

   a. new

   b. popular

   c. proud

   d. adopted

6. Congress adopted *The Star Spangled Banner* as our anthem in _____.

   a. 1929

   b. 1930

   c. 1931

   d. 1932

7. Key called America the "land of the free and the _____."

   a. home of the brave

   b. New World

   c. bombardment of Fort McHenry

   d. Hail Columbia

8. The tune of the national anthem is a well-known _____ song.

   a. American

   b. Civil War

   c. Baltimore

   d. British

Answers

1. c	**5.** b
2. a	**6.** c
3. d	**7.** a
4. a	**8.** d

Let's Write the New Words

In the blank, write the word or phrase that completes the sentence. Look at the words in parentheses. They will help you.

1. The sky is beautiful at _____. (faint light at dawn or dusk)

2. Her ring was _____ in the light. (shining)

3. The journey to America was _____. (dangerous)

4. The crowd _____ the young hero. (greeted, saluted)

5. The flag flew _____ the fort. (above)

6. We _____ watched the flag go by. (with pride and honor)

7. The _____ were under attack. (embankments around a fort)

8. The house was quiet at _____. (sunrise)

9. We _____ the exploding rockets. (looked at, observed)

10. The _____ of the song continued to grow. (approval by many people)

11. The soldiers fought _____. (bravely, courageously)

12. I like this _____. (song)

13. Banners were _____ over the street. (flowing)

14. The great victory _____ him. (moved, made emotional)

15. I looked into the _____ of the headlights. (strong light)

16. Bombs were _____ in the sky. (exploding)

17. You need _____ of citizenship. (evidence, convincing fact)

18. The _____ of the fort ended. (attack with cannons)

19. The flags _____ from the flagpoles. (flew, fluttered)

20. He was a _____ soldier. (courageous)

Answers

1. twilight
2. gleaming
3. perilous
4. hailed
5. over
6. proudly
7. ramparts
8. dawn
9. watched
10. popularity

11. gallantly
12. tune
13. streaming
14. inspired
15. glare
16. bursting
17. proof
18. bombardment
19. waved
20. brave

Some Tips About English

In many languages, *gender* is determined by the formation of the word. But in English, gender is determined by the *sexual gender* of a person or thing.

All words referring to men and boys are *masculine*. All words referring to women and girls are *feminine*. All words referring to objects are *neuter*.

Masculine	Feminine	Neuter
the father	the mother	the book
a brother	a sister	a mountain

Words that refer to professions can be either masculine or feminine.

Masculine or Feminine
the doctor
a lawyer
my teacher
their dentist

Nouns can be changed to pronouns. When this happens, a specific pronoun must be used for each gender. Masculine words change to *he*, feminine words change to *she*, and neuter words change to *it*.

Noun	Pronoun
my father	he
this man	he
her mother	she
a little girl	she
the car	it
a house	it

There is no distinction made in gender in the plural. All plurals use *they* as their pronoun form:

Noun	Pronoun
the men	they
the women	they
the books	they

Look at these example sentences to see how a noun changes to a pronoun:

Masculine		
My brother is at home.	→	He is at home.
The boy is sick.	→	He is sick.

Feminine		
His aunt is in Mexico.	→	She is in Mexico.
Your sister helped me.	→	She helped me.

Neuter		
The tree is very old.	→	It is very old.
The sky was blue.	→	It was blue.

Plural		
The dogs were playing.	→	They were playing.
Two pennies were on the floor.	→	They were on the floor.

Your Oral Interview

What You Must Know

To be a good citizen of the United States, you need to know English. It is the language used by most people in the United States. If you were not born a native English speaker, you may believe that your English is poor. Do not let that worry you. To become an American citizen, you do not have to speak and write perfect English.

Although there is no "official language" of this country, a basic knowledge of English is required to become a citizen. That is one of the reasons for the oral interview. The USCIS officer who will interview you wants to determine whether or not you can speak and understand basic English.

The personal interview will be between you and a USCIS officer. The officer will look through your Application for Naturalization (Form N-400) to see that everything is in order. He or she may ask about things in your application. Then the USCIS officer will begin questioning you to find out whether you are ready to become a citizen. The officer wants to know whether you have knowledge of American history and government. And the officer will probably ask you some questions about your personal life and about everyday life.

Dictation is usually included in the interview. The purpose of the dictation is to determine whether or not you can write simple sentences in English. These sentences may deal with history or government, your personal life, or everyday life. You may also be asked to read a few simple sentences.

If you have worked regularly with this book, you should be prepared to take your oral interview. But even with a lot of study and practice, there may be words or phrases in the interview that you do not understand immediately. Do not panic. Listen for a word or phrase that will give you a hint about the meaning of the question or sentence you heard. For example, if you hear the following:

"How many stars does the flag of the United States have?"

If you only understood "stars" and "flag," that is enough information to help you come up with an answer to the question. Take your time and think about the *likely* answer to the question. Then answer it:

"The flag has 50 stars."

Do not be afraid to guess at the answer, but base that guess on the few words you understood from the question. And do not forget: **You can ask the officer to repeat the question.**

Sample Questions

These are sample questions that you might hear at your oral interview. Remember this is an **oral interview**. Practice the questions and answers **out loud**.

American History and Government

Question: Who is the President of the United States?

Answer: George W. Bush

Question: What are the colors of the American flag?

Answer: red, white, and blue

Question: How many stars are on the American flag?

Answer: 50

Question: What is the capital of the United States?

Answer: Washington, D.C.

Question: How many senators are there in the Senate?

Answer: 100

Question: How many branches of government are there?

Answer: 3

Question: What date is Independence Day?

Answer: July 4

Question: Who was the first president?

Answer: George Washington

Question: What president freed the slaves?

Answer: Abraham Lincoln

Question: Where does the President live?

Answer: in the White House

Question: How many stripes are on the American flag?

Answer: 13

Question: What is the name of the governor of your state?

Answer: (Learn the name of the governor of your state.)

Question: What is the capital of your state?

Answer: (Learn the capital of your state.)

Question: Who is the Vice President of the United States?

Answer: Dick Cheney

Question: What year was the Declaration of Independence signed?

Answer: 1776

Question: Who is the Father of Our Country?

Answer: George Washington

Question: What branch of government can declare war?

Answer: Congress

Question: What are the first 10 amendments to the Constitution called?

Answer: the Bill of Rights

Question: Who becomes President if the President dies?

> *Answer:* the Vice President

Question: What two regions fought in the Civil War?

> *Answer:* the North and the South

Question: What branch of government makes the laws?

> *Answer:* Congress, the Legislative Branch

Question: What is the highest court in the land?

> *Answer:* the Supreme Court

Question: What document describes the American government?

> *Answer:* the Constitution

Question: What is the minimum voting age in the United States?

> *Answer:* 18

Question: What is the name of our national anthem?

> *Answer: The Star Spangled Banner*

Question: What are the two parts of Congress?

> *Answer:* the House of Representatives and the Senate

Question: Who has the power to declare war?

> *Answer:* Congress

Question: What country gave the United States the Statue of Liberty?

> *Answer:* France

Question: Why do people come to the United States?

> *Answer:* They want to live in freedom.

> *Answer:* They want to live in a democracy.

> *Answer:* They are looking for a better life.

Question: What is one of the privileges of being an American citizen?

> *Answer:* You have the right to vote.

Questions About Your Personal Life

The answers given to these questions are sample answers. More than one answer is given if there is more than one way to answer the question. You should answer according to your personal experience. Prepare your own answers if they are different from the sample answers.

Question: How old are you?

> *Answer:* I am 35 years old.

Question: What town do you live in?

    Answer: I live in Los Angeles.

    Answer: I don't live in town. I live in the country on a farm.

Question: Are you married?

    Answer: Yes, I am married.

    Answer: Yes, I have a wife (husband).

    Answer: No, I am single (unmarried).

    Answer: No, I am divorced.

Question: How many children do you have?

    Answer: I have two children. I have one son and one daughter.

    Answer: I don't have any children.

Question: What is your address?

    Answer: I live at 3450 North Park Street, Los Angeles, California.

Question: What kind of job do you have?

    Answer: I'm a waitress (waiter).

    Answer: I work in a factory.

    Answer: I'm a landscaper.

    Answer: I work in a grocery store.

    Answer: I'm a teacher.

    Answer: I'm a housewife.

    Answer: I don't work. I stay home with the children.

Question: Do you pay taxes?

    Answer: Yes, I pay my taxes every year.

Question: Have you ever had a traffic ticket?

    Answer: No, I have never had a traffic ticket.

    Answer: Yes, I got a ticket for speeding

    Answer: Yes, I got a parking ticket.

Question: Have you ever had a DUI? (**D**riving **U**nder the **I**nfluence of alcohol)

    Answer: No, I've never had a DUI.

    Answer: Yes, I once had a DUI.

Question: Have you ever been arrested?

   Answer: No, I've never been arrested.

   Answer: Yes, I was arrested for speeding

   Answer: Yes, I was arrested for a DUI.

   Answer: Yes, I was arrested for fighting.

Question: Have you ever used drugs?

   Answer: No, I've never used drugs.

   Answer: Yes, I was arrested for using drugs.

   Answer: Yes, but I no longer use drugs.

Question: Do your children go to school?

   Answer: Yes, my son and daughter are in elementary school.

   Answer: Yes, my children are in high school.

   Answer: Yes, my son goes to college.

   Answer: Yes, my daughter is in medical school.

   Answer: No, my children are too young to go to school.

Question: Why did you leave your country?

   Answer: I was looking for more opportunities.

   Answer: I had no job in my country.

   Answer: I wanted to become an American.

Question: Do you live in an apartment?

   Answer: Yes, I live in an apartment.

   Answer: No, I live in a house.

Question: Do you like sports?

   Answer: Yes, I like baseball.

   Answer: Yes, I like soccer.

   Answer: No, I don't like sports.

Question: Are you a person of good character?

   Answer: Yes, I have good morals.

   Answer: Yes, I am honest and hardworking.

Question: Do you drive a car?

    Answer: Yes, I drive a car.

    Answer: Yes, I have a driver's license.

    Answer: No, I don't drive a car.

    Answer: No, I take public transportation to work.

Question: Have you ever had your driver's license revoked?

    Answer: No, I've never lost my license.

    Answer: Yes, I once lost my license for speeding.

Question: Do you have relatives in the United States?

    Answer: No, I don't have any relatives here.

    Answer: Yes, I have a brother and a sister here.

    Answer: Yes, my parents live here.

Question: How long have you lived in the United States?

    Answer: I've lived here for 10 years.

Question: Do you want to become an American citizen?

    Answer: Yes, I want to become an American citizen.

Questions About Everyday Life

The answers given here are sample answers. Prepare an answer in advance if it is different from the sample answers.

Question: What color is your shirt?

    Answer: My shirt is white (blue, red, green, black, gray, brown).

Question: Where do you shop for groceries?

    Answer: I shop for groceries at the Safeway Store.

Question: What is the weather like today?

    Answer: It's sunny today.

    Answer: It's rainy today.

    Answer: It's hot today.

    Answer: It's cold today.

Question: How many windows are in the room?

    Answer: one, two, five, and so on

Question: Where can a person see a movie?

    Answer: at a movie theater

Question: Where can a person cash a check?

　Answer: at a bank

Question: Where can a person buy some dinner?

　Answer: at a restaurant

Question: Where do horses and cows live?

　Answer: on a farm

Question: How many cents are in a dollar?

　Answer: 100

Question: What's larger? An elephant or a mouse?

　Answer: an elephant

Question: What is the Mississippi?

　Answer: a river

Question: What statue stands in New York Harbor?

　Answer: the Statue of Liberty

Question: How do you get from one side of a river to the other?

　Answer: on a bridge

　Answer: on a ferry

Question: What is more expensive? One steak or one cookie?

　Answer: one steak

Question: How many hours are there in a day?

　Answer: 24

Dictation

The USCIS officer will ask you to write some sentences. The officer will say the sentences, and you will write them. Practice writing these sample sentences.

Officer: "The flag is red, white, and blue."
You write: _____

Officer: "This table is square."
You write: _____

Officer: "I have two children, a boy and a girl."
You write: _____

Officer: "I will vote in every election."
You write: _____

Officer: "The president must be born in the United States."
You write: _____

Officer: "There are three branches of government."

You write: _____

Officer: "Is your dress green?"

You write: _____

Officer: "I go to work on the bus."

You write: _____

Officer: "I am learning English."

You write: _____

Officer: "The children often watch television."

You write: _____

At some point in the interview, the officer may ask you to read a few lines from your Application for Naturalization (Form N-400). Or he or she may give you a sheet of paper with a few sentences on it. The officer will ask you to read what is on the paper. It will look something like this:

The American flag is red, white, and blue. It has thirteen stripes. The stripes are red and white. The flag has fifty white stars on a field of blue. The stars stand for the states. The stripes stand for the original thirteen colonies.

Naturally, these are only examples of what might occur in your oral interview. Each USCIS officer is different and will give his or her individual touch to the interview. You should be ready for anything. If you have used this book wisely, you are.

Practice Test 1

Circle the letter of the word or phrase that correctly completes the sentence.

1. The colors of the American flag are red, _____.

    a. yellow and green
    b. white and green
    c. yellow and blue
    d. white and blue

2. There are 50 _____ on the American flag.

    a. stars
    b. stripes
    c. squares
    d. lines

3. The stars on the flag are _____.

    a. blue
    b. red
    c. white
    d. red, white, and blue

4. The stars on the flag represent the _____.

    a. 50 states
    b. capital city
    c. population
    d. presidents

5. There are _____ stripes on the flag.

    a. 5
    b. 50
    c. 13
    d. 30

6. The stripes on the flag are _____.

    a. red
    b. white
    c. red and blue
    d. red and white

7. The stripes on the flag represent the _____.

    a. 13 original colonies
    b. delegates to the constitutional convention
    c. the first presidents
    d. the nation

8. There are _____ states in the Union.

   a. 13

   b. 40

   c. 50

   d. 80

9. Independence Day is _____.

   a. July 4

   b. June 7

   c. December 7

   d. March 12

10. The American colonies wanted independence from _____.

   a. Canada

   b. France

   c. England

   d. Parliament

11. We fought against Great Britain in the _____.

   a. Indian War

   b. Revolutionary War

   c. Civil War

   d. World War II

12. On the Fourth of July, Americans celebrate _____.

   a. the flag

   b. Thanksgiving

   c. Independence Day

   d. the first president

13. The first President of the United States was _____.

   a. Benjamin Franklin

   b. George Washington

   c. Abraham Lincoln

   d. Franklin D. Roosevelt

14. The President of the United States today is _____.

   a. George W. Bush

   b. Bill Clinton

   c. Jimmy Carter

   d. Ronald Reagan

15. The Vice President of the United States today is _____.

   a. Al Gore

   b. Richard Nixon

   c. Hillary Clinton

   d. Dick Cheney

16. The President is elected by _____.

    a. all the people
    b. state governments
    c. the largest states
    d. Congress

17. If the President dies, the _____ becomes President.

    a. Vice President
    b. Secretary of State
    c. Secretary of Defense
    d. Speaker of the House

18. The President is elected for a term of _____ years.

    a. three
    b. four
    c. six
    d. eight

19. The document that describes our government is the _____.

    a. Declaration of Independence
    b. Star Spangled Banner
    c. Articles of Confederation
    d. Constitution

20. A change to the Constitution is called an _____.

    a. amendment
    b. article
    c. election
    d. exchange

21. Our government consists of _____ branches.

    a. three
    b. four
    c. five
    d. seven

22. The branches of our government are Legislative, _____.

    a. the Senate, and the House
    b. and Congress
    c. the President, and the Cabinet
    d. Executive, and Judicial

23. An amendment can _____ the Constitution.

    a. produce
    b. write
    c. change
    d. establish

24. There have been _____ amendments to the Constitution.

    a. 27
    b. 22
    c. 15
    d. 10

25. The branch of government that makes our laws is the _____ branch.

    a. Legislative
    b. Executive
    c. Judicial

26. The branch of government that decides whether laws are constitutional is the _____ branch.

    a. Legislative
    b. Executive
    c. Judicial

27. The branch of government that carries out the laws is the _____ branch.

    a. Legislative
    b. Executive
    c. Judicial

28. The House of Representatives and the Senate make up _____.

    a. the Judicial Branch
    b. Congress
    c. the Executive Branch
    d. the lobbyists

29. Congress is elected by _____.

    a. a national election
    b. citizens over the age of 30
    c. the people of each state
    d. local governments

30. There are presently _____ Senators.

    a. 40
    b. 50
    c. 75
    d. 100

31. Name the two senators from your state:

If you do not know the answer to this question, learn the names of your state's senators.

32. A senator is elected for _____ years.

    a. 3
    b. 4
    c. 5
    d. 6

33. There are _____ Representatives in the House.

    a. 100

    b. 250

    c. 375

    d. 435

34. Representatives are elected for _____ years.

    a. 2

    b. 4

    c. 6

    d. 8

35. The Executive Branch of government _____ the laws.

    a. makes

    b. amends

    c. carries out

    d. changes

36. The Executive Branch _____ the laws.

    a. decides whether laws are constitutional

    b. changes

    c. carries out

    d. prepares amendments to the Constitution

37. The _____ is in the Judicial Branch.

    a. Cabinet

    b. Congress

    c. president

    d. Supreme Court

38. The Supreme Law of the United States is _____.

    a. the Constitution

    b. the Declaration of Independence

    c. the Executive Branch

    d. the Legislative Branch

39. The first 10 amendments are called _____.

    a. Congress

    b. the Articles of Confederation

    c. the Constitution

    d. the Bill of Rights

40. What is the capital of your state?

If you do not know the answer to this question, learn the capital of your state.

41. Who is the governor of your state?

If you do not know the answer to this question, learn the name of your state's governor.

42. If the President and the Vice President die, _____ becomes president.

    a. the Secretary of State
    b. the Governor of New York
    c. the Secretary of Defense
    d. the Speaker of the House

43. The Chief Justice of the Supreme Court is _____.

    a. Dick Cheney
    b. Hillary Clinton
    c. William H. Rehnquist
    d. Thomas Jefferson

44. Name the original 13 colonies:

If you do not know the answer to this question, learn the names of the original 13 colonies.

45. _____ said, "Give me liberty or give me death."

    a. Alexander Hamilton
    b. Benjamin Franklin
    c. Abraham Lincoln
    d. Patrick Henry

46. _____ were our enemies during World War II.

    a. Germany, Italy, and Japan
    b. Germany and Russia
    c. France, Spain, and England
    d. Spain and England

47. The 49th and the 50th states in the union are _____.

    a. New York and California
    b. Washington and Oregon
    c. Alaska and Hawaii
    d. Arizona and Nevada

48. A president can only serve for _____ terms.

    a. 2
    b. 3
    c. 4
    d. 5

49. _____ was a famous civil rights leader.

    a. Martin Luther King, Jr.
    b. Harry Truman
    c. Ronald Reagan
    d. Al Gore

50. Who is the head of your local city government?

If you do not know the answer to this question, learn the name of the head of your local government.

51. A person has to be _____ to become President.

    a. 21 years old
    b. a native-born American
    c. a man
    d. college graduate

52. Each state can elect only _____ senators.

    a. 1
    b. 2
    c. 3
    d. 13

53. Supreme Court justices are selected by the _____.

    a. Senate
    b. House of Representatives
    c. Chief Justice
    d. President

54. There are _____ Supreme Court justices.

    a. 4
    b. 6
    c. 9
    d. 11

55. The _____ came to America for religious freedom.

    a. Native Americans
    b. British navy
    c. immigrants
    d. Pilgrims

56. The head executive of a state government is the _____.

    a. mayor
    b. senator
    c. legislator
    d. governor

57. The head executive of a city government is the _____.

    a. mayor
    b. senator
    c. legislator
    d. governor

58. The Pilgrims celebrated _____ for the first time.

   a. Christmas
   b. the New Year
   c. Thanksgiving
   d. the Fourth of July

59. _____ was the major writer of the Declaration of Independence.

   a. George Washington
   b. Abraham Lincoln
   c. Woodrow Wilson
   d. Thomas Jefferson

60. The Declaration of Independence was adopted in _____.

   a. 1776
   b. 1781
   c. 1787
   d. 1800

61. The basic belief of the Declaration of Independence is that _____.

   a. America must become a strong country
   b. it is important to work hard
   c. America needs a new constitution
   d. all men are created equal

62. The national anthem of the United States is _____.

   a. The Star Spangled Banner
   b. America the Beautiful
   c. God Bless America
   d. The Stars and Stripes Forever

63. The words to the national anthem were written by _____.

   a. Theodore Roosevelt
   b. Robert Frost
   c. Alexander Hamilton
   d. Francis Scott Key

64. One of the rights in the Bill of Rights is _____.

   a. the minimum wage
   b. freedom of speech
   c. unemployment compensation
   d. the right to travel abroad

65. The minimum voting age in the United States is _____.

   a. 16
   b. 18
   c. 21
   d. 26

66. _____ signs bills into law.

    a. The Congress
    b. The President
    c. The Speaker of the House
    d. The Chief Justice

67. The highest court in the United States is the _____.

    a. state court
    b. district court
    c. county court
    d. Supreme Court

68. During the Civil War, _____ was the president.

    a. Abraham Lincoln
    b. James Madison
    c. Theodore Roosevelt
    d. Franklin D. Roosevelt

69. The Emancipation Proclamation _____.

    a. abolished taxes
    b. raised taxes
    c. freed the slaves
    d. declared war on Japan

70. The President is advised by _____.

    a. his political party
    b. his cabinet
    c. his lawyer
    d. former presidents

71. _____ is called the Father of Our Country.

    a. Benjamin Franklin
    b. King George III
    c. Louis XVI
    d. George Washington

72. You need Form _____ to apply for citizenship.

    a. G345
    b. N-400
    c. N-420
    d. USCIS

73. The Pilgrims were helped by _____.

    a. the English king
    b. the English parliament
    c. Native Americans
    d. Frenchmen

74. The Pilgrims sailed to the New World on board the _____.

    a. Mayflower
    b. Queen Mary
    c. Constitution
    d. Bounty

75. The 13 original states had been _____.

    a. provinces of Canada
    b. Spanish territories
    c. French possessions
    d. English colonies

76. One of the rights in the Bill of Rights is _____.

    a. the minimum wage
    b. the right to strike
    c. freedom of religion
    d. freedom from hunger

77. Only _____ has the power to declare war.

    a. the President
    b. the cabinet
    c. Congress
    d. the state governors

78. The U.S. government is a _____.

    a. democracy
    b. socialist state
    c. kingdom
    d. branch of the legislature

79. _____ freed the slaves.

    a. Woodrow Wilson
    b. Abraham Lincoln
    c. James Madison
    d. James Monroe

80. The Constitution was written in _____.

    a. 1776
    b. 1779
    c. 1781
    d. 1787

81. The Bill of Rights is _____.

    a. the first 10 amendments to the Constitution
    b. the rules of the Supreme Court
    c. the rules of the President's cabinet
    d. the Preamble to the Constitution

82. One of the purposes of the United Nations is to promote _____.

   a. good jobs
   b. peace
   c. America's policies
   d. happiness

83. Congress meets in _____.

   a. the White House
   b. Independence Hall
   c. New York
   d. the Capitol

84. The Constitution and the Bill of Rights guarantee _____ rights.

   a. the government's
   b. the Senate's
   c. the country's
   d. the people's

85. The introduction to the Constitution is the _____.

   a. Declaration of Independence
   b. First Amendment
   c. preamble
   d. the first five amendments

86. A benefit of being a U.S. citizen is _____.

   a. having the right to vote
   b. having the job you want
   c. living in a large city
   d. speaking English

87. One of the rights in the Bill of Rights is _____.

   a. freedom of the press
   b. the right to strike
   c. the right to work
   d. freedom from hunger

88. The U.S. Capitol is _____.

   a. called the White House
   b. the Supreme Court
   c. where Congress meets
   d. part of the F.B.I.

89. The President lives in _____.

   a. the White House
   b. the Pentagon
   c. the Smithsonian
   d. the Washington Monument

90. The White House is the President's _____.

    a. cabinet

    b. official home

    c. vacation home

    d. library

91. One of the rights in the Bill of Rights is _____.

    a. the minimum wage

    b. the right to strike

    c. the right to work

    d. freedom of assembly

92. The President's office in the White House is _____.

    a. the Oval Office

    b. the Blue Room

    c. the Reception Room

    d. the Cabinet Room

93. The president is the _____ of the military.

    a. captain

    b. ranking officer

    c. advisor

    d. commander-in-chief

94. The first commander-in-chief of the military was _____.

    a. John F. Kennedy

    b. George Washington

    c. George W. Bush

    d. John Adams

95. Presidential elections are held in _____.

    a. October

    b. November

    c. December

    d. January

96. The new president is inaugurated in _____.

    a. October

    b. November

    c. December

    d. January

97. A senator can be re-elected _____ times.

    a. two

    b. three

    c. five

    d. innumerable

98. A congressman can be re-elected _____ times.

    a. two

    b. three

    c. five

    d. innumerable

99. The two major American political parties are _____

    a. Republicans and Democrats

    b. Socialists and Democrats

    c. Socialists and Republicans

    d. Liberals and Tories

100. There are 50 _____ in the United States.

    a. unions

    b. mayors

    c. states

    d. districts

Now use the Answer Key at the back of this book to check your answers. The number correct will be your percentage score: for example, 80 correct out of 100 items = 80%.

Practice Test 2

Fill in the blank with a word or phrase that makes good sense.

1. The colors of the American flag are red, white, and _____.

2. There are 50 _____ on the American flag.

3. The _____ on the flag are red and white.

4. The stars on the flag represent the _____.

5. There are _____ stripes on the flag.

6. The stars on the flag are the color _____.

7. The stripes on the flag represent the 13 original _____.

8. There are _____ states in the Union.

9. Independence Day is on _____.

10. The American colonies wanted independence from _____.

11. We fought against Great Britain in the _____ War.

12. On the Fourth of July, Americans celebrate _____ Day.

13. The first President of the United States was _____.

14. The President of the United States today is _____.

15. The _____ of the United States today is Dick Cheney.

16. The President is elected by the American _____.

17. If the President dies, the _____ becomes President.

18. The President is elected for a term of _____ years.

19. The document that describes our government is the _____.

20. A change to the Constitution is called an _____.

21. The American government consists of _____ branches.

22. The branches of our government are Legislative, Judicial, and _____.

23. An amendment can change the _____.

24. There have been _____ amendments to the Constitution.

25. The branch of government that carries out the laws is the _____ branch.

26. The branch of government that makes our laws is the _____ branch.

27. The branch of government that decides whether laws are constitutional is the _____ branch.

28. The House of Representatives and the _____ make up Congress.

29. Congress is elected by the people of each _____.

30. There are presently _____ senators.

31. The two senators from my state are _____ and _____.

32. A senator is elected for _____ years.

33. There are _____ representatives in the House.

34. Representatives are elected for _____ years.

35. The Executive Branch of government carries out the _____.

36. The Judicial Branch decides whether laws are _____.

37. The Supreme Court is in the _____ Branch.

38. The Supreme Law of the United States is the _____.

39. The first 10 amendments are called the _____.

40. The capital city of my state is _____.

41. The governor of my state is _____.

42. If the President and the _____ die, the Speaker of the House becomes president.

43. The Chief Justice of the Supreme Court is _____.

44. The original 13 colonies are _____.

45. _____ said, "Give me liberty or give me death."

46. Germany, Italy, and _____ were our enemies during World War II.

47. The 49th and the 50th states in the Union are Alaska and _____.

48. A President can only serve for _____ terms.

49. _____ was a famous civil rights leader.

50. The head of my local city government is _____.

51. A person has to be born in_____ to become President.

52. Each state can elect only _____ senators.

53. Supreme Court justices are appointed by the _____.

54. There are _____ Supreme Court justices.

55. The Pilgrims came to America for _____ freedom.

56. The head executive of a state government is the _____.

57. The head executive of a city government is the _____.

58. The Pilgrims celebrated the first _____.

59. _____ was the major writer of the Declaration of Independence.

60. The Declaration of Independence was adopted in _____.

61. The basic belief of the Declaration of Independence is that "all men are created _____."

62. The national anthem of the United States is The _____.

63. The words to the national anthem were written by _____.

64. Freedom of speech is guaranteed in the Bill _____.

65. The minimum voting age in the United States is _____.

66. _____ signs bills into law.

67. The highest court in the United States is the _____.

68. During the _____ War, Abraham Lincoln was President.

69. The Emancipation Proclamation freed the _____.

70. The President is advised by his _____.

71. George Washington is called the Father _____.

72. You need Form _____ to apply for citizenship.

73. The Pilgrims were helped by _____ Americans.

74. The Pilgrims sailed to the New World on board the _____.

75. The 13 original states had been English _____.

76. The Bill of Rights guarantees _____ of religion.

77. Only _____ has the power to declare war.

78. The _____ government is a democracy.

79. President _____ freed the slaves.

80. The Constitution was written in _____.

81. The Bill of Rights is the first 10 _____ to the Constitution.

82. One of the purposes of the United Nations is to promote _____.

83. Congress meets in the _____ Building.

84. The Constitution and the Bill of Rights guarantee our _____.

85. The introduction to the Constitution is the _____.

86. A benefit of being a U.S. citizen is having the right to _____ and elect our leaders.

87. One of the rights in the _____ of Rights is freedom of the press.

88. The U.S. Capitol is where _____ meets.

89. The President lives in the _____.

90. The White House is the President's official _____.

91. The Bill of Rights is in the _____.

92. The President's office in the White House is the _____ Office.

93. The President is the commander-in-chief of the _____.

94. The first commander-in-chief of the military was _____.

95. Presidential elections are held in the month of _____.

96. The new president is inaugurated in the month of _____.

97. A senator can be reelected _____ times.

98. A congressman can be reelected _____ times.

99. The two major American political parties are _____ and _____.

100. There are 50 _____ in the United States.

Now use the Answer Key at the back of this book to check your answers. The number correct will be your percentage score: for example, 80 correct out of 100 items = 80%.

Practice Test 3

Read each question out loud. Then say the answer.

1. What are the colors of the American flag?

2. What do the stars on the flag represent?

3. How many stars are on the American flag?

4. What color are the stars?

5. How many stripes are on the American flag?

6. What is the capital of the United States?

7. What do the stripes represent?

8. How many states are in the Union?

9. What is the date of Independence Day?

10. What great river divides the United States from north to south?

11. What country did we fight in the Revolutionary War?

12. What do Americans celebrate on the Fourth of July?

13. Who was the first President of the United States?

14. Who is the President of the United States today?

15. Who is the Vice President of the United States today?

16. Who elects the President?

17. Who becomes president if the President dies?

18. How long is a president's term in office?

19. What document describes the American government?

20. What is a change to the Constitution called?

21. Over what major issue was the Civil War fought?

22. What are the three branches of government?

23. What does an amendment do to the Constitution?

24. How many amendments to the Constitution have there been?

25. Which branch of government makes our laws?

26. Which branch of government carries out our laws?

27. Which branch of government decides whether laws are constitutional?

28. What two chambers make up Congress?

29. Who elects Congress?

30. How many senators are there?

31. Who are the senators from your state?

32. For how many years is a senator elected?

33. How many representatives are there in the House?

34. For how many years is a representative to the House elected?

35. What does the Executive Branch of government do?

36. What does the Judicial Branch of government do?

37. What is the highest court in the land?

38. What is the supreme law of the land?

39. What are the first 10 amendments to the Constitution called?

40. What is the capital of your state?

41. Who is the governor of your state?

42. Who becomes president if the president and the vice president die?

43. Who is the Chief Justice of the Supreme Court?

44. What were the names of the original 13 colonies?

45. Who said, "Give me liberty or give me death"?

46. Who were our enemies in World War II?

47. Which states were the 49th and 50th to join the Union?

48. For how many terms can a president serve?

49. What famous civil rights leader was assassinated in 1968?

50. What nation was the first to land men on the moon?

51. Where must a person be born to become President?

52. How many senators can each state elect?

53. Who appoints Supreme Court justices?

54. How many Supreme Court justices are there?

55. What two oceans border the United States in the east and west?

56. What is the chief executive of a state government called?

57. What is the chief executive of a city government called?

58. Who celebrated the first Thanksgiving?

59. Who was the major writer of the Declaration of Independence?

60. In what year was the Declaration of Independence adopted?

61. What is the basic belief of the Declaration of Independence?

62. What is the national anthem of the United States?

63. Who wrote the words to the national anthem?

64. Where will you find the right of "freedom of speech"?

65. What is the minimum voting age in the United States?

66. Who signs bills into law?

67. Which court is the highest in the United States?

68. Who was president during the Civil War?

69. What did the Emancipation Proclamation do?

70. What group advises the president?

71. Who is called the Father of Our Country?

72. What form do you need to apply for citizenship?

73. Who helped the Pilgrims?

74. On what ship did the Pilgrims come to America?

75. What were the original 13 states called before the Revolutionary War?

76. Where do you find the right of "freedom of the press"?

77. Who has the power to declare war?

78. What is it called if a president refuses to sign a bill into law?

79. Who freed the slaves?

80. In what year was the Constitution written?

81. Which amendments make up the Bill of Rights?

82. What is the main purpose of the United Nations?

83. Where does Congress meet?

84. What do the Constitution and the Bill of Rights guarantee?

85. What is the introduction to the Constitution called?

86. What is a benefit of being an American citizen?

87. Where can you find the right of "freedom of religion"?

88. Who meets in the U.S. Capitol?

89. Where does the President live?

90. Whose official home is the White House?

91. Where do you find the right of "freedom of assembly"?

92. What is the President's office called?

93. Who is commander-in-chief of the armed forces?

94. Who was the first commander-in-chief of the American military?

95. In what month are presidential elections held?

96. In what month is the new president inaugurated?

97. How many times can a senator be reelected?

98. How many times can a representative be reelected?

99. What are the two major political parties in America?

100. Who was the inventor of the electric light bulb?

Now use the Answer Key at the back of this book to check your answers. The number correct will be your percentage score: for example, 80 correct out of 100 items = 80%.

Practice Test 4

Read each question carefully. Then write your answer to the question as a complete sentence.

1. How many stars were on the first American flag?

_____

2. What do the stars on the flag represent?

_____

3. How many stars are on the American flag today?

_____

4. What color are the stripes on the flag?

_____

5. Who sewed the first American flag according to legend?

_____

6. What is the capital of the United States?

_____

7. What does D.C. in Washington, D.C., mean?

_____

8. How many states are in the Union?

_____

9. What is celebrated on July 4?

_____

10. What great river divides the United States from north to south?

_____

11. What was the Boston Tea Party?

_____

12. What happened on July 4, 1776?

_____

13. Who was the first President of the United States?

_____

14. Who is the President of the United States today?

_____

15. Who is the Vice President of the United States today?

_____

16. What is the Electoral College?

_____

17. What is the Oval Office?

_____

18. What is the name of the mansion in which the President lives?

_____

19. What document describes the American government?

_____

20. What is a change to the Constitution called?

_____

21. Over what major issue was the Civil War fought?

_____

22. Which branch of government makes the laws?

_____

23. What does an amendment do to the Constitution?

_____

24. How many amendments to the Constitution have there been?

_____

25. Where is the West Wing?

_____

26. Which branch of government carries out our laws?

27. What does the President's cabinet do?

_____

28. What two chambers make up Congress?

_____

29. How long is a senator's term?

_____

30. How many senators are there?

_____

31. Who are the senators from your state?

_____

32. What is a bill?

_____

33. How many representatives are there in the House?

_____

34. For how many years is a representative to the House elected?

_____

35. What branch of government does the President head?

_____

36. What does the Judicial Branch of government do?

_____

37. What is the highest court in the land?

_____

38. What is the supreme law of the land?

_____

39. What is the Bill of Rights?

_____

40. What is the capital of your state?

_____

41. Who is the governor of your state?

_____

42. Who becomes President if the President and the Vice President die?

_____

43. Who is the Chief Justice of the Supreme Court?

_____

44. Who is President of the Senate?

_____

45. What is Patrick Henry famous for saying?

_____

46. Who were our enemies in World War II?

_____

47. Which state was the last to join the Union?

_____

48. For how many terms can a president serve?

_____

49. What happened to Martin Luther King, Jr., in 1968?

_____

50. In what year did men land on the moon?

_____

51. Where must a person be born to become president?

_____

52. What is the largest state in the Union?

_____

53. What is the smallest state in the Union?

_____

54. How many Supreme Court justices are there?

_____

55. What ocean borders the United States in the east?

_____

56. What is the chief executive of a state government called?

_____

57. What is the chief executive of a city government called?

_____

58. What did the Pilgrims celebrate with the Native Americans?

_____

59. Who was the major writer of the Declaration of Independence?

_____

60. What is the introduction of the Constitution called?

_____

61. From what colony did Washington and Jefferson come?

_____

62. What is the national anthem of the United States?

_____

63. Who wrote the words to the national anthem?

_____

64. Where will you find the right of "freedom of speech"?

_____

65. What country borders the United States in the south?

_____

66. What country borders the United States in the north?

_____

67. Which court is the highest in the United States?

_____

68. Who was president during the Civil War?

_____

69. What did the Emancipation Proclamation do?

_____

70. What is Mount Vernon?

_____

71. Who is called the Father of Our Country?

_____

72. What benefit does a person get from American citizenship?

_____

73. Who helped the Pilgrims?

_____

74. Where did the Pilgrims' ship land in the New World?

_____

75. What were the original 13 states called before the Revolutionary War?

_____

76. Where do you find the right of "freedom of the press"?

_____

77. Who has the power to declare war?

_____

78. What is it called if the President refuses to sign a bill into law?

_____

79. How did Abraham Lincoln die?

_____

80. Which president ordered the building of the Transcontinental Railroad?

_____

81. What did Thomas Edison invent?

_____

82. How did the cotton gin help cotton planters?

83. Where does Congress meet?

_____

84. What is an amendment?

_____

85. Who is the commander-in-chief of the armed forces?

_____

86. Who cannot become President of the United States?

_____

87. Where can you find the right of "freedom of religion"?

_____

88. Who meets in the U.S. Capitol?

_____

89. What is a war president?

_____

90. Whose official home is the White House?

_____

91. Where do you find the right of "freedom of assembly"?

_____

92. What is the President's office called?

_____

93. Who becomes President if the President dies?

_____

94. Who was the first commander-in-chief of the American military?

_____

95. In what month are presidential elections held?

_____

96. What occupation did most Americans have during colonial times?

_____

97. How many times can a senator be reelected?

_____

98. How many times can a representative be reelected?

_____

99. What are the two major political parties in America?

_____

100. What two regions fought during the Civil War?

_____

Now use the Answer Key at the back of this book to check your answers. The number correct will be your percentage score: For example, 80 correct out of 100 items = 80 percent.

Present Tense	Past Tense	Past Participle
am, are, is	was, were	been
bear	bore	born, borne
beat	beat	beat, beaten
become	became	become
begin	began	begun
bend	bent	bent
bet	bet	bet
bind	bound	bound
bleed	bled	bled
blow	blew	blown
break	broke	broken
bring	brought	brought
build	built	built
burn	burned, burnt	burned, burnt
buy	bought	bought
can	could	—
catch	caught	caught
choose	chose	chosen
cost	cost	cost
creep	crept	crept
cut	cut	cut
dig	dug	dug
do	did	done
draw	drew	drawn
drink	drank	drunk
drive	drove	driven
eat	ate	eaten
fall	fell	fallen
feed	fed	fed
feel	felt	felt

(continued)

Present Tense	Past Tense	Past Participle
fight	fought	fought
find	found	found
fly	flew	flown
forget	forgot	forgot, forgotten
freeze	froze	frozen
get	got	got, gotten
give	gave	given
go	went	gone
grow	grew	grown
hang	hung	hung
have, has	had	had
hear	heard	heard
hide	hid	hidden
hit	hit	hit
hold	held	held
hurt	hurt	hurt
keep	kept	kept
know	knew	known
lay	laid	laid
lead	led	led
leap	leapt, leaped	leapt, leaped
leave	left	left
lie	lay	lain
let	let	let
light	lit, lighted	lit, lighted
lose	lost	lost
make	made	made
may	might	—
mean	meant	meant
pay	paid	paid
put	put	put
read	read	read

Present Tense	Past Tense	Past Participle
ride	rode	ridden
ring	rang	rung
rise	rose	risen
run	ran	run
say	said	said
see	saw	seen
sell	sold	sold
send	sent	sent
shake	shook	shaken
shoot	shot	shot
show	showed	shown
shut	shut	shut
sing	sang	sung
sink	sank	sunk
sit	sat	sat
sleep	slept	slept
speak	spoke	spoken
speed	sped	sped
spend	spent	spent
spring	sprang	sprung
stand	stood	stood
steal	stole	stolen
stink	stank, stunk	stunk
swear	swore	sworn
swim	swam	swum
take	took	taken
teach	taught	taught
tear	tore	torn
tell	told	told
think	thought	thought
throw	threw	thrown
understand	understood	understood

(continued)

Present Tense	Past Tense	Past Participle
wear	wore	worn
wed	wedded	wedded, wed
will	would	—
win	won	won
write	wrote	written

Your New Words

abandon = quit, give up

"The North abandoned slavery after the war."

abolish = end, destroy

"England abolished all trade with the colonies."

abolitionist = someone who wants to stop something

"Abolitionists were against slavery."

achievement = accomplishment, feat

"It was the greatest achievement of his presidency."

add = join, unite

"The West Wing was added later."

admit to = allow in

"Another state was admitted to the Union."

adopt = accept

"Congress adopted the declaration in 1776."

advise = give an opinion, recommend

"Congress advises the President on some issues."

alcohol = spirits, whiskey

"You must be an adult to buy alcohol."

allegiance = loyalty, faithfulness

"My allegiance is to the United States of America."

allot = distribute, assign

"Each state is allotted a specific number of electors."

allow = let, give permission

"Mother allowed him to stay at home."

ambassador = representative to a foreign land

"Who is our ambassador to France?"

amendment = change

"The first 10 amendments are the Bill of Rights."

annexation = take possession, add

"Many did not like the annexation of the Philippines."

appeal = a request

"He made an appeal for help."

apply = use

"Not all laws are applied fairly."

appointment = selection for an office or service

"The President made a new appointment to the court."

approve = adopt, accept

"Congress approved the amendment."

aristocratic background = from an upper-class family

"His aristocratic background made him unpopular."

armed forces = army, navy, marines

"U.S. armed forces have bases around the world."

arrange = plan, settle on

"The treaty is arranged but must still be approved by Congress."

assassinate = kill

"John Wilkes Booth assassinated Lincoln."

assembly = gathering

"A peaceful assembly of people stood in front of the courthouse."

assign = transfer to, appoint to

"The bill was assigned to a committee."

Associate Justice = partner judge

"There are eight Associate Justices."

at the present time = now

"At the present time there is no need for new taxes."

attack = assault, fall upon

"The attack must be a surprise."

attempt = try

"They attempt to travel across the Atlantic."

automatically = done by a machine

"The seeds were automatically separated from the cotton."

avoid = keep away from, evade

"In the morning you should avoid the freeway."

background = area in the rear or distance

"The background of the picture is too dark."

banks = shore, area next to a river

"The house was on the banks of a river."

bear arms = carry weapons

"Who has the right to bear arms?"

because of = on account of

"Because of these rights, we have freedom of speech."

become = get, grow to be

"Benjamin Franklin never became president."

belief = idea, something someone believes

"Her belief in freedom was strong."

belong to = be a member of an organization

"He belongs to the Republican Party."

beyond = past, in addition to

"New lands were located beyond the mountains."

bill = proposed law

"The President vetoed the bill."

blockade = stopping traffic into a harbor by force

"The naval blockade lasted for two weeks."

body = official group, organization

"The City Council is a legislative body."

bombardment = attack with cannons

"The bombardment of the city began in the morning."

border = frontier

"Mexico and the United States share a border in the south."

bottom = the base, lowest point

"She signed her name at the bottom of the letter."

branch = offshoot, section, group

"There are three branches of government."

brave = courageous

"The brave soldier was called a hero."

burn = set on fire

"They burned the president's house."

bursting = exploding

"Bombs were bursting all around us."

business = commerce, trade

"Business is good at holiday time."

camp = live in tents

"The army camped at Valley Forge."

campaign = waging war

"The Cuban campaign lasted four months."

candidate = nominee, office-seeker

"Her party selected her as their candidate."

capital = city and seat of government

"The new capital was named for Washington."

capture = catch, seize

"The British wanted to capture the capital."

cargo = goods on a ship

"The men threw the cargo into the harbor."

case = example, instance

"In many cases slaves just ran away."

cast a vote = vote

"The electors cast their votes in the capital."

cause = reason

"There were three causes for the war."

cavalry = soldiers on horseback

"The cavalry attacked the enemy."

celebrate = mark with a festival

"We celebrated her birthday last Friday."

center = the middle

"Philadelphia was the political center of the colonies."

century = 100 years

"My family has lived here for a century."

ceremony = official event, ritual

"The ceremony took place in New York."

chamber = assembly of officials

"Congress is made up of two chambers."

Chief Justice = head judge

"Rehnquist is the Chief Justice of the United States."

choose = select, pick out

"Washington chose the location of the new capital."

college = assembly, gathering

"How does the Electoral College work?"

colonist = person sent to live in a new place

"The Pilgrims were early colonists of Massachusetts."

commission = payment for a task

"He received a commission to paint a picture."

committee = an official group of people

"There are five people on the committee."

community = town, neighborhood

"My community is on the east side of the city."

completed = finished

"The work was completed in two years."

conflict = struggle, clash

"The Korean Conflict followed World War II."

consent = agree to

"The Senate did not consent to the idea."

consideration = examination, evaluation

"The bill is in the Senate for consideration."

consist of = composed of, made up from

"The committee consists of five members."

construction = building

"Construction lasted seven years."

copper = reddish metal

"Copper plates cover the statue."

corrections = prison system

"The department of corrections is on the first floor."

cotton = plant used for making cloth

"Cotton was picked by hand."

cotton gin = cotton and seeds separator

"Whitney invented the cotton gin."

countries = nations, lands

"They come from many countries."

court = legal tribunal

"The courts are one branch of government."

crash = violent downfall, failure

"What year was the stock market crash?"

crisis = time of great danger

"The nation found itself in crisis."

criticize = judge, find fault with

"Mark Twain criticized the government."

cruel = severe, without pity

"His punishment was very cruel."

dangerous = unsafe and difficult

"Life was dangerous in the new land."

dawn = sunrise

"I never get up before dawn."

deal with = consider, treat

"Appellate courts deal with appeals."

death = the end of life

"Washington's death came at the end of the century."

debate = argument, to argue

"They debated the statements in the document."

decade = 10 years

"I lived in Mexico two decades ago."

decide = determine, make up one's mind

"They decided to move the capital."

declare = announce

"The colonies declared their independence."

dedicate = officially put into service

"It wasn't dedicated until 10 years later."

defeat = beat, conquer

"The enemy was defeated in 1781."

demonstration = public exhibition, mass meeting

"There were many civil rights demonstrations in the sixties."

department = division, branch

"The Cabinet consists of various departments."

dependent upon = relying on

"Children are dependent upon their parents."

depression = low economic state

"The depression lasted until World War II."

descent = ancestry, family background

"My family is of Korean descent."

describe = tell about

"The Constitution describes our form of government."

design = drawing, outline

"Washington liked the design of the house."

differ = be different, vary

"The North differed greatly from the South."

dignitary = high official from a foreign land

"We greeted dignitaries from Africa."

discover = find

"Who discovered America?"

discrimination = unfair treatment

"Dr. King fought racial discrimination."

distress = great trouble

"The nation was in a time of distress."

dominant = having the upper hand

"No branch of government shall be dominant."

double = increase twice in size

"They hope to double the harvest."

draft = a written plan

"The draft is the first copy of the resolution."

draw up = write, make

"The ambassadors drew up a treaty."

due process = appropriate method

"Everyone has the right of due process of the law."

during = in, throughout the time

"He died during the war."

early = previous, ahead of this time

"The woman came home early."

educated = learned, schooled

"My mother is a well-educated woman."

education = school system

"Education is an important part of life."

efforts = labors

"Their efforts ended in a new Constitution."

election = choosing by voting

"A presidential election occurs every four years."

Elector = someone who elects

"How many electors does your state have?"

emissary = representative to a foreign land

"Franklin was our emissary in France."

enact = put into law — "The Voting Rights Law was enacted in 1965."

enjoy = like, be fond of — "They enjoyed being planters."

ensure = make sure, guarantee — "The Constitution ensures our freedom."

enter = come in — "When did Hawaii enter the Union?"

entire = all — "The government now owned the entire region."

equal = the same, even — "All men are created equal."

equipped = having equipment — "His troops were well equipped."

erect = build — "The statue was erected in four months."

eventually = in time, later — "Washington eventually became the first president."

examine = look at carefully — "The planter examined the new slaves."

except for = excluding — "Except for Native Americans, we are all immigrants."

exist = be — "Slavery existed in America for more than two centuries."

expansion = growth — "This quick expansion made the population grow."

expedition = journey, march — "The expedition took them into unknown territory."

expert = skilled person, authority — "Experts gave their opinion about the law."

explain = tell why — "He explained why he did it."

explore = search through new land — "They wanted to explore the other side of the river."

face = look at — "Everyone faced the flag."

famine = starvation — "Many died during the famine."

farm = plant and harvest crops — "They farmed the land near the river."

field = space, land — "The stars are on a field of blue."

fighting = battle, making war — "The fighting continued for 10 hours."

final = last — "They made their final appeal in the Supreme Court."

fire department = service for extinguishing fires — "The fire department fought the blaze."

first = adjective form of 1 — "Who was our first president?"

fixed = made permanent — "The number of stripes is fixed at 13."

flag = banner — "The American flag is red, white, and blue."

flagpole = pole from which the flag flies — "There is a flagpole in front of the school."

force = make, compel — "Parliament forced them to pay taxes."

former = previous, earlier — "Guam was a former colony of Spain."

found = set up, create — "The Dutch founded New Amsterdam."

framework = scaffold, skeleton — "The framework was made of steel."

future = the coming time — "The future is unknown to us."

gallantly = bravely, courageously — "He served gallantly in the war."

generation = all people born about the same time — "Their generation is old-fashioned."

gentleman = fine and educated man — "Southern gentlemen were often planters."

glare = strong light — "The glare of the sun almost blinded me."

gleaming = shining — "The stars were gleaming brightly."

global = worldwide — "Pollution is a global problem."

glory = splendor, grandeur, fame — "They were proud of the glory of the nation."

gradually = slowly, little by little — "They gradually understood the problem."

guarantee = promise of security — "The Constitution guarantees our rights."

guide = lead, steer — "Washington guided the nation as the first President."

hail (hail'd → hailed) = greet, salute	"The crowd hailed the returning soldiers."
half-staff = halfway up the pole	"The flag flew at half-staff."
harass = torment, annoy	"The Americans began to harass the enemy."
harbor = port, anchorage	"There were two ships in the harbor."
harsh = cruel, severe	"Some masters were harsh with their slaves."
harvest = things grown on farms	"Farmers take the corn harvest in the fall."
head = leader, highest official	"Who is the head of Homeland Security?"
head of state = nation's leader	"The President is our head of state."
heal = make better, improve health	"It was hard to heal the economy."
heaven = sky, Elysium	"I believe people go to heaven after death."
highest (high, higher) = uppermost, having the greatest authority	"The highest court is the Supreme Court."
hunt = search, look for	"The men were hunting deer and bears."
ignorance = having no knowledge	"The slaves were kept in ignorance."
ignore = leave unnoticed, disregard	"If he ignores the bill, it's a *pocket veto*."
illegal = against the law	"It was illegal for a slave to read and write."
immigrant = newcomer from another country	"I came to America as an immigrant."
imperialism = belief in a growing empire	"Some in America believed in imperialism."
in addition = also, too	"In addition, you have to wash the dishes."
in order to = for the purpose of	"You must be a citizen in order to vote."
inaugurate = admit to office in a ceremony	"Lincoln was inaugurated in 1861."
include = make a part of, enclose	"Free speech is included in the Bill of Rights."
increase = become larger	"The states in the Union have increased to 50."
indivisible = cannot be divided	"The nation is forever indivisible."
inspiration = influence, arousal	"The flag is the inspiration for *The Star Spangled Banner*."
inspired = moved, made emotional	"The victory inspired him to write the poem."
instead of = in place of something	"I buy a truck instead of a car."
interests = things that are interesting	"His interests were science and the arts."
introduce = bring in, make known	"A senator introduced the bill."
invalid = no longer in force	"The eighteenth amendment is no longer valid."
invention = unique new device	"Edison had many inventions."
involve = be about, comprise	"Some cases involve civil rights."
is said = people say	"This hill is said to be the site of a great battle."
island = land surrounded by water	"Puerto Rico is an island."
journey = a trip	"The journey from Spain was long."
jury = citizens who decide a court case	"She became a member of the jury."
labor = work	"Slaves were used as cheap labor."
landowner = a person who has land	"Washington was a rich landowner."
largest (large, larger) = biggest	"Alaska is the largest state."
later (late, latest) = afterward	"Later she worked as a doctor."
law-making = creating laws	"Congress is a law-making body."
leader = conductor, guide	"The Founding Fathers were our first leaders."
league = club, organization	"What baseball teams are in the National League?"

legend = a fable, folk story

"There are many legends about this old house."

legislature = elected officials who make laws

"Our national legislature meets in the Capitol."

level = part, category

"The court system has three levels."

liberty = freedom

"Patrick Henry said, 'Give me liberty or give me death.'"

library = collection of books

"The new library is on Main Street."

limit = hinder, hold back

"The states cannot limit a citizen's right to vote."

located = situated, found

"The factory is located in the city."

location = place, site

"The location of the capital was on the Potomac."

long distance = very far

"It's a long distance between Boston and Miami."

lower = bring down

"We lower the flag at sundown."

loyal = true, faithful

"She is a loyal American."

maintain = keep

"Maintaining good streets is a big job."

major = great, important

"It was a major defeat for Spain."

majority = the greater number of people in agreement

"A majority voted for the new law."

mansion = large grand house

"The White House is a mansion."

manufactured goods = things made in a factory

"Our company makes many kinds of manufactured goods."

market = shop, stalls for selling goods

"There were slave markets across the South."

material = goods, products

"He found money and material for the war."

memorize = put in your memory

"I want to memorize *The Pledge of Allegiance*."

met = assembled, encountered one another

"The delegates meet in Independence Hall."

migrate = move from one place to another

"Some birds migrate south for the winter."

military = referring to an army or soldiers

"Who has enough military experience?"

military arts = science of war

"Officers were schooled in the military arts."

minority = the smaller number of people in agreement

"A minority was against the war."

missile = rocket

"The U.S.S.R. placed missiles on the island of Cuba."

mistake = error, something done wrong

"Parliament made many mistakes."

mostly = principally, for the most part

"The slaves mostly worked on plantations."

mourning = time of grieving after a death

"A period of mourning followed his death."

move = relocate, transfer

"In 1800 the capital was moved."

native = born in a place

"Many native Africans became slaves."

navigation = travel by boat

"Free navigation of the river was important."

negotiate = bargain

"Two men were sent to negotiate with Napoleon."

network = rail system

"The railroad network spread westward."

newcomer = new arrival

"The newcomers finally arrived in New York."

nickname = pet name, special name

"The flag's nickname is *Old Glory*."

north, south, east, west = the four points on a compass

"Which direction should we go? North, south, east, or west?"

o'er (o'er → over) = above

"The flag flew over the fort."

oath = vow, word of honor

"He took the oath of office in 1789."

obey = comply with, yield to

"The child does not obey his parents."

obey = listen to, comply with, yield

"The colonists did not obey the king."

omit = leave out

"He omitted a few words from his speech."

original = the first one, genuine — "This is an original painting by Picasso."

outlaw = forbid, make illegal — "The Constitution outlaws slavery."

oval = elliptical, egg-shaped — "The new office was shaped like an oval."

overcrowding = excess population — "They left Italy because of overcrowding."

overseas = in foreign lands — "Some soldiers are serving overseas."

oversee = manage, control — "What department oversees new construction?"

paint = coat or brush on color — "They painted the walls white."

palace = castle, royal building — "The king lives in a palace."

parade = ceremonious procession or march — "The parade went down Main Street."

parliament = legislature of England — "Parliament governed the colonies."

participate in = take part in — "Not everyone participated in the convention."

partner = colleague — "She had a new business partner."

party = political organization — "There are two major parties in the United States."

pass = win the vote — "The bill passed with a simple majority."

passenger = traveler — "The boat carried 10 passengers."

patriot = loyal citizen, nationalist — "Patrick Henry was a famous patriot."

pedestal = base, stand — "The statue was put on a pedestal."

perfect = finish, make perfect — "Bell finally perfected his telephone."

perilous = dangerous — "It was a perilous time for the nation."

period = time, era — "The period of war was over."

permanently = forever — "Slavery cannot remain permanently in the nation."

petition = formal request or application — "We have the right to petition our government."

piece of land = property — "The District of Columbia is a piece of land in Maryland."

pine tree = evergreen, fir tree — "A pine tree stood in the center of the garden."

plan = scheme, proposal — "He had a plan for the new capital."

planet = satellite of the sun, such as Earth — "We live on planet Earth."

planning = preparations, design — "Many helped in the planning of the capital."

plantation = large farm — "He grew tobacco on his plantation."

planter = farmer, someone who plants crops — "Washington was a planter like his father."

pledge = promise — "I pledged $50 to help his family."

poll tax = money paid in order to vote — "Some southern states had a poll tax."

popular = from the people at large — "He won the popular vote."

popularity = approval by many people — "Her popularity helped her win election."

population = number of people — "The population of Chicago is about four million."

possession = something owned — "The colonies became American possessions."

powers = authority, control — "Each branch of government has its own powers."

Preamble = introduction — "The Preamble begins the Constitution."

present = show, give — "The bill was presented to the House."

present time = now — "Who is President at the present time?"

preserve = keep safe — "Lincoln wanted to preserve the United States."

press = media that produce newspapers and magazines — "Freedom of the press is guaranteed in the Constitution."

pressure = moral force — "The protests put pressure on the government."

279

primarily = fundamentally, mostly

"Many people were primarily planters."

principle = basic truth or rule

"I believe in the principles of democracy."

prison = jail

"They built a new prison."

process = method, procedure

"The legal process is sometimes long."

produce = make, write

"James Madison helped produce the Constitution."

profitable = earning money

"Soon the plantations were profitable again."

proof = evidence, convincing fact

"He needed proof to believe her story."

protest = complain

"The colonists protested the unfair taxes."

proudly = with pride and honor

"He proudly showed me his diploma."

provide = prepare, supply

"The Constitution provides us with certain rights."

punishment = discipline, beating

"The punishment for a slave was often harsh."

purchase = buy

"It cost millions to purchase the land."

rails = long iron bars

"Iron rails stretched from coast to coast."

raise (money) = find, arrange for

"We have to raise more money."

rampart = embankment around a fort

"The soldiers were running toward the ramparts."

ratify = accept, approve

"The delegates ratified the constitution."

rattlesnake = a poisonous snake with a vibrating tail

"Careful! There's a rattlesnake under that bush!"

raw materials = things used to make a new product

"Wood and steel are some of the raw materials we use."

rebuilt = built again

"The house was rebuilt after the war."

recommendation = statement that something is favorable

"They studied the President's recommendations."

regarding = about

"They hear cases regarding federal laws."

region = area, territory

"The Louisiana Territory was a large region."

register = sign up

"You can register to vote at the state DMV."

relationship = connection or bond with someone

"The relationship between England and the colonies was growing weak."

release = set free

"The bill will be released tomorrow."

rename = give a new name

"They renamed our school John F. Kennedy High School."

repeal = revoke a law

"Prohibition was repealed in 1933."

replace = take the place of

"The Vice President could replace the President."

represent = to act on behalf of

"Ms. Brown will represent us in Congress."

require = demand, need

"My landlord required payment today."

reserve = set aside, keep as one's own

"Certain powers are reserved for the states."

resident = a person who lives somewhere

"I am a resident of the United States."

resolution = a statement, document

"They called for a new resolution."

responsibility = accountability, burden

"Congress has the responsibility of making laws."

retain = keep

"I retained the bills you sent me."

retire = resign from work

"He and Martha retired to Mount Vernon."

revenue = income

"Most revenue comes from taxes."

revision = a change

"Jefferson wanted several revisions."

rights = guaranteed privileges

"Each citizen has certain rights."

role = part, participation

"The role of Congress is to make laws."

route = road, way

"I travel this route to work."

rural = of the country

"Even rural towns had a railroad station."

safeguard = ensure, protect, keep safe

"The new law safeguards civil rights."

sail = travel by ship

"Columbus sailed west."

sale = selling

"For more than a decade the sale of alcohol was illegal."

sanitation = hygiene, maintaining cleanliness

"Good sanitation means good health."

sculptor = artist who works in stone and metal

"The sculptor made a statue out of stone."

season = time of year, spring, summer, fall, winter

"What season do you like best?"

seat of government = central location of government

"Philadelphia was the seat of government."

secede = leave, abandon

"South Carolina was the first to secede."

second = adjective form of 2

"John Adams became the second U.S. president."

secretary = officer in the president's cabinet

"Who is the Secretary of Defense?"

seek = look for, search

"He is seeking help with his problems."

seizure = taking, confiscation

"Seizure of private property is not allowed."

select = choose, pick out

"The delegates selected the members of the committee."

separate = divide, detach

"Church and state are separated."

serve = give service, aid

"The President serves the country."

serve as = act as

"Washington served as President for eight years."

services = work performed for the benefit of others

"What services does the city provide?"

sew = stitch, attach with needle and thread

"They say Betsy Ross sewed the first flag."

sewer = underground drain

"The rainwater flowed into the sewer."

show = display, demonstrate

"The flag shows a snake in the center."

sign = write your name on a document

"Each delegate signed the declaration."

simply = merely, easily

"They simply wanted to be free."

sinking = destroying a ship and making it sink

"The sinking of the *Maine* shocked America."

slave = servant in bondage

"There were slaves in America for many years."

slightly = a little bit

"The original version is slightly different."

spangled = covered, adorned with glitter

"The flag is spangled with 50 stars."

special = distinct, uncommon

"The President lives in a special house."

spelled out = clearly written

"The people's rights are spelled out in the Constitution."

sponsor = promote, arrange

"They sponsor a debate before the election."

spread = stretch, extend

"Settlers began to spread into the western territories."

square mile = 1 mile × 1 mile

"The town is located on five square miles of land."

stand for = represent

"The flag stands for the Republic."

statement = something said in words

"His statement was simple but clear."

statewide = across the whole state

"Statewide elections were held in November."

steam = vapor from boiling water

"Steam power ran the Clermont."

stimulate = arouse

"Immigration stimulated population growth."

stood for = represented

"The Declaration of Independence stood for liberty."

streaming = flowing

"Banners were streaming down from the buildings."

stretch = reach, spread, extend

"The mountains stretch a hundred miles from north to south."

strike at = hit hard

"They struck at the enemy at night."

stripe = a band, streak, line

"The American flag has 13 stripes."

struggle = battle, violent effort

"The struggle for freedom had ended."

study = learn

"He had to study science and languages."

successful = reached a goal

"They made a successful voyage in 1807."

succession = following in order

"Do you know the order of succession?"

suffer = undergo pain, tolerate

"The dog suffered from the heat."

supervise = oversee, control

"He supervised the work on the house."

support = uphold

"He supported the Declaration of Independence."

surprise = amazement, wonder

"It was a surprise when he agreed to sell the land."

surrender = give up, yield

"The general did not want to surrender."

surrounded = in a ring, encircled

"Cornwallis was finally surrounded."

survive = live through

"My son survived a terrible accident."

swear into office = take an oath

"The President was sworn into office at noon."

symbol = sign, something representing something else

"The bald eagle is an American symbol."

symbolize = represent something else

"The statue symbolizes liberty."

table = stop an action, avoid

"They tabled the bill."

take place = happen

"The test took place in Room B."

tax = money owed the government

"I pay my taxes every year."

teach = instruct, educate

"No one would teach them to read and write."

term = time in office

"A president's term is four years."

therefore = for that reason

"Therefore, you must register if you want to vote."

threat = warning, menacing statement

"Their threats did not frighten her."

threaten = make threats

"The South threatened to leave the Union."

throughout = in every region

"Every slave throughout the land was free."

time-consuming = using much time

"The work was time-consuming."

tobacco = plant for making smoking material

"These planters grow tobacco."

together = as one, united

"The states were together in one Union."

top = highest point

"There is a large bird at the top of the tree."

trading post = a small colonial store

"I buy tools and grain at the trading post."

traffic = movement of cars and trucks on a street

"Traffic is slow today."

tragically = sadly

"Tragically, many soldiers died in the war."

trained = prepared, taught skills

"The British soldiers were trained better."

transport = carry, move

"They were transported by ship."

transportation = movement of cargo or passengers by vehicle

"What form of transportation do you use?"

trap = catch, ensnare

"They trapped a young fox."

treasury = money storage

"There is no money in the treasury."

treaty = peace document

"The delegates signed the treaty in Paris."

trial = a case in court

"Her trial began in July."

tune = song

"This is a happy tune."

twilight = faint light at dawn or dusk

"The sky is beautiful at twilight."

unexpectedly = as a surprise

"The attack came unexpectedly."

unknown = no one knows about this

"The answer is unknown to me."

unreasonable = irrational, unjustified

"An unreasonable search of your home is outlawed."

until = up to the time

"They were not free until the end of the war."

upper = above, higher than something else

"My friends live on an upper floor."

upside-down = up is down, down is up

"The picture is hanging upside-down."

use = employ, utilize

"This big car uses too much gas."

violence = fury, dangerous and unlawful force

"Violence broke out in the streets."

volunteer = a soldier serving willingly

"The minutemen were volunteers."

voter = a person who votes

"The voters have elected a new senator."

wager = make a bet

"I wagered five dollars in the card game."

wages = pay, salary

"She wanted better wages."

was born = came into the world by birth

"He was born in Virginia in 1732."

watch'd (watch'd → watched) = looked at, observed

"He watched the rockets explode."

wave = fly, flutter

"A flag is waving over the entrance to the museum."

wealthy = rich

"Washington was a wealthy landowner."

were brought = were shipped

"Many slaves were brought to America."

western hemisphere = continents of the New World

"Canada is in the western hemisphere."

win = gain, secure

"The colonies wanted to win their independence."

worsen = become worse

"The patient's health began to worsen."

yield = harvest

"The cotton yield this year was good."

A Timeline of American History and World Events

Use this timeline of history to learn how America evolved and what people took part in that history. Compare American history with what was going on in other parts of the world at the same time.

Year	History of America	People	World Events
1000	Scandinavians come to North America.	Leif Erikson	
1066			Normans conquer England.
1350			Bubonic plague hits Middle East and Europe.
1492	Spain sends an expedition across the Atlantic in search of Asia.	Christopher Columbus	The New World is discovered.
1588		Elizabeth I	English fleet defeats Spanish Armada.
1602			Dutch East India Company founded.
1607	Jamestown Island settled. Start of the Virginia colony.	Captain John Smith	
1614	Dutch found New Nederland.	Henry Hudson	
1620	Pilgrims land at Plymouth Rock.		
1625	New Amsterdam is founded.	Peter Stuyvesant	
1755	French and Indian War begins.		
1763	French and Indian War ends.		
1773	Boston Tea Party		
1775	Revolutionary War begins.		
1776	Declaration of Independence is written. George Washington becomes commander-in-chief of American forces.	Thomas Jefferson	
1783	Revolutionary War ends. Treaty of Paris is signed. Britain cedes all territory west to the Mississippi. 80,000 loyalists emigrate to Canada.		
1784	Bifocal eyeglasses invented.	Ben Franklin	
1788	Constitution is ratified.	James Madison	
1789	George Washington becomes first President.		French Revolution begins.
1791	Creation of the first 10 Amendments: The Bill of Rights.		

(continued)

Year	History of America	People	World Events
1792	First U.S. mint.	Alexander Hamilton	
1793	Invention of the cotton gin.	Eli Whitney	King Louis XVI is executed.
1798			Napoleon invades Egypt.
1800	Library of Congress founded.		
1803	Louisiana Purchase.	Thomas Jefferson	
1804	Lewis and Clark Expedition		Napoleon wages war in Europe. Napoleon becomes emperor of France.
1807	Voyage of the steamboat *Clermont*.	Robert Fulton	
1811	First steamboat voyage on the Mississippi to New Orleans.		
1812	War of 1812 against England	James Madison	Napoleon defeated in Russia.
1814	British burn President's Palace. Treaty of Ghent ends War of 1812. *The Star Spangled Banner* is written.	Dolley Madison Andrew Jackson Francis Scott Key	
1815			Napoleon defeated and exiled from France. Queen Victoria is born.
1817	Construction of the Erie Canal.		
1820	Missouri Compromise. Congress prohibits importing slaves.	Henry Clay	
1823	Monroe Doctrine issued.	James Monroe	
1830	Spoils System is created.	Andrew Jackson	French invade Algeria.
1833			Santa Anna elected President of Mexico.
1837	Telegraph is invented.	Samuel F.B. Morse	
1838	Trail of Tears begins.	Cherokee Indians	
1846	Founding of the Smithsonian Institution		
1848	Gold discovered in California.		Upper and Lower Canada united.
1853			Crimean War begins.
1854	Republican Party formed.		
1855			Crimean War ends.

Year	History of America	People	World Events
1861	Kansas admitted to the Union. Confederate States of America. Southern states secede. Civil War begins.	Abraham Lincoln	Unification of Italy.
1862	Transcontinental Railroad begun.		
1863	Emancipation Proclamation.		Austria's Maximillian made Emperor of Mexico.
1865	Lee surrenders to Grant, ending the Civil War. Lincoln assassinated in Ford's Theater. 13th Amendment outlaws slavery. Reconstruction of the South begins.	John Wilkes Booth	
1867	Purchase of Alaska from Russia.		
1868	First impeachment of a president.	Andrew Johnson	
1870		Otto von Bismarck	Franco-Prussian War. Dominion of Canada formed.
1871	Great Chicago Fire.	Kaiser Wilhelm II	Algeria becomes French territory. Germany unified.
1876	National Baseball League founded. Custer defeated at Little Big Horn. Invention of telephone is patented.	Alexander Graham Bell	
1877	End of Reconstruction.		
1879	Invention of electric light bulb.	Thomas Edison	
1881			French occupy Tunisia.
1882			British occupy Egypt.
1886	Haymarket labor riot in Chicago. Geronimo surrenders.		
1893	Columbian Exposition in Chicago.		
1896	Supreme Court rules for "separate but equal" in segregation.		
1898	Sinking of the battleship *Maine*. United States declares war on Spain. Spain is defeated and her territories annexed.		
1901	President McKinley assassinated.		

(continued)

Year	History of America	People	World Events
1903	Wright brothers successfully fly their airplane at Kitty Hawk.		End of Victorian Era with death of queen.
1904		Theodore Roosevelt	Panama Canal is begun.
1905		Albert Einstein	Russo-Japanese War. Theory of Relativity.
1914			Franz Ferdinand is assassinated in Serbia. World War I begins.
1917	United States declares war on Germany.	Lenin	Russian Revolution.
1918			Czar and family are executed.
1919			U.S.S.R. formed. Versailles Peace Treaty. League of Nations formed.
1920	18th Amendment ratified. Women receive the right to vote. 19th Amendment ratified: Prohibition.		
1924			Lenin dies. Stalin takes power.
1929	Stock Market crash.	Herbert Hoover	
1933	Start of the New Deal	Franklin Roosevelt	Hitler comes to power.
1935	The Social Security Act.		
1939			Hitler attacks Poland. World War II begins.
1941	Japan attacks Pearl Harbor. United States enters the war.		
1942	Navajo Indians used as "Windtalkers."		
1944	Normandy invaded.		
1945	United States drops atomic bombs on Hiroshima and Nagasaki. Japan surrenders.	Harry Truman	Germany is defeated in May. United Nations formed.
1947			India becomes India and Pakistan.
1948	Start of the Cold War.	Stalin	
1950	Marshall Plan inaugurated.		Start of the Korean War.

Year	History of America	People	World Events
1953			Stalin dies.
1955	African-Americans boycott buses in Montgomery. Supreme Court orders desegregation of schools.	Rosa Parks	
1957			Soviets launch Sputnik.
1960	John F. Kennedy elected President. Start of the Civil Rights movement.	Martin Luther King, Jr.	
1962	Cuban Missile Crisis	Nikita Khrushchev	
1963	John F. Kennedy assassinated.	Lee Harvey Oswald	
1965	Protest against the Vietnam War.	Lyndon Johnson	
1967			6-day Israeli War.
1968	Robert Kennedy assassinated. Martin Luther King, Jr., assassinated.	Sirhan B. Sirhan James Early Ray	
1969	Men land on the moon.		
1974	President Nixon resigns over Watergate.		
1975			South Vietnam surrenders to North Vietnam.
1979			Americans held hostage in Iran. Soviet troops invade Afganistan.
1983	President Reagan proposes "Star Wars."		
1989			Berlin Wall comes down.
1998		Mikhail Gorbachev	*Glasnost.*
1991	First Gulf War.	George Bush	Iraq invades Kuwait. End of Cold War.
1999	U.S. budget goes into surplus.	Bill Clinton	
2000	George W. Bush elected president.		
2001	September 11 attack on World Trade Center. Start of U.S. global war on terror.	George W. Bush	Taliban removed from power.
2003	United States forces invade Iraq.	Sadam Hussein	
2005	Pope John Paul II dies. Pope Benedict XVI appointed.		

Answer Key

Pre-Test

Part One

1. c. 50
2. a. 13
3. d. 50
4. c. England
5. a. July 4
6. a. amendment
7. b. three
8. d. Senate
9. c. Congress
10. a. the President
11. d. California
12. b. a civil rights leader
13. a. two
14. b. The Supreme Court
15. c. laws
16. a. the Bill of Rights
17. d. Preamble
18. d. 100
19. a. 18
20. d. Native Americans

Part Two

21. Cabinet
22. 1776
23. January
24. Congress, the House of Representatives and the Senate
25. Bill of Rights
26. Abraham Lincoln
27. 50
28. governor

29. *Spangled Banner*

30. Thomas Jefferson

31. George Washington

32. Congress

33. Alaska and Hawaii

34. Washington, D.C.

35. people

Part Three

36. George W. Bush

37. the Pilgrims

38. nine

39. four

40. red and white

41. the Vice President

42. they represent the 50 states of the Union

43. July Fourth

44. Germany, Japan, and Italy

45. Dick Cheney

46. It makes the laws.

47. six

48. 435

49. Learn the capital of your state.

50. Learn who the governor of your state is.

Practice Test 1

1. **d.** white and blue

2. **a.** stars

3. **c.** white

4. **a.** 50 states

5. **c.** 13

6. **d.** red and white

7. **a.** 13 original colonies

8. **c.** 50

9. **a.** July 4

10. **c.** England

11. **b.** Revolutionary War

12. **c.** Independence Day

13. **b.** George Washington

14. **a.** George W. Bush

15. **d.** Dick Cheney

16. **a.** all the people

17. **a.** Vice President

18. **b.** four

19. **d.** Constitution

20. **a.** amendment

21. **a.** three

22. **d.** Executive and Judicial

23. **c.** change

24. **a.** 27

25. **a.** Legislative

26. **c.** Judicial

27. **b.** Executive

28. **b.** Congress

29. **c.** the people of each state

30. **d.** 100

31. Learn the names of your state's senators.

32. **d.** 6

33. **d.** 435

34. **a.** 2

35. **c.** carries out

36. **c.** carries out

37. **d.** Supreme Court

38. **a.** the Constitution

39. **d.** the Bill of Rights

40. Learn the capital of your state.

41. Learn the name of your state's governor.

42. **d.** the Speaker of the House

43. **c.** William H. Rehnquist

44. Connecticut

    Delaware

    Georgia

    Maryland

    Massachusetts

New Hampshire

New Jersey

New York

North Carolina

Pennsylvania

Rhode Island

South Carolina

Virginia

45. d. Patrick Henry

46. a. Germany, Italy, and Japan

47. c. Alaska and Hawaii

48. a. 2

49. a. Martin Luther King, Jr.

50. Learn the name of the head of your local government.

51. b. a native-born American

52. b. 2

53. d. president

54. c. 9

55. d. Pilgrims

56. d. governor

57. a. mayor

58. c. Thanksgiving

59. d. Thomas Jefferson

60. a. 1776

61. d. all men are created equal

62. a. *The Star Spangled Banner*

63. d. Francis Scott Key

64. b. freedom of speech

65. b. 18

66. b. The President

67. d. Supreme Court

68. a. Abraham Lincoln

69. c. freed the slaves

70. b. his cabinet

71. d. George Washington

72. b. N-400

73. c. Native Americans

74. a. Mayflower

75. d. English colonies

76. c. freedom of religion

77. c. Congress

78. a. democracy

79. b. Abraham Lincoln

80. d. 1787

81. a. the first 10 amendments to the Constitution

82. b. peace

83. d. the Capitol

84. d. the people's

85. c. preamble

86. a. having the right to vote

87. a. freedom of the press

88. c. where Congress meets

89. a. the White House

90. b. official home

91. d. freedom of assembly

92. a. the Oval Office

93. d. commander-in-chief

94. b. George Washington

95. b. November

96. d. January

97. d. innumerable

98. d. innumerable

99. a. Republicans and Democrats

100. c. states

Practice Test 2

1. The colors of the American flag are red, white, and **BLUE**.

2. There are 50 **STARS** on the American flag.

3. The **STRIPES** on the flag are red and white.

4. The stars on the flag represent the **STATES**.

5. There are **13** stripes on the flag.

6. The stars on the flag are the color **WHITE**.

7. The stripes on the flag represent the 13 original **COLONIES/STATES**.

8. There are **FIFTY** states in the Union.

9. Independence Day is on **JULY 4.**

10. The American colonies wanted independence from **ENGLAND/GREAT BRITAIN.**

11. We fought against Great Britain in the **REVOLUTIONARY** War.

12. On the Fourth of July Americans celebrate **INDEPENDENCE** Day.

13. The first President of the United States was **GEORGE WASHINGTON.**

14. The President of the United States today is **GEORGE W. BUSH.**

15. The **VICE PRESIDENT** of the United States today is Dick Cheney.

16. The President is elected by the American **PEOPLE/NATION.**

17. If the President dies, the **VICE PRESIDENT** becomes President.

18. The President is elected for a term of **FOUR** years.

19. The document that describes our government is the **CONSTITUTION.**

20. A change to the Constitution is called an **AMENDMENT.**

21. The American government consists of **THREE** branches.

22. The branches of our government are Legislative, Judicial, and **EXECUTIVE.**

23. An amendment can change the **CONSTITUTION.**

24. There have been **TWENTY-SEVEN** amendments to the Constitution.

25. The branch of government that carries out the laws is the **EXECUTIVE** branch.

26. The branch of government that makes our laws is the **LEGISLATIVE** branch.

27. The branch of government that decides whether laws are constitutional is the **JUDICIAL** branch.

28. The House of Representatives and the **SENATE** make up Congress.

29. Congress is elected by the people of each **STATE.**

30. There are presently **ONE HUNDRED** senators.

31. The two senators from my state are _____ and _____.

    LEARN THE NAMES OF YOUR SENATORS.

32. A senator is elected for **SIX** years.

33. There are **FOUR HUNDRED THIRTY-FIVE** Representatives in the House.

34. Representatives are elected for **TWO** years.

35. The Executive Branch of government carries out the **LAWS.**

36. The Judicial Branch decides if laws are **CONSTITUTIONAL.**

37. The Supreme Court is in the **JUDICIAL** Branch.

38. The Supreme Law of the United States is the **CONSTITUTION.**

39. The first 10 amendments are called the **BILL OF RIGHTS.**

40. The capital city of my state is _____.

    LEARN THE CAPITAL CITY OF YOUR STATE.

41. The governor of my state is _____.

    LEARN THE NAME OF THE GOVERNOR OF YOUR STATE.

42. If the president and the **VICE PRESIDENT** die, the Speaker of the House becomes president.

43. The Chief Justice of the Supreme Court is **WILLIAM H. REHNQUIST.**

44. The original 13 colonies are:

Connecticut

Delaware

Georgia

Maryland

Massachusetts

New Hampshire

New Jersey

New York

North Carolina

Pennsylvania

Rhode Island

South Carolina

Virginia

45. **PATRICK HENRY** said, "Give me liberty or give me death."

46. Germany, Italy, and **JAPAN** were our enemies during World War II.

47. The 49th and the 50th states in the Union are Alaska and **HAWAII.**

48. A president can only serve for **TWO** terms.

49. **MARTIN LUTHER KING, JR.** was a famous civil rights leader.

50. The head of my local government is _____.

LEARN THE NAME OF THE HEAD OF YOUR LOCAL GOVERNMENT.

51. A person has to be born in **AMERICA** to become president.

52. Each state can elect only **TWO** senators.

53. Supreme Court justices are appointed by the **PRESIDENT.**

54. There are **NINE** Supreme Court justices.

55. The Pilgrims came to America for **RELIGIOUS** freedom.

56. The head executive of a state government is the **GOVERNOR.**

57. The head executive of a city government is the **MAYOR.**

58. The Pilgrims celebrated the first **THANKSGIVING.**

59. **THOMAS JEFFERSON** was the major writer of the Declaration of Independence.

60. The Declaration of Independence was adopted in **1776.**

61. The basic belief of the Declaration of Independence is that "all men are created **EQUAL.**"

62. The national anthem of the United States is **THE STAR SPANGLED BANNER.**

63. The words to the national anthem were written by **FRANCIS SCOTT KEY.**

64. Freedom of speech is guaranteed in the Bill **OF RIGHTS.**

65. The minimum voting age in the United States is **EIGHTEEN**.

66. **THE PRESIDENT** signs bills into law.

67. The highest court in the United States is the **SUPREME COURT**.

68. During the **CIVIL** War Abraham Lincoln was president.

69. The Emancipation Proclamation freed the **SLAVES**.

70. The president is advised by his **CABINET**.

71. George Washington is called the Father **OF OUR COUNTRY**.

72. You need Form **N-400** to apply for citizenship.

73. The Pilgrims were helped by **NATIVE** Americans.

74. The Pilgrims sailed to the New World on board the **MAYFLOWER**.

75. The 13 original states had been English **COLONIES**.

76. The Bill of Rights guarantees **FREEDOM** of religion.

77. Only **CONGRESS** has the power to declare war.

78. The **AMERICAN** government is a democracy.

79. President **ABRAHAM LINCOLN** freed the slaves.

80. The Constitution was written in **1787**.

81. The Bill of Rights is the first 10 **AMENDMENTS** to the Constitution.

82. One of the purposes of the United Nations is to promote **PEACE**.

83. Congress meets in the **CAPITOL** Building.

84. The Constitution and the Bill of Rights guarantee our **RIGHTS/FREEDOMS**.

85. The introduction to the Constitution is the **PREAMBLE**.

86. A benefit of being a U.S. citizen is having the right to **VOTE** and elect our leaders.

87. One of the rights in the **BILL** of Rights is freedom of the press.

88. The U.S. Capitol is where **CONGRESS** meets.

89. The President lives in the **WHITE HOUSE**.

90. The White House is the president's official **HOME/RESIDENCE**.

91. The Bill of Rights is in the **CONSTITUTION**.

92. The President's office in the White House is the **OVAL** Office.

93. The President is the commander-in-chief of the **ARMED FORCES/MILITARY**.

94. The first commander-in-chief of the military was **GEORGE WASHINGTON**.

95. Presidential elections are held in the month of **NOVEMBER**.

96. The new president is inaugurated in the month of **JANUARY**.

97. A senator can be reelected **INNUMERABLE** times.

98. A congressman can be reelected **INNUMERABLE** times.

99. The two major American political parties are **REPUBLICAN AND DEMOCRAT**.

100. There are 50 **STATES** in the United States.

Practice Test 3

1. What are the colors of the American flag? (RED, WHITE, AND BLUE)

2. What do the stars on the flag represent? (THE STATES)

3. How many stars are on the American flag? (50)

4. What color are the stars? (WHITE)

5. How many stripes are on the American flag? (13)

6. What is the capital of the United States? (WASHINGTON, D.C.)

7. What do the stripes represent? (THE ORIGINAL 13 COLONIES)

8. How many states are in the Union? (50)

9. What is the date of Independence Day? (JULY 4)

10. What great river divides the United States from north to south? (THE MISSISSIPPI)

11. What country did we fight in the Revolutionary War? (GREAT BRITAIN/ENGLAND)

12. What do Americans celebrate on the Fourth of July? (INDEPENDENCE DAY)

13. Who was the first President of the United States? (GEORGE WASHINGTON)

14. Who is the President of the United States today? (GEORGE W. BUSH)

15. Who is the Vice President of the United States today? (DICK CHENEY)

16. Who elects the President? (THE PEOPLE)

17. Who becomes President if the President dies? (THE VICE PRESIDENT)

18. How long is a president's term in office? (FOUR YEARS)

19. What document describes the American government? (THE CONSTITUTION)

20. What is a change to the Constitution called? (AN AMENDMENT)

21. What was a major issue why the Civil War was fought? (SLAVERY)

22. What are the branches of government? (LEGISLATIVE, JUDICIAL AND EXECUTIVE)

23. What does an amendment do to the Constitution? (IT CHANGES THE CONSTITUTION)

24. How many amendments to the Constitution have there been? (27)

25. Which branch of government makes our laws? (LEGISLATIVE)

26. Which branch of government carries out our laws? (EXECUTIVE)

27. Which branch of government decides whether laws are constitutional? (JUDICIAL)

28. What two chambers make up Congress? (SENATE AND HOUSE OF REPRESENTATIVES)

29. Who elects Congress? (THE VOTERS OF EACH STATE)

30. How many senators are there? (100)

31. Who are the senators from your state?

    Learn the names of your state's senators.

32. For how many years is a senator elected? (6)

33. How many representatives are there in the House? (435)

34. For how many years is a representative to the House elected? (2)

35. What does the Executive Branch of government do? (IT CARRIES OUT THE LAWS.)

36. What does the Judicial Branch of government do? (IT DECIDES WHETHER LAWS ARE CONSTITUTIONAL.)

37. What is the highest court in the land? (THE SUPREME COURT)

38. What is the supreme law of the land? (THE CONSTITUTION)

39. What are the first 10 amendments to the Constitution called? (THE BILL OF RIGHTS)

40. What is the capital of your state?

Learn the capital of your state.

41. Who is the governor of your state?

Learn the name of your state's governor.

42. Who becomes President if the President and the Vice President die? (THE SPEAKER OF THE HOUSE)

43. Who is the Chief Justice of the Supreme Court? (WILLIAM H. REHNQUIST)

44. What were the names of the original 13 colonies?

Connecticut

Delaware

Georgia

Maryland

Massachusetts

New Hampshire

New Jersey

New York

North Carolina

Pennsylvania

Rhode Island

South Carolina

Virginia

45. Who said, "Give me liberty or give me death"? (PATRICK HENRY)

46. Who were our enemies in World War II? (GERMANY, ITALY, AND JAPAN)

47. Which states were the 49th and 50th to join the Union? (ALASKA AND HAWAII)

48. For how many terms can a president serve? (2)

49. What famous civil rights leader was assassinated in 1968? (MARTIN LUTHER KING, JR.)

50. What nation was the first to land men on the moon? (THE UNITED STATES)

51. Where must a person be born to become president? (IN THE UNITED STATES)

52. How many senators can each state elect? (2)

53. Who appoints Supreme Court justices? (THE PRESIDENT)

54. How many Supreme Court justices are there? (9)

55. What two oceans border the United States in the east and west? (ATLANTIC AND PACIFIC OCEANS)

56. What is the chief executive of a state government called? (GOVERNOR)

57. What is the chief executive of a city government called? (MAYOR)

58. Who celebrated the first Thanksgiving? (THE PILGRIMS)

59. Who was the major writer of the Declaration of Independence? (THOMAS JEFFERSON)

60. In what year was the Declaration of Independence adopted? (1776)

61. What is the basic belief of the Declaration of Independence? (ALL MEN ARE CREATED EQUAL)

62. What is the national anthem of the United States? (*THE STAR SPANGLED BANNER*)

63. Who wrote the words to the national anthem? (FRANCIS SCOTT KEY)

64. Where will you find the right of "freedom of speech"? (IN THE BILL OF RIGHTS)

65. What is the minimum voting age in the United States? (18)

66. Who signs bills into law? (THE PRESIDENT)

67. Which court is the highest in the United States? (THE SUPREME COURT)

68. Who was President during the Civil War? (ABRAHAM LINCOLN)

69. What did the Emancipation Proclamation do? (IT FREED THE SLAVES.)

70. What group advises the president? (THE CABINET)

71. Who is called the Father of Our Country? (GEORGE WASHINGTON)

72. What form do you need to apply for citizenship? (N-400)

73. Who helped the Pilgrims? (NATIVE AMERICANS)

74. On what ship did the Pilgrims come to America? (THE MAYFLOWER)

75. What were the original 13 states before the Revolutionary War? (13 ENGLISH COLONIES)

76. Where do you find the right of "freedom of the press?" (IN THE BILL OF RIGHTS)

77. Who has the power to declare war? (CONGRESS)

78. What is it called if a president refuses to sign a bill into law? (A VETO)

79. Who freed the slaves? (ABRAHAM LINCOLN)

80. In what year was the Constitution written? (1787)

81. Which amendments make up the Bill of Rights? (THE FIRST 10 AMENDMENTS)

82. What is the main purpose of the United Nations? (TO PROMOTE PEACE)

83. Where does Congress meet? (IN THE CAPITOL)

84. What do the Constitution and the Bill of Rights guarantee? (THE PEOPLE'S RIGHTS)

85. What is the introduction to the Constitution called? (THE PREAMBLE)

86. What is a benefit of being an American citizen? (YOU HAVE THE RIGHT TO VOTE.)

87. Where can you find the right of "freedom of religion"? (IN THE BILL OF RIGHTS)

88. Who meets in the U.S. Capitol? (CONGRESS)

89. Where does the president live? (IN THE WHITE HOUSE)

90. Whose official home is the White House? (THE PRESIDENT'S)

91. Where do you find the right of "freedom of assembly"? (IN THE BILL OF RIGHTS)

92. What is the President's office called? (THE OVAL OFFICE)

93. Who is commander-in-chief of the armed forces? (THE PRESIDENT)

94. Who was the first commander-in-chief of the American military? (GEORGE WASHINGTON)

95. In what month are presidential elections held? (NOVEMBER)

96. In what month is the new president inaugurated? (JANUARY)

97. How many times can a senator be reelected? (INNUMERABLE TIMES)

98. How many times can a representative be reelected? (INNUMERABLE TIMES)

99. What are the two major political parties in America? (DEMOCRAT AND REPUBLICAN)

100. Who invented the electric light bulb? (THOMAS EDISON)

Practice Test 4

1. There were 13 stars on the first American flag.

2. The stars represent the states in the Union.

3. There are 50 stars on the flag today.

4. The stripes are red and white.

5. People believe that Betsy Ross sewed the first American flag.

6. The capital of the United States is Washington, D.C.

7. D.C. means District of Columbia.

8. There are 50 states in the Union.

9. Independence Day is celebrated on July 4.

10. The Mississippi divides the United States from north to south.

11. The Boston Tea Party was a protest against the tax on tea.

12. The Declaration of Independence was introduced on July 4, 1776.

13. George Washington was the first President of the United States.

14. George W. Bush is President today.

15. Dick Cheney is Vice President today.

16. The Electoral College is the gathering where the states' Electoral votes are counted.

17. The Oval Office is the President's office.

18. The President lives in the White House.

19. The Constitution describes the American government.

20. A change to the Constitution is an amendment.

21. The Civil War was fought over slavery.

22. The Legislative branch makes the laws.

23. An amendment makes a change to the Constitution.

24. There have been 27 amendments to the Constitution.

25. The West Wing is in the White House.

26. The Executive branch carries out the laws.

27. The cabinet advises the President.

28. Congress is made up of the House of Representatives and the Senate.

29. A senator's term is six years.

30. There are 100 senators.

31. Learn the senators from your state.

32. A bill is a proposal for a new law.

33. There are 435 representatives in the House.

34. A representative is elected for two years.

35. The President heads the Executive Branch.

36. The Judicial Branch decides whether laws are constitutional.

37. The Supreme Court is the highest court in the land.

38. The Constitution is the supreme law of the land.

39. The Bill of Rights is the first 10 amendments to the Constitution.

40. Learn the capital of your state.

41. Learn the name of the governor of your state.

42. If the President and the Vice President die, the Speaker of the House becomes president.

43. William Rehnquist is the Chief Justice of the Supreme Court.

44. The Vice President is the President of the Senate.

45. Patrick Henry said, "Give me liberty or give me death."

46. Our enemies in World War II were Germany, Italy, and Japan.

47. Hawaii was the last to join the Union.

48. A president can serve for two terms.

49. He was assassinated.

50. Men landed on the moon in 1969.

51. A person must be born in the United States to become President.

52. Alaska is the largest state in the Union.

53. The smallest state is Rhode Island.

54. There are nine Supreme Court justices.

55. The Atlantic borders the United States in the east.

56. The chief executive of a state is the governor.

57. The chief executive of a city is the mayor.

58. They celebrated the first Thanksgiving with the Native Americans.

59. Thomas Jefferson was the major writer of the Declaration of Independence.

60. The introduction to the Constitution is the Preamble.

61. They came from Virginia.

62. The national anthem is *The Star Spangled Banner.*

63. Francis Scott Key wrote the words to the national anthem.

64. The right of "freedom of speech" is found in the Bill of Rights.

65. Mexico borders the United States in the south.

66. Canada borders the United States in the north.

67. The Supreme Court is the highest in the land.

68. Abraham Lincoln was President during the Civil War.

69. It freed the slaves.

70. Mount Vernon was Washington's home in Virginia.

71. George Washington is called the Father of Our Country.

72. American citizenship gives someone the right to vote.

73. Native Americans helped the Pilgrims.

74. The Pilgrims landed at Plymouth Rock.

75. Before the Revolutionary War, they were British colonies.

76. The right of "freedom of the press" is in the Bill of Rights.

77. Congress has the power to declare war.

78. If the President refuses to sign a bill, it is a veto.

79. Abraham Lincoln was assassinated.

80. Abraham Lincoln ordered the building of the Transcontinental Railroad.

81. Edison invented the electric light bulb.

82. The cotton gin doubled the cotton yield.

83. Congress meets in the Capitol.

84. An amendment is a change to the Constitution.

85. The President is the commander-in-chief.

86. A person born outside the United States cannot become president.

87. The right of "freedom of religion" is in the Bill of Rights.

88. Congress meets in the Capitol.

89. A war president is one who serves as president during wartime.

90. The White House is the home of the President.

91. The right of "freedom of assembly" is in the Bill of Rights.

92. The President's office is the Oval Office.

93. If the President dies, the Vice President becomes president.

94. Washington was the first commander-in-chief.

95. Presidential elections are held in November.

96. Most Americans were farmers.

97. A senator can be reelected innumerable times.

98. A representative can be reelected innumerable times.

99. The two major parties are the Democrats and the Republicans.

100. The North fought against the South during the Civil War.